NOTES
FROM
THE CUBE

a year in the office

by

THE CUBE

Published by Red Frog Media Publishing,
a division of
Red Frog Media.
Visit our website www.redfrogpublishing.com

DISCLAIMER: This is not a work of fiction – but, in all cases, no person, places, events or companies depicted are based entirely upon a specific person, place, event or company. All names have been changed. Any 100% resemblance to a specific person, place, event or company is purely coincidental, without malice, and unintentional. The only intent was to describe generalized persons, places, events and companies that would be recognizable by persons in almost any work environment involving cubicles.

Nonfiction/Humor   First Edition

ISBN 13: 978-0-9845933-9-2   ISBN 10:098459339X

PROFILE

The Cube. The cubicle. Where you work. Where you live. It's a beautiful world we live in . . .

Occupation: Inside The Cube

Location: Anywhere & Everywhere

About THE CUBE:
Well, we work together, don't we? You've seen me and I've seen you - and We see what goes on around us. It's funny how they write about us - the business journals, the newspapers, the MBA programs - but they're on the outside looking in. We're here. Looking at what goes on.

TABLE OF CONTENT

May

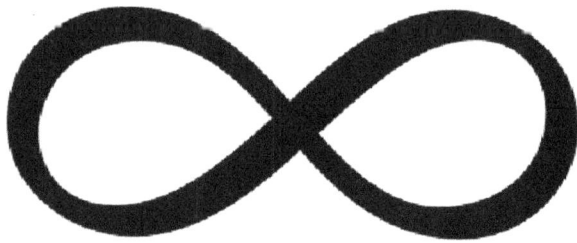

Thursday, May 12

Zero Tolerance

The Zero Tolerance Policy.
aka An admission that we don't have the wisdom
to figure out what to do on a case by case basis.
aka Failure of Authority and Common Sense.

Friday, May 13

The ECO

ECO - Engineering Change Order. Ah, it's called other things in other places, but it's always the same:

The Document That Must Be Approved
For Things To Happen.

Well, of course, when Approval is needed and things must Happen, you need an Approval Process and a Review.

And a Standard.

'Mustn't forget the Standard.
We'll use ISO - the International Standards Organization - because, doncha know?, it's *international* and it's a *standard.*

And let's just give our Review a full-fledged Board to make it sound official and have Authority. And an acronym - you've got to have acronyms - something like CCB: Change Control Board.

Now let's all sing:

Let me see your ECO.
Let me see your change.
The CCB will probably say "No,"
But write it anyway.
Who decides, we just don't know -
Submit it just the same.
That's the rule, follow ISO,

It's called the Paper Game.

Chorus:
Check-Mark!
Fill the box!
Complete the form
And pray:
A miracle may happen
They'll approve it
Any Day!
Hey!

Saturday, May 14

Meetings: a haiku

If you have
a meeting
And no one
listens
Does it count?

Sunday, May 15

The Alzheimer's Executive

Tragicomic moment. The first "Employees First" meeting after laying off 20% of the workers. The President stands in front of the assembled crowd, annoyed that so few are in attendance...

Monday, May 16

The Blame: Justification #1

He (nervously/confidently) walks into the meeting and sits down in front of his staff. He has been with the company ten years and, with the new executive management, now has five people working under his supervision. He's not quite sure what all of his reports do, but he was assured by the (new) Vice President that he could "manage." His first management task is to inform his "team":

"First on the agenda, as you may have already heard, XXX and YYY are no longer with us. It was decided, what with the new direction the company is taking, that we need people on the team who are fully committed to that vision and, well, they weren't."

Old Hire: "Vision?"

"Vision... yes, *vision*. We can be part of the team, finding solutions – or a negative influence, finding obstacles."

New Hire: "Yeah, XXX was definitely an obstacle."

Old Hire: "Did you ever work with him?"

New Hire: "No, but I heard what he was doing."

5

Old Hire: "What about YYY – she probably knows more about this biz than anybody?"

He looks at the Old Hire (sympathetically/with panic in his eyes/sternly): "They were obstacles to the vision of the new direction."

The New Hire and the Old Hire both turn to their team leader for support. He knows that what he says next will be reported back upstream.

(In the back of his mind, calmly,/With barely concealed panic,) he thinks: "They have to have been doing something wrong. Otherwise it makes no sense. Otherwise I make no sense still being here. They have to have been doing something wrong."

But he says: "Let's move on to the next agenda item."

Tuesday, May 17

Fortune's Fables: The Deadline

Bear with us. In the spirit of Aesop and La Fontaine (without the furry little creatures), an allegorical fable witnessed from The Cube ...

Once a king he did decree
"Of course my son will follow me.
And now it is important, son,
To defend ourselves against the Hun."

The Hun, you see, was a raging force
Sweeping the world and, of course,
It's threat pressed closer day by day.
So the prince set out without delay

To the farthest castle, the border's end
Where stood a pass they could defend.
"Build up the walls," was his first command.
"This is where we make our stand."

Then every knight, serf, freeman and slave
To this task their efforts gave
And the walls did rise, day by day,
Ahead of the Hun – the land would be saved.

But –

The prince was smart and he did see
Improvements needed for the wall-to-be:
"This tower's too short, this gate too thin.
To make this wall great, begin again."

Well, he was right, he surely was, sir,
And even though the Huns drew closer,
The people tore their new walls down,
Then built them again to defend their town.

But –

The prince was smart and he did see
A weakness in the walls-to-be:
"The mortar's slack, the bricks ill-formed.
The walls might tumble if we are stormed.

"Rip them down and start again:
To save our lives we must do it right, men."

Well, he was right, no doubt of that.

(Though the Huns were storming down the pass.)
Still the prince was firm, he shouted out:
"We want strong walls, without a doubt!"
So the walls were tumbled from within
And they started building yet again.
But the Huns attacked before they were done:
Without defense they were overrun.

The kingdom was lost with the prince defeated,
The people enslaved, the king unseated.
And the castle wall? Never completed.

Moral:
Sometimes decisions – right or wrong, first or last,
Mean nothing when the deadline's passed.

The Line

Thank God for the Line: they keep on making product despite us.

Wednesday, May 18

Bland Boys and Marshmallow Men

Bland Boys and Marshmallow Men. That just about says it all, doesn't it...

No, there's a lot to say. Not now, though. We'll get back to them in time, just had to make the observation while it's fresh.

Thursday, May 19

An Apology

As you may have noticed, The Cube likes poetry - at least The Cube's poetry, ego-bound as that may sound. (This is a plea: please do not send in angst-filled verses.)

Once upon a time, The Cube wrote a report and was reprimanded for calling the Company's product what it was: a genitally-related term that was medically accurate. Apparently, though, delicate ears in More Powerful Cubes did not want to hear that term.

Oddly enough, we create euphemisms for what we make, for what we do. The Cube now assumes that a garbage collector prefers "disposal agent." We no longer die, we "pass." And one should definitely not say that the Company's piss-passing portals connect to the ! @ & * !

The Cube was astounded and amused by the objection. While familiar with the concept of Virgin Birth, the idea of penis-less urinary release was a novel idea. But The Cube was also not pleased with the Official Reprimand. The Cube now had a Record in The Files.

The Cube felt it diplomatic to apologize to the More Powerful Cubes, to wit:

> **I**f we writers have offended
> **T**hink but this and all is mended:
> **S**ince the words I did last profess
> **F**ell on your ears with such distress
> **U**nder-thought and over-ripe they
> **C**ould not a simple joke convey.
> **K**now this, know this: 'tis me to blame
> **I**nsisting that my humor's sunny.
> **N**ot you: you rightfully felt shame
> **G**iven such a dismal pun, we
> **S**houldn't have to hear jokes lame,
> **H**ilarity requires thoughts funny.
> **I**n conclusion here's a word from me:
> **T**he word's to you -- Apology.

Yes, the first word in every sentence was made bold. No, five years later no one has yet noticed. Yes, The Cube did give it to the More Powerful Cubes. No, The Cube did not get fired – yet.

Great quote from Hagakure: The Book of the Samurai –

"The end is important in all things."

Friday, May 20

Job Perceptions: The Sales Field Rep

The young moth was a go-getter, getting out of his co-coon before the others, flexing his wings, flying from the garden into the house to check out the opportunities. He smelled linen and cotton and rich tasty cashmere – and he smelled it in there.

Yes, he was far ahead of the other moths, just struggling out of their cocoons as he returned from the house, all of them eagerly asking: "How'd it go?"

"It was a fantastic success!" he replied. "Everyone was clapping for me!"

Courtesy Andrzej Mikos

Saturday, May 21

Bland Boys & Marshmallow Men: Recognized

A correspondent from Canada, Pierre Dolet, writes:

I know them, the Bland Boys and Marshmallow Men. They're the executives with soft, perpetually friendly smiles and neutral eyes. There is no anger, no emotion, to their decisions. You can't argue with them, not on substance, because they won't disagree – but you won't necessarily know what they agree with, either. Management books are written for them, because they can quote an opinion and use its printed existence as justification – and always, just the same, have a distance from that opinion. Consultants are their messenger angels – again because its an outside opinion that they can use for justification, while keeping distance from the results. They will have flavor-of-the-month words from the business journals they read or the seminars they attend: flat world economy, granular, crisp. They are, always, "Professional" management.

The Cube cautions:

Be careful, Pierre Dolet, because you sound dangerously unaware of their Power. Don't pass them off with easy sarcasm. These are the ones in control.

Or, to use a political Bland Boy term: the ones with the "mandate."

Sunday, May 22

"An ISO Certificate of Democracy"

Lest we feel alone in our cubicles, there are others who see the same things we do in the larger view, aka The World.

"An ISO Certificate of Democracy" -- an article headline that The Cube came across this weekend.

Pretty much says it all... Nothing left to add.

Meetings: a haiku - Response: It's Training

A correspondent, Citrom, responds to May 14th's "Meetings: a haiku":

Perhaps they can call it a Training Session.

To which The Cube adds:

Only if they don't require an Evaluation: Training works best when no one is accountable for anything -- especially for what they learned.

Monday, May 23

Executing Plans #1

What surprises you is how much is improvised. Great beautiful plans are drawn up by the hundred: general, schematic, detail, detail of detail.

And then, in reality, the plans don't necessarily show you how to do the damn thing. What steps to take, in what order, how – to – do – it. Sure, there are logical orders, but not as many as you'd think.

Imagine assembling a Christmas bicycle – 10-speed, no parts pre-assembled – with only the parts list and a schematic drawing, no step-by-step instructions. Multiply this by ten thousand (because, really, a bike is so pitifully simple compared to a company's business operations). Now add in one more factor...
Sometimes the plans are wrong...

Tuesday, May 24

Executing Plans #2

...Sometimes the plans are wrong.

The plans are based on an ideal, without necessarily having knowledge of inconvenient facts.

Or, just as often, the plans are based on other plans and the planners don't feel it necessary to ask those down below, those who do, how real are the plans.

"We want solutions, not obstacles" – and the simplest solution is not to bring up obstacles.

Wednesday, May 25

In the end: Control

In the end, it's all about Control, isn't it...

Thursday, May 26

Redline

Spent a lot of time recently on the "new" management style, so here's a nostalgic trip down memory lane ...

Show me what you've written
I'll redline how you're wrong
I'll bog you down in shit and
Make your project long.
I do not trust your judgment.
(I do not know my mind, but)
I call it "check-and-balance"
(Though it looks like ass behind).
The rest of you don't know a thing,
Only I am right: I am - the - king.

Well, obviously, not so "memory" after all, since it goes with any management style, depending on the mind behind the smile or frown or, possibly worst, the blank expression of "objective" evaluation. 'Have a nice day, luv!

Friday, May 27

The Smile

The Smile - an executive strategy? - 'probably exists on several levels, but this is how The Cube has been watching it lately. *No, this is not a poem, it just seemed easier to write it this way...*

The Smile displays an even disposition that says
"I am your friend."
That Smile does not say "I understand" or
"I am going to support you."
It does say "I agree with you," though.

Agreement.
The Smile will never disagree in public.
With anyone.
"Let's take it offline, one to one."
And then the Smile will agree with you – one to one –
And you –
You, too.

Or, maybe, have unavoidable schedule issues which
Keep preventing that particular one to one.
Until the problem goes away.
Or is ignored.
Or isn't, but
Is avoided.

The Smile is very good at bringing
Peace to the organization.
Very good at avoiding conflict.
Very good at avoiding.

Until the Smile gets what it wants
Whether or not the conflict
Conflict –
"Are you an obstacle or part of the solution?" –
Conflict –
Don't want that –
Can't have that in this organization –
Whether or not the conflict brings up an
Uncomfortable truth,
Because
Truth is maybe not what the Smile cares about.

Not when the Smile is in charge.
The Smile wants results.
The Smile's version of results.
We all want results,
Don't you agree?

Coda: There are moments in life when The Cube is very glad not to be the one paying the Smile for screwing off with my money. But, probably, I wouldn't notice: the Smile is so friendly and persuasive that it's dazzling.

Saturday, May 28

White Wall #1

White wall
Empty
like the heart
Killing lives
unseen by the bottom linc.

Sunday, May 29

White Wall #2

White wall empty
Hum
Carpet dim footsteps
Voices flat
Breaking dreams.

The Ballad of Phil's Fortune

You know the tune; if not, fake it . . .

Let me tell you all a story 'bout a man named Phil
He built himself a business from a tiny molehill
Then one year after working quite a while
He said to himself, "Hey, I've built me up a pile."

Now his friends all said, "Phil, you've gotta have a Board.
If you wanna grow, you gotta know how to go forward."
So he brought on three Directors from all across the land
And he paid 'em all big bucks to give him a hand.

Big bucks – to advise
Because their CVs said: these guys are wise
And smart
And been around
Around.
Yeah.

Well the first Director said, "Phil, you need a consultant."
While the second one said, "And of course a President."
And the third one said, "With my colleagues I agree,
So we made a Search Committee and the President is me."

The new President he said, "Phil, I need a free hand
And so the Board has voted, I hope you understand
That we'll keep you on the Org Chart high and pretty
But really all decisions now they're really made by me."

The President, top man
Promised money in Phil's hand
In a while
It takes time
To plan.
Yeah.

Now the President he brought in all of his new Team
Looked an awful lot like his old company
He said to Phil, "Your old crew, they have gotta go:
We need new blood and anyway it's my choice you know."

And he gave them all great salaries, big bucks for each man
And they made pie charts and tall graphs they called The Super Plan
And they promised Phil more money than he would ever want
As he sits in his big office growing old and looking gaunt.

Phil, that is – alone now
Everyone else is new
Laid off the old crew
And the factory too
Offshore.
Yeah.

Well now this is where we say goodbye to our friend Phil
The President and Board have bulldozed Phil's molehill
The Super Plan went a-bust and led to bankruptcy –
But they all had golden parachutes and are happy as can be.

The Board and President and New Team Super Plan!
Heading on to New Horizons!
Brought to you by the cash flow from Phil's molehill
And all those managers and workers and friends
Who put in twenty years on that molehill
And now have –
Yeah.

$$$

Tuesday, May 31

No Responsibility, No Accountability

The old saw "No Guts, No Glory" has a new face:

No Responsibility, No Accountability.

No, of course: it's not so new. Peasants in every feudal/ caste system in history and privates in every army of the world figured that out eons ago. It's corollary is "keep your head low" and "only those who dare to look up lose their heads."

And the Communist bureaucracies perfected the appa- ratchik mentality of hiding behind the rule - oh so many rules - to disguise incompetence and, equally often (if not more) fear.

No Responsibility, No Accountability.

What's new (and, again, maybe older than history) is that the sentiment of NR,NA is traveling from the top down these days.

The Cube doesn't care about top-dog corporate execs to- day - hell, NR,NA is what they pay million dollar lawyers to convince juries was their "true" situation while raking in billions in (oh how sadly) government-frozen "perfor- mance" bonuses and faux dividends.

But, if one believes in the intrinsic capability of the Mid- dle tiers - and The Cube is tiered smack in Middle - then one has to be appalled by a recent experience - which The Cube, eyes newly opened, is seeing played out again and again.

And again.

No Responsibility, No Accountability.

It plays out like this:

We are setting up a new operation. Not too simple, since it's both new and requires coordination among 3 - 4 departments. Somewhere in the setup, The Cube notices that part J doesn't link up with part K like it's supposed to. A little closer look discovers that quite a few little C-Ds, O-Ps and X-Y-Zs exist but they aren't connected. Logic says they should be linked, somehow, and when The Cube investigates - asks some simple questions like "Why this?" and "What is that for?" - the answers confirm logic. So The Cube informs the Management and other Do-ers of the Middle tier.

To discover that no one wants the Responsibility of connecting those links - and maintaining them.

The conversations become surreal: voices acknowledge the issue, while eyes look in different directions, embarrassed, as if we were discussing genital warts. And no one - not one of three, four, five Managers wants to touch the issue --- even though it will affect the operation we are putting together. No one wants the Responsibility. No one wants to be held Accountable.

It would be easy to say that "this reflects upper management style and temperament," but The Cube has noticed that there is not such a direct correlation. Yeah, Responsibility-ducking Tops spawn like-minded Middle children --- but The Cube has seen great things come from the Middle and the Line in spite of such skewed Toppers --- and has seen, is seeing, NR,NA Mids spreading like cancers under the sightlines of some pretty solid, standup Tops.

No Responsibility, No Accountability.

The Cube is feeling rather ashamed these days. It's easy to see how the Top - both the competent captains and the ambitious greedy bastards who certainly want The Credit - look down on the Middle.

June

Wednesday, June 01

Random

The Cube sat in three different meetings today - which certainly puts a dent in productivity (although the profile was amenably high). Anyway, with so much verbal priority, there was little time for making more than these few short observations:

Meeting #1: There is a thin line between documentation and meaningless paper.

Meeting #2: It's good for all the department personnel to see how confused it is at the top - it's not just their manager ordering them around.

Meeting #3: Remember to speak with a British accent - it makes you sound very important.

Thursday, June 02

Meetings and Goals

As noted in the last posting, The Cube spent many an hour in meetings yesterday - and today looks like more of the same.

Many Folks From The Cube think that meetings are a waste of time, specifically *their* time.

Not so.

Meetings are an ideal opportunity to perfect:

* The discipline of meditation: sleeplike state of being that is yet alert;
* One's graphic talents: the doodle you make can
  great art fake; and - perhaps most importantly –
* Your organic farming skills: bull___ is *very* essen-
  tial to preservation of the environment - especially
  within the confines of the hothouse business cli-
  mate.

The Cube has been to many valuable meetings, just not
lately, or often, or with unadulterated pleasure. It is a
Goal to be Sought: the Perfect Meeting - timely, to the
point, with meaning for all participants.

It is an admirable Goal, and The Cube is not sarcastic
about that - only a bit forlorn at its rarity.

Friday, June 03

Answers You Shouldn't Give

It is naturally expected that a question seeks an answer
- that a statement demands a response - that a business
runs on rapid response.

The Cube warns: *Not so fast.*

Through sad experience, The Cube has learned to treat
almost all questions, statements and Pay Attention To
Me management comments as *rhetorical* - as in "Listen
only to what I say - no matter the what, regardless of the
facts - *do not answer* - because I want to hear the sound
of my own voice."

This knowledge was not learned overnight, and The Cube admits to many an unintended career change as a result of answering some of the following:

> Director: "This report for the Board: keep it simple."
> Cube: "For simple minds."

Observation: Correct analysis, wrong to say it aloud.

> VP: "Just because it was in the Review agenda doesn't mean you gave it enough emphasis."
> Cube: "Look, I'm sorry you didn't do your part of the job, but the rest of us–"

Observation: 'Never got to finish the sentence - don't tell a VP he's a slacker.

> New Pres: "We have to up the profit margin by reaching for the low-hanging fruit."
> Cube: "Grab us by the balls, cut benefits and lay off entire shifts."

Observation: Correct forecasting does not prevent personal castration. We are all "fruit."

Saturday, June 04

The Vital Few

And the President addressed the Staff:
"We are the vital few
Who will save this business."

And each member of the Staff knew:
"I am one of the vital few
Who can run this business."

And they made their lists
To cut down the crew
Decisions were made
By the vital few.

And then the Staff was reduced
To skeletons too

Remainders
Survivors
But each one knew -

(Or prayed that the President knew)
"Those others they weren't
The vital few."

Fortune's Fables: In The Name of the

Micro-Management Father

Malinka the Milkmaid loved her cows
Stephan the Shepherd loved his sheep
Together they cared for their little flocks
Better than Boy Blue or Bo-Peep.

Lawrence the Landlord loved to order,
And order and order he did:
"Plow the fields, mend the mill,
Shoe the horse, feed the kid."
(Goats, that is.)
Lawrence gave order to all that he did.

Still the farm was so big, so much to be done,
That Larry got lost sometimes
He'd say, "Stop." Then say, "Go."
Then say, "Catch-up, slowpoke.
We've got to get this done on time."

Larry depended on Stephan and Mallie
To do their jobs well anyway.
"They know what they're doing and if I forget
Then they'll tell me and not go astray."

Which would have been fine, but apparently not,
For as Malinka would say:
"When my boss tells me 'Do',
I do without thought,
For thinking is not what I'm paid."

29

Stephan was different, he thought all the time,
But he thought like a lawyer in heat:
"If I do what he says and it's not what he wants,
Or do what he wants and it's not what he says,
Or go to the left when he says 'To the right' –
Oh lord, it's hurting my head!"

Which brings us now to Warren the Wolf,
As hungry a beast as could be.
When he saw what was what
He knew what was not:
That decisions were never to be.

So he went to the cows and he went to the sheep
And he said to Malinka and Stephan:
"Lawrence the landlord wants me to be fed
Bring me lamb chops and steak by eleven."

Now Stephan he knew that this was a crock
And Malinka she said, "This is crazy."
But Warren the Wolf, he huffed and he puffed:
"This is what Larry said. Don't be lazy!"

Despite both knowing the Wolf's words made no sense,
The name of "Lawrence" was uttered:
And so though they knew that disaster'd ensue,
They served him steaks and chops in hot butter.

Moral:
If there's no common theme, there's no self-defense
When the shepherds behave like the sheep.
So masters beware, craft your orders with care:
For consequences to be what you mean.

Eh?

Crisp it up, Jack
Granularity is needed
The world is flat
Give me a Super Plan!

Tuesday, June 07

Two Meetings

So Don sits down at the Review. Quiet guy, easily ignored. Does his job and, now, a half dozen other departments are going to sign-off on the project - or find reasons to object and require changes for things that Don overlooked or otherwise missed.

But here is the beauty moment:

"I have to object, Don, because there's not enough data on the Triple Y process. Re-verification will be needed."

Don's soft eyes harden, his voice gets softer - and steely: "Page 7."

"But it's not -" and you can tell that the page is being opened for the first time, even though the Review Report had been circulated a week earlier, "it's not-"

"It's right here. Three passes. Each one exceeding published requirements." And you can see that Don is prepared. That he has actually preempted every possible objection by that old reliable: professionalism.

And his voice never raises, and he's till the pudgy, unassuming man sitting at the end of the table, and he shoots down every objection with facts and full disclosure.

Buck was brilliant at the meeting, dominating it in fact.

His strong-voiced comments forced them to reconsider the proposal's merits and to delay what - as Buck so powerfully observed in that good-humored way of his - what would have been a certain disaster.

Later, discussing the proposal with his assistants, Buck was overheard to boast: "Naw, I never read the thing. Who has time for that crap?"

Wednesday, June 08

Smart People

Hank Gerber writes to The Cube ...

Smart people are great people to work around.

It's awful fun to watch smart people strut their stuff.

Never liked school much, the formal learning thing, so it's a gas to have an unintentional "teacher" to watch and learn from.

Best experience recently: Sitting in on a phone conference while two different lawyers argued - one pro, one con - about some IP the company owned. Their arguments were cogent, pointed and logical. I'm not a lawyer, nor an expert in intellectual property, and I could follow what they were saying, where they were leading. Then, at one point, they switched sides: not as an intellectual game, but with each one playing Devil's Advocate to his own arguments.

Love that kind of casual intelligence: the Accountant who knows her numbers - not like a geek or a bean counter, but with a functionning comprehension of the underlying theory of organization; the Marketing Manager who understands the human psyche and its relationship to the Company's product - and how no advertising word should be just "there" as filler; the Veep with the elephant memory remembering the *reason* behind institutional decisions made fifteen years earlier, and prepared to learn from past mistakes - even from new people; the Board Director with the years in venture capital, sharing a doctoral level of experience and insight in a review of what was supposed to be a simple "leave behind" white paper.

Casual intelligence - not show-off. Smart people, not those who end an argument with the meant-to-impress "I know better than anyone else in this room."

That Engineer with the eye of an artist and the mind of Leonardo. The Manager with the accomplishments of Patton and the style of Mother Teresa. The Receptionist who can make everyone feel at home and in a serious place of business at the same time. The Operator who knows the machine like a cowboy knows his horse, responds to pressure like a Zen samurai, and can fix the Line problem with a minute's thought and a moment's right action.

Smart people are sure worth being around.

Thursday, June 09

IOAD

It's Only A Demo - IOAD.

Nifty way to keep paperwork off your back and standards out of the picture. Too bad it sounds like an obscenity.

IOAD.

'Hope they don't accidentally sell any of them there IOADs.

Ooops!

Friday, June 10

The List

The List is very important.

"Put it on The List," is a regular command at meetings. That is why it is so very important: we have acknowledged that it must be Listed.

The List is an object of worship - an icon - it exists in and of itself.

When placed on The List, "it" becomes a identified, deified, untouchable.

Untouchable. That's the most important part about The List: that - whatever is put on The List - has now been dealt with. "It's taken care of: it's on The List. Let's move on to the next issue."

Yes, Action has been taken: "it" is on The List. Do you want more done? What are you - an obstacle or a problem-solver?

Let it be for now: it's on The List.

The Good Lieutenette

She's quick and smart, ready to produce what her Captain of Industry needs. Supportive.

On the old ship, when the Captain was the Crusty Mariner, she understood.

"He's a take-charge guy. Some people fear him, but they shouldn't : not if they've done their job. He wants straight talk, information, not words just for the sake of wind. He's always accessible to people with solid thoughts and ideas. People who know what they're doing, they have no problem."

But, as time passes, all ships must be re-fitted, and the Good Lieutenette was set to serve a new Captain, The Smile.

The Smile was smooth and friendly and didn't give a damn about what you knew or the contents of your thought - as long as you agreed with him and were dimmer than the light of his Smile. It was a radiant light - and she understood.

"He's accessible, not like the Crusty Mariner, who was distant. The Smile reaches out - and people appreciate that: it's truly refreshing after the Crusty Mariner who, you have to admit, people were afraid of. People who know how to be team players, they have no problem."

The Good Lieutenette is quick and smart, ready to produce what her Captain of Industry needs. Supportive. Maybe not totally honest with herself, but that's certainly not a requirement for successfully serving Captain Smile. She's a team player now, basking in the radiance of The Smile, and that's what counts.

Sunday, June 12

Godot Done Left

Finished the project yesterday. Six months, half a mil, twenty productive souls' efforts.

Brought it to Doc Control, ready to go. Countdown, Start the engines. Make the product, GO!

The pile was 6" high. A wary eye looked at it.
"Um, not me."
Four blank faces.
A sign: "On vacation - back in 2 weeks."
Four blank faces.
"Put it on that desk."
It sits.

Monday, June 13

Faith-Based Marketing

It has been decided to make and sell a faith-based product.

No one has developed Marketing Specs yet. Or defined the product - beyond a vague wish list of options that sounds a lot more coherent after three drinks. (Your choice: well or call.)

Oh, we used to do that stuff. Boring stuff, tedious - got in the way, really, slowed us down: all the *paperwork,* and *market research and financial projections...*

"Streamline the bureaucracy!" says the New Management - and we do.

("Besides," and this is the dirty little secret whispered by the remaining Old Management, "we mainly faked those numbers anyway.")

Does anybody want it? Even if not now, is there an emerging market?

Color? Size? Weight?

F-U-N-C-T-I-O-N-?

Dunno. 'Heard it from a guy, who knows another guy, that this could be really **BIG.**... (Oops, sorry: was at the track yesterday - wrong slang crept in... Sort of... not really...shit!)

It must be faith-based marketing -

Dear God, I *pray* it is –

- because we've been developing it for the past six months and it rolls out Monday.

Tuesday, June 14

5S - The Saga Begins

Pierre Dolet writes to The Cube ...

We are beginning a new program: 5S - a Japanese management system transplanted to America and, in our factory, to be imposed on an employee base that is 80% Mexican.

This should be fun.

The Cube expands ...

Pierre Dolet, do you know anything about 5S - what it stands for, how it got started, what it does? Please keep me posted... Oh, and it will be "fun." I mean, after all, Japan's economy has only been in recession for 15 years, so it makes sense to adopt their workplace models now.

Wednesday, June 15

5S: The Team Descends (The Saga Continues)

Pierre Dolet sends another Note to The Cube about his company's 5S implementation ...

They developed a Core Team or a Tiger Team or a Softball Team (they're all wearing blue polo shirts and baseball caps, so...) - a group of people who disappear for half the day, every day, with the 5S consultants. This went on for a week.

And then The Team descended on us.

Suddenly, there are RED TAGS everywhere. My cubicle looks like a Christmas tree or a fire sale advertisement. I'm not sure why. Nobody has spoken to me - I wasn't there at the time - they just swarmed into the space, attached their tags, and left. "Don't touch the tags" was the only direction I received, after the fact.

It was too late: I had already removed a few - the tags were in my way and on some stuff I was working with. But The Team said, "Don't touch" - so I lied.

What does it mean?

Will I go to hell?

The Cube answers: Probably.

Thursday, June 16

5S Explained (Sort of)

Pierre Dolet wrote a Note to The Cube yesterday about his company starting up a "5S" program. What is a 5S program? Well, a simple link for those who do not trust the Cube's interpretation is

http://en.wikipedia.org/wiki/5S

And a (very) brief summary of the 5Ss would be:

> *Seiri* - Sort
> *Seiton* - Set in Order
> *Seiso* - Shine
> *Seiketsu* - Standardize
> *Shitsuke* - Sustain

For those who do trust The Cube's spin on things ...

5S is one of those "workplace 'philosophies' " (and the word 'philosophy' is double-quoted with reason) that seek to provide guidance on organization principles that can make things work smoother and more efficiently. Much like the Judeo-Christian-Islam evolution, this philosophy has its own progression: 5S - Lean Manufacturing - Six Sigma. Much like all of the religious phi-losophies, the origins were humble and well-meaning -- while the descendants have become, well, contentious in their divisions between fundamentalist blind adherents and those who try to understand the spirit of the thing. Both have their true prophets and hypocritical leaders - ah, but which is which?

The humble origin: Japan, bombed to rubble, turned to its traditional backbone characteristics of discipline, order and minimalism to rebuild the nation's industrial base. There were also assumptions of hierarchical loyalties and paternalism left inherently intact, if unsaid, but a key one was: you give your all to the company, the company is your home until you retire. Much like the U.S. auto industry -- until the 1970s.

So Japan's economic success was apparent to all in the 1970s and 80s, losing some of its shine starting in 1990 or thereabouts when it hit a recession which traditional answers have not found a way of resolving so far. But, by then, the American business management books had already been written for a decade about the "secrets" of Japan's economic success – written and taught in the MBA programs for a decade or more. And, now, those MBAs are the Captains of Business & Industry, taking what they learned...

Now, trust the Cube for a moment, this is not a slam on the 5S-and-descendants philosophies – but the Cube does note that those books and MBA programs tried to have the best of both worlds without really understanding either.

In America, for instance, the common phrase "Get a life" means that the job isn't everything and immediate self-gratification is part of the commercial equation – and everyone buys into the concept of Democracy (whether or not we practice or understand its full implications). In Japan, those just weren't part of the equation when these workplace philosophies were developed: there were (still are) class divisions - and self-sacrifice for the larger goals of the group is intrinsic. Pierre Dolet, in his Note yesterday, mentioned that 80% of his company's manufacturing workforce is Mexican: still another psyche stirred into the melting pot of ideas.

But our MBAs and business books took only the form of the 5S philosophy, without questioning the underlying assumptions.

Drama - or comedy - ensues ...

Friday, June 17

5S - Blind Faith

For the past couple of days, The Cube has been following up on Pierre Dolet's questions about his company entering a 5S program ...

5S - according to those folks who make a bundle providing consultation services on the matter - is self-described as a "philosophy."

As philosophies go, 5S is fairly simple, boiling down to: Clean up your act and keep it clean.

Had 5S been Yiddish and not Japanese in origin, it would have been called the Momma Says Clean Up Your Room philosophy.

OK, so most folks aren't going to argue with the "Cleanliness is next to godliness" line of reasoning - and the Protestant work ethic that governs the American workplace likes godliness.

Where we fall apart is in the execution.

5S, for all its rules on red-tagging unnecessary things, SORTing out the trash, SETting IN ORDER and STAND-ARDIZing (3 of the 5Ss), sort of relies on that non-philosophical thought pattern called Common Sense.

Oy, Common Sense! That doesn't fit into a $35.00 business book, a $350/day consultancy or a $35,000/year MBA program - those rely on a certain mysterium, magic and miracle to justify their hefty price tags.

Common Sense - OUT!

Definitive Leadership - IN.

"I have paid, therefore I have learned, therefore It Must Be!"

Bzzzzz - it's also a buzzword among the other Captains of Industry.

Ommm - it becomes a mantra among the middle management, those who are mere Ensigns of Industry.

5S - It Be Good. It Be the Only Way. It Be -

Blind Faith.

Do what you're told.

A Consultant, a Captain, a Book, an MBA has said "This Must Be."

Around the Kernel of Common Sense grows the Hard Shell of Dogma.

"This Must Be."

Advice from The Cube to Pierre Dolet: Do not read or learn about 5S - ignorance is bliss and, by invoking the Original Philosophy, you may be burned as a heretic.

𝕾

Saturday, June 18

**Fortune's Fables: The Exec Team
(Nostalgic Memories)**

Say Nothing Nick was mighty quick
With a smile or a shrug or a frown
If you said "Yes," he'd never say "No"
But he'd look thoughtfully at the ground.

I-Gotta-Plan Pete had his words down neat
About how everything could be
Fixed with a plan: "Gotta have a plan, man,
Just don't leave the details to me."

Quality Sue was a bit of a shrew
'Cause she knew what her word would mean:
"I'll set the bar, I'll shoot down your star,
If you don't meet the standards of – me."

Heavy Harry was extremely wary
Of anyone else but himself.
Don't try to make a plan without this man
Or you'll find it stuck on the back shelf.

Anxious Anne had never met a man
She couldn't bust with an harassment suit.
Though rarely used, it was much abused
By Anne's threat of intended use.

When Nick 'n Pete, Sue, Harry & Anne
Met to make their plans -
Nick said nothin' and Pete he blustered
And the others just waited to damn.

Well this went fine for a mighty long time
'Cause they'd once been first with the best
But now they weren't so and as everyone knows
It's tough standing out from the rest.

Still they didn't change and the meetings they made
Went from long to boring to bland,
Till the company died and the team they sighed
With their golden parachutes in hand.

And the moral: it's neat – just grab a seat
And I'll tell you what you need to know:
That if you're gonna to do nothing
Make sure you've got $omething
To take out the door when you go!

Sunday, June 19

Sunday Night Memo for Monday Morning

To Do Tomorrow:

* Activity v Productivity - keep moving

* New Ideas - write a bullshit memo

* Ongoing - find someone who is always trying to get noticed and lay off the drudge work to 'em. (Note to Self: Stamp PRIORITY on the top page)

* Planning - schedule an emergency meeting for the afternoon, when not everyone one can attend at such late notice, cancel at the last minute and complain about lack of commitment to the company.

Monday, June 20

Monday Review

Per yesterday's To Do memo:

* Productivity v Activity: Failed to keep moving - got stuck with job I would have easily ducked with a little speed.

* Bullshit memo: Excellent idea - set up an email string that went around and back to me five times from seven people: 35 emails on one fake idea. 'Looked really productive for setting that one up.

* PRIORITY stamp: Actually needed it, damn!

* Planning: eh?

Tuesday, June 21

The Recycled Meeting

Ever go to a meeting that you swear you've been in before?

Sat down with a dozen others, meeting leader began talking, other people began responding, back-and-forth, issues raised, objections voiced ...

I was there last week.

Not *deja vu*. Not boring impression that "All meetings are alike."

No: this one had real issues - and the calendar said "today" - and, and –

And I looked in my notebook and realized that we actually *had* this *exact same meeting seven days earlier.*

It was as if twelve people had done absolutely nothing between then and now - and no one was self-conscious about that, or apologetic, or acknowledged it. No one had thought about it during the interim, not a whisper of a thought, an inkling of an idea. And, now, a collective amnesia.

I have been here before.

Wednesday, June 22

Mother Cube Nursery Rhymes: Priority

There once was prez who said "Do it.
And by 'Do it' I mean 'Now.'"
So you've wasted your night, just screwed it:
But he forgot he wanted it - Ow!

That is what we mean by "Priority":
For others to set for you and me.
Don't ever take it personally:
They haven't thought it through, you see.

Thursday, June 23

The Pass-Off

A recently learned lesson from a MarCom executive:

It is very important to pass-off your responsibilities and tasks.

Remember: You never know when you will run out of time. Therefore, whenever possible, point out that you and your department have "a number of deadlines in the pipeline" and set a meeting to "discuss priorities" and, if you delay long enough, the requesting party will run out of time and do it themselves.

Which they could have done all along.

Actually, you are helping the Company to streamline the workflow.

Friday, June 24

Bend with the Wind

Yes, of course: it's easier.

So easier: You get the order - it makes no sense. Endless complications of a simple operation. Information wanted that no one will read. Three different directives that add up to a mélange of data impossible to decipher - without another report to decipher the first report.

Or, more probably, sit on a corner pile orphaned and neglected.

So why do you go along with it? Theoretically you're paid

for your skills and expertise in, at the very least, *this* small matter? Why did you spend yesterday and today mindlessly filling in a spreadsheet that you know reflects no reality - just because someone or two or three managers gave you a half-formed thought that included a binder filled with pretty, multi-colored pages filled with numbers and words?

The Chinese or somebody have a proverb about the weak grass and the mighty oak: one bends with the wind, one breaks. So The Cube understands why you bend. You are grown from seeds planted by a reward system that favors compliance and activity.

Question to Adam Smith: Does capitalism ever mow the lawn?

Saturday, June 25

5S: Go Team!

Pierre Dolet, our erstwhile correspondent from a company going "5S," writes again...

So I walk in to work and suddenly the Company has what looks like a softball team walking around the halls and factory floor-

Everybody in the core group that has been studying/ implementing the 5S program - "The 5S Team" - is wearing matching polo shirts and baseball caps. In baby blue.

And they have a cheerleader.

A real, honest-to-goodness cheerleader - roaring with every "success" they have (they haven't told us what they're supposed to be doing, so I can only guess it's a success). They stand in a big room together and chant & clap the 5Ss in unison: "Sort - CLAP! - Set - CLAP! - Shine - CLAP! - YEAH!!!

(I know, only three Ss. I guess that's how far along they've gotten to date.)

The Cube responds...

It's sort of cute, isn't it?, watching them all dress up like Little Leaguers - because, let's be honest, not everyone should be wearing a cap. Ever. The Look of Authority loses some of its power to Impress when the Accounting Manager's ears are sticking out in that dorky kid fashion some people outgrew - and some didn't.

Look for the Fashionable Woman Exec in her high heeled pumps, biz dress and 5S Team uniform: that will be one outfielder unhappy with her position.

But, y'know Pierre Dolet, in 5S it's important for everybody to "buy in." And what better way to prove your purchase than to wear the receipt?

Sunday, June 26

Two Days Late & I Know Better

Phenomenon noticed of late:

The semi-important person who waits until a day or two after the deadline for feedback - when lots of time and effort have now been expended on the "finalized" version - and now has important information on What Is Wrong.

Monday, June 27

Survival Mantra: If There's A Deadline...

If There's A Deadline -
It *Will* Break Down.

☞

Tuesday, June 28

Survival Mantra: Your Best Friend Is...

Your Best Friend Is -

The Night Cleaning Lady
Who knows where every supply is.

Wednesday, June 29

Survival Mantra: After 4 PM...

After 4 PM -

No One else cares if you have a Deadline.

Thursday, June 30

Survival Mantra: After 6 PM...

After 6PM -

The food in the refrigerator is *yours*. Take it.
It would probably have been thrown out anyway.

July

Friday, July 01

Oh That Archangel Understood

What is it - Why - does this meeting, this training session, reek with such self-righteousness? They know better. And, I have to admit, They may even be - right. It's just that, it's just that ...

> *Oh that Archangel understood*
> *Why God's right*
> *Required rebellion.*

Very bad attitude. Why? I don't know.

From my side or theirs? I don't know.

Meeting: THE ATTENTION

Excellent meeting yesterday. I'm sure we scared the hell out of the Chinese.

Wanting to do business on The Mainland - aka outsource our manufacturing operations - we are desperate to find a partner in the Land Of The Red to pony up the cash that will allow our rinky dink operation to gear up to full speed and sell in massive quantities the sort of cheapjack rip-offs of our own products that we accuse others of doing in violation of the trade laws, our patents, and good ol' American patriotism.

So far, we have hired three Chinese-speaking consultants who talk among themselves and tell whoever is listening either: (a) whatever the listener wants to hear, or (b) how "This is difficult, y'know, I need this company's *commitment* (aka more $$$ for me) if you want results." So, far, many many trips.

Oh, and the consultants have convinced the execs that the Chinese-speaking employees already on staff should be let go as "negative influences." I supposed their *feng shui* aura was bad. (Or they understood what the consultants were *really* saying on the phone and... Nope: must have been the *feng shui.*)

But, even phony rainmakers' gobbledygook gesticulations even-tually coincide with precipitation, and so it is now with our con-sultants and some real "Chinese business-men." I can't give short shrift to the Chinese bizmen: they're real. 'Even have a website in English and a lotta lotta presence in the U.S. stock market. I think they could eat us for breakfast without too much heartburn.

So, yesterday, we brought them to our facilities. We have 700 employees, so it ain't a shabby sight - especially not with the brand new coat of paint slapped on last fall. And we make pretty decent product. Great product, actually.

But we've got "Date sweat." *Maybe* a little over-anxious. *Maybe* a little worried that the exec bonuses paid out the past three years have been based more on phantoms than fact. *Maybe* we really really need this deal... Soon.

Or maybe the Creator has a great sense of visual humor.

It was great fun watching the little Chinese bizman step out of the block-long black limo we sent for him. It was a bit frightening (from a medical perspective) looking at our five overweight sausages stuff themselves into tight suits and ties, their faces turning red, looking just like they probably did on Junior Prom night.

Most beautifully bizarre, though, was the four-hour mar-athon meeting, where the Chinese businessman had to be scared out of his wits.

We could watch it all, like on a huge wide-screen TV. They

all sat in a large conference room, glass wall open to the White Collar Floor. (Yes, we were all dressed up, too.)

Hands were shaken with increasing fervor on our side. Presentations were thrown up on the wall, each succeeding speaker trying to top the one before in enthusiasm. Eyes began to bulge from the efforts to illuminate the businessman in the wonders of our company. From what little I know of Chinese mythology, I believe the businessman realized fairly early that he was dealing with earth-bound Demons.

Most unsettling of all, however, must have been The Attention.

The Attention. For the entire afternoon, every one of our five execs sat forward in their chairs, eyes virtually glued on the Chinese businessman, their breaths in sync with his, the Prez literally leaning-in to drink in every word the man uttered: sincere, oh so sincere in his attention to the man's needs, desires, thoughts, breaths - heartbeat.

Oh, and they forgot to ask for the food to be brought in. The poor man was probably starved and thirsty by the end of this marathon, but we - like Greek gods punishing Tantalus - kept an array of delicious foods, prepared by an excellent deli, sitting in a closet ... waiting ... just out of reach.

It was, they reported later, "a good meeting."

⌘

Saturday, July 02

Maybe Management Will Understand

A follow-up to yesterday's "rebellion" ...

Maybe Management will understand that How you convey directives is as important
as What is inside the words?

Is it necessary to provoke unnecessary resistance?

Do even they see it ... ?

Sunday, July 03

Do They Know What They Said?

The Cube is obsessed with the "rebellion" string of the past two days ...

It hit me, after yesterday's thoughts, that maybe Management actually has no idea What is inside its words.

Monday, July 04

Independence Day or Rebellion - Depends on your POV

Polishing off this "rebellion" string ...

Well, of course stupid me, I know why now The Cube's been obsessed with "rebellion": it's the 4th of July weekend.

Small historical side note: In America, it's a celebration of the "American Revolution" - in England it's dissed as the "American Rebellion." It all depends on where you're looking from.

The Cube sits in an odd position: somewhere between the ordered and the order-givers, i.e., frequently, Responsibility without Authority.

To get things done, The Cube must generally use persuasion and logic to effect cooperation. This makes The Cube very aware of when there is no logic behind an order that The Cube must get others to implement.

Sometimes humor is used as a persuasive tool, too - especially when the logic is thin but the "get it done" imperative is mighty - but The Cube has noticed that some Management distrusts humor as subversive.

(NOTE to self: Remember - don't use big words in memos - stay away from dictionary. Rely on the word "impact" and let it go at that.)

So... now we go back to our original "rebellion" of three days ago, when Management so blithely spent two hours of our lives in a mandatory-attendance "Team-Building Seminar" where we learned a dozen new "Success Goal Stepping Stones." So far so good ... The Cube likes to learn. Really. No sarcasm intended.

And there was nothing actually wrong or onerous about the Stepping Stones - beyond a terribly trying trend toward tongue-twisting alliteration. The Cube, for one, believes that we should "Cooperate - Innovate - Initiate."

The problem is: these are Slogans Without Substance.

We spent two hours repeating the slogans, with no time given to exploring the implications of such change from "vertical hierarchy to lateral teamwork." Nowhere did the program indicate that Management would give up its hierarchical, top-to-down directives in deference to a "Team-generated initiative." These were words repeated without meaning - by both Management and Staff. Yes, we repeated and repeated, chanted and clapped our hands, rah-rah-RAH, TEAM! What does it mean?

Since today is the 4th of July, we'll play political analogy and reference this to the Pledge of Allegiance (choose your own version, with or without "under God") ...

The Pledge is a curious phenomenon. We all learn it in grade school, recite it a million times - and then understand the Pledge so little that most of us can hardly say it without either: (a) 2 or 3 other people saying it with us, or (b) repeating it fast and rhythmic so that the words come out automatically, on their own.

But what does the Pledge mean? And why do we say it?

Oddly enough, it can be read as a pretty scary statement. If The Cube were a Southerner or a Conservative or a Libertarian or any combination of the three (and The Cube has tendencies towards all three at times), then the Pledge certainly sounds very "Soviet" in its collectivization and definitely anti-States Rights. As a Religious - leaning person, The Cube might feel uncomfortable pledging allegiance to "the Flag ... and to the Republic for which it stands" instead of to the principles of the Republic. And where is the word "democracy" in that there Pledge? Finally, as a Democracy, it's uncomfortable that we are the only Democracy that sort of forces our people to pledge to a Flag. The Sons of Liberty, throwing tea overboard in Boston Harbor because it was the symbol of taxation and faceless government, might have a problem with this Pledge.

But, in the end, The Cube just doesn't think that much about it, puts hand over heart, and says the words in rote repetition like everybody else. I dunno, though: is that what we're *supposed* to do?

Same question goes for business and our chanted Stepping Stones: rote repetition without meaning - is that what we're supposed to do?

Tuesday, July 05

Ring Around The Rosie

Yes, The Cube *knows* what the old nursery rhyme means:

> Ring around the rosie
> A pocket full of posies
> Ashes, ashes
> We all fall *down!*

It's about the Black Death and other horrible things from the Middle Ages.

Now it's back - the horrible things - and it's a-ringing around.

The Cube refers, of course, to the Memo Denial Circle.

Jayzus H. Kuh-righst!, can't people pay attention to what they're saying the *first* time they say it?!?

No, of course not, that would mean that they are thinking things out instead of speaking from their ass.

Ah, but if it would only end *there* ...

First, the Asinine Memo.

It is key to the Asinine Memo that a Self-Important Person, or SIP, send it to a Less Important Person (LIP).

But, sometimes, the memo goes astray. Maybe the SIP mistakenly CC'd a VIP in addition to the LIP. Or the LIP did a FWD to a VIP as an FYI.
So the VIP memos the SIP asking "What is THIS?" To which the SIP replies to the VIP, "I didn't say that" - but forgets that the LIP was CC'd and, to PYA, the LIP FYIs the VIP a CC of the Asinine Memo. But the VIP, who wasn't paying much attention to the first CC, has already CC'd another VIP, usually the SIP's VIP, with   an FYI and a "What do you mean the SIP says you said?" So the 2nd VIP responds to the 1st VIP, while the SIP sends the   LIP a clarification, which is really a denial, and the denial gets into the Asinine Memo Stream and now everyone is part of the big ASS-E-9 Memo Circle of Denial that goes round and round...

And round and

round.

Wednesday, July 06

Says It All #2

Bullets.

●

●

●

●

●

Thursday, July 07

5S and Streamlining

It's been a while since one of our correspondents told of us of his company and it's adventures with "The 5S system for Workplace Organization." Here is his latest.

Pierre Dolet asks –

Streamlining: explain the appeal in working hard to obsolete your own jobs.

The Cube answers –

Everyone is sure "It won't be me."

Friday, July 08

Transaction

And so she leaned upon the door
Looking
Longing
Needing more.
"Tell me, Purchase Order Man:
Can this be bought?"

"The BOM-" he began.

"The BOM be damned!"

Within his cell
The said Man's smile
Glowed.
To her:
"Wait awhile."

"But now, the BOO," she whispered,
"-Now."

"BOM – BOO – Yes, do!" he gloated,
"Do! ...
Make – your – order."

"Do? And–?"

"And wait awhile –
Or –
Do you expect my attention in this hell?"

She sighed within the door frame,
"Yes,"
And stepped within his cell.

"Oh," he answered, "What is this?"
His hand held up the yellow form.
"Your P.O.'s next."

"Come closer, Next."

The walls closed in on her.

Saturday, July 09

The Never-Read Memo

The Never-Read Memo takes it's place in business an-
nals as *The* most popular of literary forms. It is important
to write a memo, necessary to receive a memo – but certainly, most assuredly, redoubtably crucial to enterprise
and the survival of the free market system to never, ever,
neverwhatsoever do you read the damned things.

This makes communications oh so much easier.

Sunday, July 10

You're Right

You've gotta be right!
Even when you're wrong
You're right!
It doesn't matter
If you should have done it right:
Now it's so screwed up, don't admit a mistake
You're right!

You've gotta be right!
Don't face the music, you're right:
Just
Deny the fact
And
Shift the blame
To every other thing in sight
'Cause everyone knows

Everyone knows
You're right -

Yes, you've gotta be right.

Damn, you've gotta be right.

Well, there's no argument here
'Cause everyone knows ---
You're right!

Monday, July 11

Self-Righteous Indignantly Wrong

Al Mann, reading yesterday's Note, adds:

He's a self-righteous indignantly-wrong man
Trying to make a living off of what others can -
When there is an excuse
Then he is your man
He's self-righteously indignantly wrong.

Went into the review unprepared, yes
Tried to finesse it past the others there
Understood that they don't
Ever really care
Passed the buck and let the blame be shared.

66

He's a self-righteous indignantly-wrong man
Waiting for the shit to hit the fan.
When it finally splatters
He's hiding safely and
He's a self-righteous indignantly wrong man.

Tuesday, July 12

When You're Gone #1: Sick

When you're not at work unexpectedly - sick - it can usually be counted on that:

a) You missed the important meeting that was circled twice on your calendar;

b) You have been needed *at least* twice by higher-ups who don't notice you any other day;

c) You did not get any of the free food doled out after the Executive Lunch was cancelled (sometimes related to b), above);

d) You get emails expressing sympathy from coworkers that it's "too bad you're 'sick' today (heh, heh)";

e) You receive phone calls from work asking "Can you just take care of *this?*" that always come during those few moments of relief when you are not wishing you were dead and are vulnerable to guilt feelings (Note: timing is often coupled with shame that you are enjoying the TV soap operas) - you foolishly agree and work harder from your sickbed than if you'd been at the office;

f) You didn't miss anything at work, despite all of the above; and

g) You go back to work a day too early to show that you are "responsible" - thereby either:

***   spreading your disease amongst co-workers, or *if you cover up your misery with good cheer,*

***   confirming to coworkers that you really were "sick" yesterday.

Wednesday, July 13

When You're Gone #2: Vacation

It can be safely assumed that, if you plan a vacation, every report, quarterly meeting, project deadline and company party - *anything* that affects you - will be scheduled during that time.

Consequently, when planning vacations of a week or more, you have only a few options:

1) Hope that your company is one of those that never plans in advance, so you don't *know* about everything due.

2) Hope that your supervisor(s) are the kind who don't look at their calendars and notice what you have due.

3) Pretend that you didn't know that anything was due.

4) Kill yourself getting everything ready before you go on vacation, thereby assuring that everything presented under your name will be premature, outdated by the time it is presented, unpolished, and easily attacked in your absence. You will also be volunteered for several new tasks because of by your combined attributes of Responsibility and Non-Presence.

Thursday, July 14

When You're Gone #3: Never Coming Back

If you quit your job, you will be missed.

If you are laid off as part of a downsizing or shifting political winds, you will be missed, but no one will admit it out loud.

If you are fired, even if deserved, you will be missed - sometimes with relief.

Once you are gone, no matter how important you were to the workings of the company, things will go on.

Friday, July 15

When You're Gone #4: STOP! - Don't Leave

A Friday Inspirational Message from The Cube -

DISCLAIMER: The following Note is not intended for incompetents, asses or others who make life generally miserable for their coworkers. It is furthermore recognized by The Cube that these people do not know who they are. Such is the tragedy of life - I know no solution...

Well, the last few blurbles have been about your absence from work. Here's a twist: Don't Go.

Now - and this has been observed - there are people (we won't say whom) that the Company would like to leave on their own. Let's be generous and just say "for a variety of reasons."

69

Leave but not be fired or laid off - "for a variety of reasons" (usually dealing with "excessive" integrity or competency, shifting office politics, or potential whistleblowing - i.e., the designated leavee is usually right and to zap him/her/them would leave the Company open to some expen$ive liabilities, settlement issues, 401k co-pays, unemployment, potential lawsuits and maybe an OSHA inspection or two.)

Anyway, the Company is making this person's life at work a living hell - or at least a Sisyphean nightmare. What to do, what to do?

Obviously, the intelligent thing is to "move on": find another job, a better job somewhere where you are appreciated and not under so much unwarranted pressure and stress.

Less obviously, try sticking around.

But relax and ENJOY it!

Look at 'em, trying, hoping, pushing for you to leave - and you're still there, doing your best, which is a sore stone in their shoes.

Hang in there, buddy! Stay the course, gal! Your existence in their lives is the best revenge *and* it's cheaper than a lawsuit.

Friday Inspiration from The Cube...

Saturday, July 16

Easy Shot #1

Intestinal Fortitude: Eating from the roach coach.

(Note to Myself: This subject deserves more attention, as it touches upon sado-masochistic subliminal desires within so many of us.)

Sunday, July 17

Easy Shot #2

Intestinal Fortitude: Taking the "healthy" selection from the lunchroom junk food machine.

(Second Note to Myself: Needs no further explanation or follow-up - we are all self-delusional when Hunger meets Guilt at 3:30 PM.)

Monday, July 18

Monday Morning Reflection: The Saturday-Sunday 12-Day Week

Once again The Cube has gotten suckered by a failure to add up the numbers.

This is not an Accounting failure - heck, does anyone care if the Company loses another $100K due to a misplaced decimal point or juxtaposition of 6 and 9? (Well, anyone beyond federal auditors, stockholders and, perhaps, the Controller up on Floor 23 ripping his eyes out in disbelief.)

No, this is the kind of addition failure that hits where it hurts - me. I agreed to work over the weekend. Again.

Let's put this in perspective. The Cube likes the work. The Cube's ego loves the attention that goes with "Only you can do it." And, back when The Cube was hourly, the concept of OverTime tripping gaily into DoubleTime was an absolute ecstasy!

And, to be candid, The Cube's social life ain't so hotcha these past few months, so we're not talking loss of Quality Time here. The Cube, too, can rent a DVD online and over the mail: there's no need to sit in a cinema, alone, among squalling babes and make-out middlebrows to watch... well, *anything.*

But today - this Monday morning - after two fulfilling days of productive enterprise witnessed by only myself and the cockroach in the corner, The Cube is driving to work realizing that "I didn't work an extra two days - I'm working 12 days straight!" It's Monday morning and I wanna go home. I wanna take a day off. I wanna see *daylight.*

I wanna knock myself in the head with a ballpeen hammer and remind myself for the twenty-fourth time: Live a Life!

The Cube is even growing nostalgic for the sound of cellphones ringing in a darkened theater.

Tuesday, July 19

Easy Shot #3

Status: The middle-aged middle-management Mustang driver. Polished. BRIGHT red.

Convertible, of course.

Wednesday, July 20

No One's To Blame

Yesterday a meeting was set-up, yes:
There was no agreement but "We'll make it work."
Now out-of-sight the principals are where? - Guess:
They're all somewhere but anywhere but here.

And the meetings, they go round-and-round
And the heads go nodding up-and-down
It's easier to pass the buck: "Next time."
We can't escape, we can only shake
Our heads: We're fooled again -
And go round-and-out-and-down
No one's to blame.

Thursday, July 21

What's The Outlook?

What's the Outlook?
Lotus Notes:

Our Project
From Excel
Blessed be the Oracle
The message of PowerPoint
The power of Access
In Linux as it will be networked
And lead us not into Word tables
But deliver us from DOS keystroke commands

For this is the paperless, the powerful, the Office
Today.

Friday, July 22

Adverse

Adverse

(No, not Ad-Verse: The Cube has nothing to do with commercial jingles - yet. This is a career world where training in 10-key data entry can lead to.... Oz?)

Adverse

We had a group-think meeting yesterday. It was explained to us that Conditions were "adverse to the health of the Company." This we knew, since anyone with eyes (sighted or un-) could see that the Company lost $$$ the last quarter. I understate: the Company lost $$$$$$$$$ last quarter.

In fact, that was the topic of our group-think: to develop contingencies that we ourselves could implement to stop the hemorrhaging. ("We-O" being the middle-management who live in closed-door confines, on down the food chain to the cubicle dwellers of the open range.) First, though, we needed some Facts to work with, and we asked-in the Top Dogs to fill us in on the Facts.

Facts. Much like Conditions , Facts are apparently "adverse to the health of ---" Who?

Hmm.

Hmmmmm.

Never quite heard a Fact uttered: heard about "adverse Conditions," saw a Chart with a beautiful (Beautiful!) matrix-type Chart indicating the "adverse pattern of interlinked Factors (unspecified, tho' several were red), learned how our "efforts are appreciated"...

In sum: Nada. Nothing.

Well, in fact, not totally nada Nada -

Somewhere in the subtext - and remember: subtext is never   spoken out loud - we nascent problem-solvers understood that "Conditions" was a code-word for "Decisions," as in "Decisions were made adverse to the health of the Company."

And Who made the adverse Decisions?

Remember: Subtext is never spoken out loud.

I saw Mommy kissing Santa Claus
Underneath the mistletoe last night
....
Oh what a joy it would have been
If only Daddy'd been there to see
Mommy kissing Santa Claus
Last Night

© 1952 J. T. Connor

Saturday, July 23

Bureaucracy 1-2-3

1 is an Entrepreneur.

2 is a Team.

3 is a Bureaucracy.

(The Cube would like to hear from others how and why a bureaucracy is.)

Bureaucracy: It Is Written, So It Is

[The "Bureaucracy" correspondence begins on July 23rd. Begin there for context.]

Pierre Dolet writes:

We have, mais oui, the bureaucracy of my cousins in France:

It Is Written, So It Is.

Henri, my cousin, and his dear wife, Henriette, need to update their travel documents – they are French citizens resident in America. This is a regular occurrence (fortunately, not a frequent regular occurrence) and it necessitates the submission of new lifedata change information (if any), new fee payments (always and ever-growing) and new photographs (a sometime traumatic experience, especially for Henriette – Henri, fortunately. having achieved the visage of aged wisdom at the tender year of 24 and remained ever constant ever since).

Eh bien, they present themselves at the consulate, they complete the forms, they provide the pictures – and, several days later, they receive the documents.

Ah, the documents ...

But – before we look at the documents, we should look at the consulate. This is not a busy consulate. There are no long lines, no masses of émigrés pushing at the doors for their life-saving visas. No real– (well, for lack of a better word) No real work to do. Except for these small, routine and infrequent tasks.

Simple tasks.

... documents the, Ah

Beautifully bound little Papers Official, these documents, a tribute to the standards of the professional diplomatic class manning French consulates worldwide.

Which is why, of course, Henri's photograph is in Henriette's documents – and vice-versa.

There has been, equally of course, an attempt to return the documents with the opening phrase "I am afraid that there has been a mistake" – but, that is not a phrase that can be heard, because it immediately encounters an upraised hand and the Phrase Official: "Procedure has been followed, there have been no mistakes."

Missing from the Phrase Official was the Act Logical: to look at the documents.

This cannot be allowed.
This cannot be allowed.

For to allow this would be to admit that, throughout the seventeen-hundred-and-forty-five Officially Decreed Steps for processing this document, no one thought to look at what he or she was doing and to make note (let alone correct) the photographic mismatch. Henri/Henriette – so obviously clear that Henriette has a beard and moustache, that Henri has a feminine side expressive in his rouged and lipsticked visage.

The Steps Official have been followed, the document issued: It Is Written, So It Is.

Vive La France!

*The Cube respo*nds:

Do not be so harsh on your French brethren – The Cube was once listed as a "Malamute mix" in the local town census – a mistake repeated ad infinitum by direct mailers for ten years. Small town bureaucracy teamed with mass advertising business smarts: we American can

match and surpass anything the French nation can con-
jure. As a side note: The Malamute mix was quite incensed
that I had stolen her identity.

Monday, July 25

What Didn't They Know & When Didn't They Know It

One of the biggest lessons we in the cubicles experience
early in the days of inhabiting our flexiwall spaces is that
thems above us don't know what's happening.

Oh, this isn't a general indictment of management. In
fact, it's not an accusation against middle management
at all: I see too too clearly that my immediate supervisor
knows what is going on in our area. And, by the way,
"What's going on" isn't necessarily a whistleblower alarm,
either.

It is, literally, What – Is – Going – On.

Things happen in a company.

Usually because we do them.

Without activity, there is no business.

But you'd think sometimes that the executive team
doesn't quite realize this.

We are, for example, building a serializer. This involves
Engineering. This involves several engineers. And equipment. And money to pay for the engineers and equipment. This serializer – and, for the record, The Cube has
no idea what a serializer is/does/looks like (sounds cool,
though, yes?) – this wonder of modern technology will
be installed on the production floor, where the Operations group will inherit Engineering's brainchild and ex-

ploit the living daylight out of its muscular qualities and boundless youthful energy. Ta-Da!

So it was with a sensation of disconnect that I came across a memo left lying on a copier (left-behind memos are a great source of company news), a correspondence to the effect that Operations had just paid out $XX,XXX for a serializer...?

"Perhaps Operations is paying for the Engineering project?" mused I – but since I knew that the Engineering serializer added up to $YY,YYY, the X and Y of this knowledge did not add up to a coherent Z.

Being a nosy Cube, I "returned" the forgotten memo to the VP of Operations, casually mentioning the Engineering serializer almost-completed.

"Really?" said VP/Ops. "Who's that for?"

Emmm.

I believe we can all see where this is going.

Despite the fact that every Friday middle management reports to its Veeps – and every Monday the Veeps share donuts with the Prez – somehow, someway VP/Eng and VP/Ops – sitting a looooong five feet apart at the executive conference table – were unable to communicate their knowledge of what their individual departments were doing. Or perhaps the VP/$$$ might have notice the parallel expenditures and brought it up???

Or maybe they had no knowledge of what their Depts were doing: The Cube isn't at those Exec Status Meetings, nor inside the Veep thought waves.

What didn't they know and when didn't they know it ...

Tuesday, July 26

Bureaucracy: Cross-Cultural Administration

[The "Bureaucracy" correspondence begins on July 23rd. Begin there for context and continue on.]

Abdullah O'Rourke writes:

As the son of an expatriate Irishman married into a Saudi family of Bedouins years before things turned fundamental in our Kingdom, I grew up learning of the bureaucratic perils of:

Cross-Cultural Administration.

Insh'Allah, you have to know that we in the Empty Quarter were once a nomadic people, bound only by the wind, the sun and the shifting desert sands. And then the black pearl of Oil was discovered and the Americans came with their wildcatting ways – and then the British with their colonial ways – and then the Sa'udis with their family ways. (For, don't you know, we are Saudi Arabians now, but we are not all *Sa'ud* – a difference.)

There was room, in the beginning, for all three. The Americans built their little enclaves of Southern California suburbia and laid-back administration. The British set up their hidden stills and class-based middle management. And, as long as the income rolled in, the Sa'udi family was content to build their capital in Riyadh, separate from the worker bees and, since their power was based on royalties, becoming ever-more royal themselves.

As for the Yanks and Brits: sure they despised and contradicted one another, but there was so much moolah to mulch that they squashed it between their expat toes like jellyfish on the beach and just spent more moolah to cover up the inconsistencies in everything from bookkeeping to equipment quality standards.

Oi, but the greed of some a the Oil Giants stepped onto the Kingdom's black pitch shores and threw it all off-kilter. When the infamous Oil Embargo of the 1970s occurred, the Oil Giants took a gander at the Sa'udi indignation over Israel's once-again-we've-beaten-your-pants-off performance against her neighbors in the Yom Kippur War (never mind that the Sa'udis weren't too friendly with those neighbors either) and the Oil Giants converted the Embargo into a giant Cash Cow.

At that point, King Faisal noticed that his indignation still only owned a pitiful percentage of that Cash Cow and started buying back some of the "Arab" oil producing company from the Americans and British. The goal was to reach the 51% mark, which happened sometime in the mid-1980s. By that time, though, Faisal was assassinated by a disco-loving nephew and the other Sa'udi family members failed to catch on to where the real royalties were buried: not under the desert sands, but in the offshore refineries that the Oil Giants still possessed – elsewhere.

But that's a different story. What happened as part of this history is that the Kingdom realized that it did not know how to run its own business: everything was handled by Brits and Yanks – or "Other Arab" expats trained in Brit/Yank yank-both-ways-at-once ways.

So it came to pass that, as the Kingdom gradually came to own its own resources, someone – we'll call him the "Prince" since there were 70-odd Sa'udi princes to choose from – the Prince proposed that "Why don't we show the

Americans and the British, arrogant bastards that they are, that we can use traditional Middle Eastern administrative techniques to run our chief national resource, the Petroleum Industry."

Huzzah!, went the cry around the campfires. (Well, truly, it was more of a Laa, Insh'Allah, pass the hummus around the air-conditioned banquet tables of the Riyadh Palace, but ...) *We shall build our bureaucracy on our native standards!*

Not to put it too delicately, but our native standards were Bedouin and, love my grandfather's tribe as I do, organization is not our focus in life. Ask a man for charity – it's yours. As a woman with your dying wish to raise your children – she's their mother. Fly a falcon, cross the unmapped desert, drive a hard bargain in the souk – come to visit Bedu-land.

Sit at a desk and push a pencil –

I, personally, leave it to my Paki houseboy. He is educated, he is polite, he has patience. He is, in short, not a Bedouin.

Which is not to say that the Kingdom lacked for Middle Eastern administrative role models. The Ottoman Empire had ruled over us all for half a millennium – but that memory was too recent, many of our grandfathers having still the scars from Turkish boots along their spines. Besides, when Ottoman administration had really worked, it was the result of their policy of putting foreign administrators over us: mainly Mediterranean Jews and Balkan Christians. So, while Israel's economy was the success story of the Middle East, there were few followers of the Koran looking towards Jerusalem for role models.

"Egypt!" the Prince decided. "Egypt was the Cradle of Civilization – the oldest continuous government – the oldest continuous government administration – indeed, Egyptians have administered their country continuously from the time of the Pharaohs, through the Greeks, Romans, Arabian, Ottoman, British and now, again, Egyptian rule."

Egypt. Our role model.

And so, in the emerging affirmative action program of let Saudi Be Saudi, the Kingdom imported Egyptian consultants and their administrative models and their business standards, and we became...

A twelve thousand year old bureaucracy.

Yes, the one fly in the ointment, donkey in the stable, fox in the henhouse and other abominable clichés of glitch that, Insh'Allah, it became our fate to experience was the sad old cliché that: Just Because It's Always Been Done That Way Doesn't Make It Good.

Egyptian administrative techniques had been founded twelve centuries ago – outliving even their ancient Chinese contemporaries. But, if you look at history, you'll see that once Egypt developed its Pharaonic (rhymes with "ironic") administrative bureaucracy, it stagnated at that same place for ten millennia until the Alexander the Great brought in Hellenic energy and innovation – until Egyptian bureaucracy infiltrated their ways and dragged them down to a standstill until the next conquerors, the Romans, roamed in. And then the Arabian jihad and ...

And we invited them in.

Sp, please, come and visit: In this corner, you' find an

American "manager" who knows his techno-duties and doesn't understand people. In that corner a British ex-sergeant major runs "his" sand niggers about as he sees fit – no matter what anybody else needs, asks for or expects. And, in every office, you will find a taste of old (Old, OLD) Civilization administration, slowly clogging our arteries with the Bureaucracy of the Ages.

The Cube responds:

Abdullah, your "note" is practically a book, but The Cube is familiar with the practice of cross-cultural bureaucracy: at a recent multinational corporate gig, in Atlanta of all places, an American consultant was advising Dutch corporate management on how to implement a Japanese manufacturing system – at our cross-border plant in Mexico. I truly think the African influence is under-represented.

Wednesday, July 27

An Appreciation of Executive Ignorance

What didn't they know
and when didn't they know it ...

There are, lately, some high profile criminal cases going on where the top execs of certain scurrilous companies plead ignorance to the illegal activities of their underlings and same-level colleagues.

Much as The Cube, whose early-career pension plan went down the tubes in one such scam, would love to see those Top E's taken down, it has to be admitted that they may have a point -

- as The Cube must confirm, having stepped into this situation a few too many times when the company's left hand doesn't know what the company's right hand is doing. We see it on the floor every -

What didn't they know and when didn't they know it ...

They may have a point.

What didn't they know...

And, of course, who can tell when executive incompetence is used to mask willful ignorance? It is not a crime to be a fool. "Fool" is a harsh word, but it is what so many of these bright and brilliant Captains of Industry now claim. And one of them, so far, has gotten off on that defense.

Billions made and a Fool.

This Note, then, is *truly* an appreciation of executive ignorance.

Thursday, July 28

The Good Employee

Her eyes say it all:
something is wrong.
The papers in her hand insist:
something is wrong.
But she is only a clerical -
- and this is Big.
Big.
Beyond her department.
Big.
Beyond her reach.
Big.
It will embarrass or anger
BIG PEOPLE.
And she is only a clerical.
But the papers in her hand insist:
something is wrong.
What if they are mad,
BIG PEOPLE, mad
At her?
She is only a clerical.
It is not her responsibility.
She has been told that often:
"It is not your responsibility,
Not your department,
Not your business
Or pay scale
To think
About."
She binds the papers in her hand
As told
Into a large anonymous file folder
As told

She has done her job
As told
And the day is over,
She goes home.
Overtime has not been authorized,
The deadline for filing was already set.
No time, really,
To bring this up.
No time:
Overtime has not been authorized.
The file was put in its place
On time
Goals met.
She is a Good Employee.

yet ...

Friday, July 29

Acronyms: M

MIT - Most Important Task

MOW - Movie Of the Week

MOS - Mit Out Sound

MOO

Saturday, July 30

Bureaucracy: Communist-Style

[The "Bureaucracy" correspondence begins on July 23rd. Begin there for context and continue on.]

Bartek Wolodyjowski writes:

In my native Poland, before freedom, democracy and Pizza Hut replaced the communist regime, we had our own brand of bureaucracy, embodied in the "Biurwa" (byourvah).

Biuro – an office or administrative section
+
Kurwa – a whore or prostitute
=
Biurwa – Cholera!, she really made your day.

The Biurwa, sadly, alas, and tragically, was not the office slut. She was, instead, the System's Bitch: screwed daily by a System that had neither logic, reason nor goodwill behind it, she nevertheless was its love slave.

Do you need a permit? The Biurwa is the one who will stand in your way. Not because she is personally or politically oppressive or antagonistic towards you, but because "Those are the rules, panie, the rules."

Maybe you need to know what "the rules" are, since so many in the West think that godless, oppressive communism "ruled" every aspect of our lives. I am not to speak for the Soviet Union, but in Poland this was not so.

We were fairly lazy communists, oppressive to no one unless you were a Jew in '68 through '72 or a thinking intellectual or sometimes one in the same. God forbid if you were actually a practicing big-C Communist. Those people pointed out things like corruption and vestigial class divisions and started things like the Solidarity trade union movement and demanded equality of Worker and Red Bourgeoisie pay! (We didn't have a "Religion" problem, since almost everyone in the country was a Roman Catholic, even the Party chiefs, and the Soviets be damned about that.)

But communism was our "System" (officially "socialism," but we all knew we weren't Swedes) and our System had a rule for everything. You see, in a communist system, ideally, every problem has a solution and we need only make a rule to address that problem/solution.

Now, along the way, sometimes it was "diplomatic" to prefer certain solutions over others. One of the key diplomatic initiatives in the early days of post-World War II "liberation" by the Red Army was to avoid being purged for accidentally-made pro-bourgeois/anti-socialist administrative decisions.

In a brilliant series of maneuvers by committees of anonymous geniuses, we developed The Rule That Makes No Sense But Looks Good On Paper policy. This was coupled with the Do What You Need To Do But Write Up What They Want To Read unwritten rule-of-thumb.

These two guiding principles built us up from the rubble of War and persuaded the Soviets that they could largely leave us alone, confining their "protective" forces to a few self-contained bases – looking West.

A good programme, yes – but they had forgotten to calculate the Biurwa into the equation.

The Biurwa – ah, she of little influence and infinite pedestrian power.

The Biurwa, unthinking whore to the System.

She was not a True Believer in communism. She could never understand an inkling of Marx's philosophy and certainly did not think of herself as a "worker of the world, unite(d)." "Worker?" – Pah! That would spoil her fingernails and muss her makeup.

But she had a charismatic faith in her rules and regulations and papers.

Those rules. Those regulations. Those papers. True Bureaucracy. Unthinking, dronelike, without recourse to common sense. True Bureaucracy.

Do you want to know what killed communism? Forget popes and presidents and premiers and politics.

It was the Biurwa.

Marx could call it any name:
Kapital, Communist, all the same.
Bureaucracy, it rules the game.

The Cube responds:

Ummmmm.......... Sounds like ISO, 5S, Lean Manufacturing and Six Sigma gone awry. But we're not communists, are we?

Sunday, July 31

Acronyms: A

ASAP – As Soon As Possible

ANSI – American National Standards Institute

AMA – American Medical Association

ASS

August

Somebody To Blame

An Ode to the new Exec Management on
It's 2nd Quarter Negative Profits

Your plans, your chart projections
They reached so high, it seemed.
But some people said "That's not right"
You fired the ones who said that:
"We need a positive team."

Now your lies, I say your lies
They look so fine.
But as the numbers come in
They're nowhere near what you said:
It really is a crime.

Don't you want somebody
To blame
Don't you need somebody
To blame
Wouldn't you love somebody
To blame
You'd better find somebody
To blame

Sales are falling
Falling right through the floor
And though you always know what is "best"
It seems you don't know what we do yet
You really should be shown the door.
Don't you want somebody
To blame

Don't you need somebody
To blame
Wouldn't you love somebody
To blame
You'd better find somebody
To blame

And now, well yes, just now
You've found a goat.
You've brought in a third party
A highly paid consultant
Now it isn't your fault.

Don't you want somebody
To blame
Don't you need somebody
To blame
Wouldn't you love somebody
To blame
You'd better find somebody
To blame

Blame is falling
Falling all around the shop
You've laid off all the 3rd shift
Now working on the second
God knows when you're going to stop.

Now you've found somebody
To blame
More than one somebody
To blame
Anybody but your body
To blame
And you're glad there's someone
To blame.

Tuesday, August 02

Acronyms: F

FYI - For Your Information

FEMA - Federal Emergency Management Agency

FICA - Federal Insurance Contributions Act

FUBAR - F***ed Up Beyond All Repair

Wednesday, August 03

Easy Shot #4: Cynicism

Cynicism is an easy out. The "knowing" shrug, raised eyebrow, cocked head. And, of course, the sarcastic joke - sometimes even funny.

How do you get past cynicism?

Like to think that the joke masks a "We'll do it, no matter what" sentiment.

Hope it does.

It's easy to slide into attitude as an excuse.

Thursday, August 04

The Knowledge/Action Disconnect

Just one of those democratic questions unfettered by job title, pay scale, collar color or profession...

Person sees that something isn't happening the right way, maybe needs a little straightening out, maybe needs a little investigation - maybe it's OK or maybe it's the tip of the iceberg for a problem - doesn't matter: it's definitely seen and just as definitely passed-on as if nothing was there.

Why?

Can't say that it's the product of a hostile or oppressive work environment where no one sticks their necks out for fear of having their heads lopped off.

True enough in those places, but it happens elsewhere as well.

Not particularly talking about those times when it's RE-ALLY BIG, when the "Uh-Oh" moment would require whistleblower fortitude and strength of character.

Just the ordinary, everyday knowledge/action discon-nects that add up over time...

Why?

Sorta lost on the answer to this one.

Friday, August 05

Crippled: How to Document

The workflow crippled by How To Document.

Sat in on a meeting where a full hour was spent on trying to figure out how to give a Part Number to a product component. I had no idea what they were talking about, since I was there as a fill-in for something else that was supposed to be covered by the meeting ('never was) but here is the apparent problem as Noted:

There needs to be a WIP in Department A but an FG in Dept B . Before that can happen, a PO must be generated - which can't happen until there is an approved ECO for the BOO, BOM, PS, MS, ES, PLS, DPS and Rat-a-tat-tats: no one quite knew which was needed for what and what went where. The product component was completed, verified, validated and qualified - no arguments there, no disagreements, no Quality "Yes, but..." - but everyone seemed to be bewitched, bothered and bewildered on how to document it to get it properly "into the system."

Also: Dept A thinks Dept B should be WIPped, too, to which B said "FG you!" and refused to talk about it. QA said "Let's take this offline" and calmed them down.

Oh, and they didn't come up with a solution, either.

The component missed its scheduled release. It was sold, but could not be delivered.
There is a meeting scheduled Monday with Sales & Marketing to discuss how to get the product component released.

Latchkey Leadership

It's cute, really, watching the kids play, pretending they're executives with power, earnestly discussing "key" issues and "strategies." Very impressive, all the card castles and Popsicle stick constructs they're gluing together –

– And they're not even teenagers: y'know, those upper-middle-managers who have been there and done that and still aren't executives. Oh, those teens were too expensive to keep around as babysitters. Teenagers, phoo!, always questioning authority by bringing up things like facts and statistics and, and Experience. Like they have Executive Experience in running an entire company. Read a book!, why don't you?

But the kids now, they're very serious, talking long and intensely about things they've never done before but are really really really excited to be doing now – the occasional weary joke from shared exhaustion – inventing "solutions," missing Memorial Day weekend, the 4th of July, the– well, their families will understand, these kids are busy sweating out deadlines, bottom lines and organizational fault lines…

The President & CEO is starting his vacation tomorrow. Two weeks. 'Haven't seen the Vice President of Engineering for a while, I think he has a mountain cabin that needs fixing up a little. The VP/Production is … somewhere.

No matter.

The latchkey kids are doing a real good job of pretending they're grown-up executives with real power.

Sunday, August 07

Fortune's Fables: Turf

Once there was a tavern,
By the name of "Barney's Bay".
The owner retired to baron's life
And was often far away.
So he left the bar and the land and the inn
In the care of his five sons
And they worked together and fought together
And rarely acted as one.

Still —

Barney's Bay it was a success,
Built on the family's toil,
For the service it was mighty good,
The location on good soil.
The food they served was excellent,
The wine it was quite fine.
And when you looked at the accounting books,
My how they did shine!

Still —

Other taverns started to build
In the neighborhood one day:
They were small and not so good as Barney's,
But they wouldn't go away.
One place it made a dessert,
Just as grand as you could eat.
Another place was not so clean but,
Man, it sure was cheap.

Still —

Barney's stayed at Number One,
The place you'd want to stay.
(Though #1 was not so tops
Today as yesterday.)
The father said to the brothers,
"Swat these flies down, do it now."
So they put their heads together
To devise a big plan How.

Still —

Barney was still absent a lot,
Gone on his long trips.
And the brothers were so long in-fighting
They'd forgotten what it is
To plan as one and share their thoughts
And bring their work together:
So the inn did rock and slip its dock
Like a ship befouled by weather.

Still —

Barney's Bay stayed #1,
There's no denying that.
While the flies grew into vultures
That were eying Barney's ass.
For #1 in an empty port
Is a ship that is marooned.
And all could tell that Barney's
Was a-sinking very soon.
The tavern it grew emptier,
More hollow day-by-day
As guests departed everywhere,
No one could make them stay.
Though the inn still made great coffee,
The beds laid with precision:
The brothers they had turfed so long,
They could not make a decision.

Moral:

Owners they should stay at home
And watch how things are run so
That managers who carve their turf
Should be the first to go.

Afterward: This tale of Barney's Bay is not related to the
Latchkeys of yesterday - tho' absentee leadership is the
theme of both: one is purposeful, one neglect. Maybe they
both end up with the same result, but the Cube dinna
ken if tha's so, laddies 'n ladies, The Cube dinna ken,
since it's Life now without end yet in sight.

In fact, tho', the tale of today - of Barney's - was the road
that led to the Executive change that found us the Latchkey of yesterday's observationing.

There's a little more to it than that, tho', and someone be
sure to remind me to tell some of the intervening tales
of Giants and Bland Boys and Marshmallow Men, of
the slain Teenagers of upper-middle-Management who
served faithfully as retainers and paid the prices of their
jobs as the Vice-Princes, er, Presidents, of both regimes
hide golden eggs in their turf-built nests.

Monday, August 08

On a Meeting with the Mountains in View

Mountains loom behind the glass-walled conference room
Where sleepy faces not their heads and argue
The subject is a product with a future filled with gloom
And the voices coarsely insist, "Take the long view."
But here there is no thunder. Here there is no heat.
Here there is no reason to believe in what is seen.

Here there is no present. Here there is no past.
Here there is no passion in the dream.
When the rust light slants across
The distant mountain range
The conference descends into the night.
Epiphany achieved within the profit gain,
Congratulations light up eyes now bright.
For now they're going home,
Now they're leaving here.
The meeting now is over,
There is great good cause for cheer.

Tuesday, August 09

All 4 One $

Pierre Dolet writes ...

So, as a follow-up to one step in our 5S re-organization, we have posters put up all over the place:

ALL FOR ONE MILLION $$$

They took lots of pictures of lots of smiling faces - ours - and placed them over a map of the world: WE are going to conquer the world with our joint effort, bumping up the quarterly net profit by ONE MILLION DOLLARS!

In an unrelated side note, the 3rd shift was laid off last week. It seems they aren't part of the effort anymore. Unfortunately, the posters were made before the layoffs and - God knows why - all the ladies with the friendliest smiles were on the 3rd shift. They look goooood in the photos.

Wednesday, August 10

Deadline Press

Isn't it fun, when the deadline's almost come, when:

* The hourlies take their breaks like clockwork.

* The execs take their vacations on time.

* The managers schedule meetings about nothing.

* Your stomach is not feeling very fine.

Thursday, August 11

Deadline Press 2

Yes, a deadline is approaching, it's coming down to the wire - AND, of course:

* There is probably a family event this week.

* The coffee machine is empty.

* The network's running slow.

* Your prime application hangs up.

* A crash, somewhere, sometime, after hours & during prime time.

* You realize that you are falling asleep - standing up - at noon.

* The printer is out of ink.

* There is a suspicious spot on your face that looks suspiciously like stress-activated acne - or SOMETHING LE-THAL (!!!) - but there's no time to check it out.

* The copier says "Toner Low" - which doesn't matter because its jammed - which doesn't matter because it's almost out of paper anyway and - you're not going to get more before the deadline hits because - the paper order has been delayed by the holiday weekend that you're working through.

Friday, August 12

Deadline Press 3: Frozen

Yes, the deadline is coming on and you are frozen.

It is now Day 3 of talking about The Deadline - and you have done Nothing.

Zilch.

Nada.

Rien.

Niets.

Nic.

No-Thing.

Nope.

Zero.

It's getting down to the wire and you have given yourself Friday, Saturday & Sunday to shut yourself in - you have no one, nobody, no nothing around to distract you - and now you will finish this baby in a great, glorious burst of concentrated, hardworking energy.

You will.

Saturday, August 13

Deadline Press 4

It's

not

happening.

Sunday, August 14

Deadline Press 5: Haiku

Sunday
and the intestines
tremble.
The Deadline
Monday
will still
come.

Monday, August 15

Deadline Press 6

False hope or satisfaction?

The time in the deadline rush where you've put in hours and hours of work - some of it even good (damn good!) - and you're still not finished, may not finish on time - but you see some light ahead, and a lot of distance behind, and it looks like there's a decent chance ...

Well, it looks that way. It's Monday morning and, against all better judgment, you're filled with optimism and - dare one say it? - a feeling of "We can do it."

Now, if the rest of the day is as positive as the first five minutes have been...

Tuesday, August 16

Deadline Press 7: Last Night

This is the end - almost
This is the end - near
This is the end - when
Now
Ow
This is the end
First thing in the morning
This is the end
When it's over
It's gone
Now
Ow
8 AM - OK
9 AM - Too Late
It's 11 PM - Don't sleep
Midnight now - Awake
1 AM - Coffee
3 AM - Speed
5 AM - Hyper
7 AM - Please
We're almost there
Please
The end is near
Please
Don't interrupt
Please
8 AM
We're there.

Wednesday, August 17

Deadline Press 8: Over

The deadline was met. The company was saved. (The job, too.) Everyone's needs and requirements were fulfilled. A leviathan effort. Hours, days, weeks, months of effort culminated in -

Delivery of a six-inch package of documents that means a product is ready to be manufactured and can be released and sold and -
Today there is another priority.

Another deadline.

Another -

S***!

Thursday, August 18

Deadline Presssss: Epilogue

We are lost again, unable to understand ...

The Deadline, which started out as observation and evolved into participation – has now devolved into exasperation.

The Deadline was met. The Cubes in this quadrant have moved on to other horizons. But, looking back, it is Noted that ---

That ---

It's just sitting there.

The Deadline Project, that is.

The "DealBreaker-if-not-finished," "Layoffs if not shipped," "Bankruptcy if not completed":

Is

Just

Ignored.

It seems that the President and the 3 key Vice-Presidents have gone on vacation:
Product Development, Marketing and Manufacturing.
Somewhere, somehow, someone said to somebody: "We have to do B as a top priority" - forgetting to add "- once A is completed."

So, now, all of the minions of Marketing left for out-of-town to lay the groundwork on Project B - and all of masses of Manufacturing are moving things around to prepare for working on Project B - and all of the product, shipments, orders, documentation and profits of Project A are sitting in a corner.

They obey, these minions and masses. They have no leaders and, apparently, no thoughts of their own. Their priorities have been re-set: they do not question, ask or offer feedback - they obey.

"They" are Us, of course: Fellow Cubes.

We are very very smart, up-and-down the line.

Friday, August 19

How Can You Smile That Way?

Pierre Dolet writes ...

Wipe the smile off your face when confessing failure.

There's a wry smile that permeates the "team," a sense of "Who cares" and "That's the way it is" that apparently allows one to mitigate the sense of responsibility with a shoulder shrug and a "knowing" grin.

Oh, they know all right: the Powers That Be never defined what they wanted adequately, didn't give enough resources, set an unrealistic deadline - and probably won't sell any of the stuff we make to justify having done it all anyway. So our failure was a set-up. Someone will pay. They'll probably lay off another 5 or 10 line workers to justify the shortfall. We failed.

So don't smile, wryly knowing or not, when confessing failure.

Saturday, August 20

Self-Made Rules

Citrom writes ...

This is about Mitch, in the cubicle across the aisle.

I've sat across from Mitch for about two years now; he's a quiet person, but considered very hardworking. Recently, I've had the opportunity to work with Mitch on a few different projects, and I can add the words "competent" and "intelligent" to the description. It's very much a pleasure working with Mitch.

Except for his Rules.

Mitch, in his own way, is a subtle "anarchist": if there is a Company rule that stands in the way of what needs to get done, Mitch will ride over that rule without regard. Does the Purchase Order require 5 copies, 3 of which everyone knows nobody will read? Mitch writes up 2 copies and lets the nobodies notice and follow-up with him to press their point. So far, nobody knows nothing, does nothing, cares. So Mitch's point is made: it was a useless rule without sense, therefore it is senseless to follow it. And so on. I cannot argue: I follow every rule and feel trapped by the arbitrary nature of so many of them. Mitch is free.

Or so I thought.

But then, as I wrote earlier, there are Mitch's Rules.

It seems that, to get a grasp on things, Mitch has created a subset of mini-rules that guide him through any project. This is how he thinks, therefore, these are the Rules that must be followed to guide the thoughts toward successful completion of the project. I don't even think Mitch considers them Rules, but he follows them with the rigid adherence of self-discipline just the same. And they lead him to understanding the project, and that project is successfully completed.

But they are, just the same, arbitrary Rules: self-made, true, but Arbitrary just the same.

Why does this matter?

It doesn't, if you work in a vacuum. It doesn't, if you work alone. It doesn't, if your way is the only way.

But it's not. It never is. Never do you get all three of those conditions, together.

It doesn't even matter if you have conditions one and two - independence and sole control over the project - it doesn't matter because the sadness of watching Mitch work is that his self-made Rules stop on that one step before being truly creative: he only can do things one way - his way or no way.

This is the dictatorship of Self-Made Rules: for all their internal logic and usefulness, they create a wall - a cattle chute, if you will, that guides thoughts and activities down a predetermined path as surely as if hemmed in by Arbitrary rules, Bureaucratic Rules, Obsolete Rules or plain, old-fashioned Stupid Idiot Rules.

As the mini-tragedy of people like Mitch - hardworking, competent, intelligent people - Self-Made Rules mean that there will never be a breakthrough or "Eureka" moment: there can only be a repeat of what was learned, re-applied again and again. This will serve most instances, it will satisfy most needs. It will never innovate, always replicate.

And, meanwhile, the anarchist Mitches and their more silent kin rebel against the Company-imposed Arbitrary Rules that make their worklife miserable, building their own cell walls willingly.

Sunday, August 21

**The Tragik Komedy of Precision Ben
Part I**

*I will make my name in futures
I will forget the past*

I.

Precision Ben, proud
   handsome man
   boldly charismatic and
   smart damn smart
   fucking smarter than me
Set the pace, the race
   early on:

*I will make my name in futures
I will forget the past*

God, it was a beautiful start

We ran & ran & ran
Man, he could design and plan
Damn!, they told us we can't
And they were almost right
What a fight!
What a fucking damn fight!
When they closed us, abused us,
Certainly misused us
Stopping us
In the middle of the day

Scoffing us

I can still hear them say:
"Boys, go home and play
You're too young

Boys, go home and stay
Out of our way, go on."
And only Precision Ben
   stood in their way
To say:

I will make my name in futures
I will forget the past

And we won.

For awhile.

Monday, August 22

Ambition

Slim writes from Texas...

Ev'rybody wants to be what they are not
And of course to have what they ain't got
Pretty faces
Pretty souls
Another million
A new Rolls
Ev'rybody needs an awful lot.

Tuesday, August 23

The Opinion That Must Be Listened To

[Just a little follow-up to an earlier Note - don't remember exactly where: it must have been brilliantly stated, though, 'cause someone else remembers, obviously:]

Kyra writes ...
Jackie came into my office - well, my to my desk standing in the middle of a room with 5 other desks, actually, all working together: we are the Ops Support Team (formerly Administrative Support Department, but everyone is a "team" now) - to tell me that I must change the report that we 6 desks had spent 7 weeks compiling. Change it significantly.

"Why?" I asked. We had done our homework. Say what you like about LisaJoyAngieMarieBill and me, but the word "drone" has been applied to our antlike persistence more than once and we take pride in our accuracy, no matter how colorless or dull the result.

"Because," said Jackie. And then there was silence.

"Yes...?" said I, waiting for some details on our erroneous ways that I could learn from and correct.

"That's all you need to know," said Jackie walking away, "I think it should be changed, like I told you."

And Jackie - who, because she is a "Supervisor" and I a mere "Team Leader," carries some weight behind her thoughts, whether backed up by fact or no - has an Opinion That Must Be Listened To.

116

Wednesday, August 24

The Document That Lies There

We placed it on the desk on time:
an IN box for the department to Process.
Not our department:
we cannot touch it more.

It lies there:
untouched.
It lies there:
they know what it is.
It lies there.

To say more would be
Unpolitic,
Pushy,
Crossing lines.

We must wait,
and become Buddhists
in our patience.

Thursday, August 25

Salesman's Lament

I couldn't reach your number
The number that you gave me was wrong
It was a mistake what you told me
Or maybe you were lying all along.

I tried to call you this morning
I tried how I tried all afternoon
Your eyes were so honest
When you said that you loved it

How could you have forgotten so very soon?

This is all premature
It's an over-reaction
I'll wait for you to call.
If you don't call soon
Then I'll know it's no mistake
I really mean nothing to you at all.

But you ate my freebie luncheon
You drank my paid-for beer
You listened to my sales pitch
And you promised that you'd hear.
And when I asked you for your number
You said "This is my di-rect line."
But now I'm talking to an 800 number
And I'm starting to think you lied.

I'll try dialing you just one more time.

Friday, August 26

**The Opinion That Must Be Listened To -
Why? I'll Tell You.**
[This refers to a Note from August 23rd]

Hank writes to Kyra ...

You write that this Jackie Supervisor's "Opinion Must Be
Listened To" even though you know your report is accurate - why?

This is what ticks me off about the office: everyone keeps
their mouths shut even when they know something is
wrong.

Kyra answers Hank ...

You weren't paying attention: Jackie had said "Because - this is what I think."

That's all she is required to say. She's a boss, I'm a peon. That's her attitude and she makes the rules in our little world. When Jackie "thinks," it is The Opinion That Must Be Listened To."

Saturday, August 27

Acronyms: P

PO - Purchase Order or Post Office
PPO - Personal Physician Option (as opposed to HMO)
PPV - Pay Per View
PYA - Protect Your Ass

Sunday, August 28

**The Tragik Komedy of Precision Ben
Part II**
[Part I in on Sunday, August 21st.]

II.

We dived into the
    daily battle
Carved our modest place
Where, really, no one cared to settle
Where plastic dominated metal
Where small was large
    and death could still rattle
Where they recognized your face.

Precision Ben knew he didn't need me.

"Since we were boys," he joked ,
"You've looked back
Or you look straight down.
Me -
I will make my name in futures
I will forget the past."

So I left
Because
Fifteen years was not
   enough
To make me lose my hope
   in me.

Ben was on his own
   with the others
They argued & yelled like
   the unequals of before
Gave Ben their hearts.

He needed more, of course,
And when his brilliance
   burned a thousands suns
Drove them to new heights
And dreams
Faster than reality could
   support.
For five years, nine years,
   I forget how many
They lost most every penny
And owned their small world.

Do you wanna come back?"
   he growled to me,
"You know the value of
   a dollar."

And I did.

And did.

Monday, August 29

The Opinion That Must Be Listened To - Here's What You Do. I Don't Think So.

[This started on August 23rd and continued on August 26th]

Hank writes ...

So your Supervisor gives an order to change a report that you know is accurate - no reasons: just because "I think, therefore it is." And I understand that you won't challenge this Supervisor because she makes the Rules for her reports.

But why not go to her Manager to correct the mistake? After all, blame drips down, and if this report screws up something later on, then sooner or later it falls on you.

Kyra answers ...

Our company is very hierarchical: one is not appreciated for "speaking above your pay level."

We practice a lot of PYA around here: trust me, there was a memo from me "confirming" the changes that my Supervisor wanted me to make.

And if The Opinion That Must Be Listened To originally came to my Supervisor from her Manager, then I am as certain as I am in the existence of Taxes that there is a PYA memo from her to him.

Tuesday, August 30

Acronyms Errors To Avoid

Sometimes our fingers slip while typing. Sometimes our minds wander into the subconscious, revealing the sub-texts we mean but should not say aloud. Sometimes we just screw up. Do NOT make typo errors on the following homonyminous acronyms:

PS/BS
This would change your Post Script comment into Bull Shit - a frequent literary occurrence, but not one to be openly identified.

See also PS/TS - where it's truly Tough Shit that this happened, but not a good idea to include this observation in a letter to the President of the firm your Company is trying to woo.

PO/BO
While Purchase Orders frequently bear the stench of graft, corruption and waste, in polite society the Body Odor associated with the writer of the PO should not be referred to.

FAQs/FAGs
In our world of tolerance, the most Frequently Asked Questions should probably not be directed to one's sexual preference, especially using a derogatory term.

FYI/PYA
For Your Information may include veiled references to another party to Protect Your Ass, but do not announce this in the subject line of the memo or letter.
Bad diplomatic move.

Wednesday, August 31

Meetings: Faces We Make

Some facial expressions noticed at this morning's meeting ...

Interested - This is my meeting. I'm sure that everyone is as interested in this topic as I am.

Too Interested - I'm the new kid in town here, so let me catch somebody in a mistake and then I'll say something really impressive.

Alert - My report is up next!

Relieved - It's over and nobody said anything too bad about my report.

Anxious - I can't believe I screwed up my report in front of so many people.
Maybe I can patch things up right after the meeting, if only it will finish on time, so I can write it during lunch and then ...

Satisfied - I'm the new kid in town here and I just zapped that guy's report.

I'm looking good.

Too Satisfied - Okaaay: I gave my report and they bought that bullshit.

Bland - Sure, this directly impacts my department, but it's really too much trouble to listen. I'll review the minutes when they come out and see what was said. If the minutes are not too long. I hate long minutes. We were at the meetings, we don't need to read about it later.

Glazed - I've got nothing to report, why am I at this meeting? Why am I at any meeting? When is my next vacation again?

Preoccupied - So I'm the President, and I've made my appearance but, c'mon, I'm not interested in these details: let's see if I can eText my wife for a lunch meeting under the conference table here while nodding my head every now and then to indicate interest.

Very Satisfied - My meeting is going fantastic! I can see the President nodding in agreement with everything I've lined up.

September

Thursday, September 01

BS not PS

Today The Cube had the pleasure of adding the following Management-dictated Post Script to a letter being written to another company:

We are formulating a considered response
in light of recent information.

Translation: Even though this is our business, we've never bothered to think about that and, wow!, now that you bring it up --- we still won't, but buy this stall for now.

Friday, September 02

Absolute Minimum - Explained

Pierre Dolet writes ...

As I have Noted to The Cube a few times, our company has had a fairly recent change of executive management, followed by 5S and Lean Manufacturing programs, and so on. (Actually, the Lean Manufacturing has sort of been forgotten mid-way through, but it may rear its head again: you never know.)

Having pitched out most of my paper trails during the 5S era (it's been mostly forgotten, too, except for the fading posters and occasional visits from a "5S Review Team" that seems to change composition every time it comes around - we ignore their memos, nothing happens, and life goes on), I was surprised to come across my little top-bound steno notebook from the time when our new President first arrived. I love those little top-bound steno notebooks: reminds me of grade school without the bulkiness of a 3-ring binder to go with it. Oh, we have 3-ring binders here, too, but I have so far avoided them. My last one was in high school, held together with plastic tape to get it through the entire school term because it was bulging like a pregnant pause by year's end. Here they use them to file reports in, label them, put them on shelves and let them look impressively pristine and unread - until the 5S slaughter hacked them into red-tagged debris. Oddly enough, we never needed them until they were gone.

My steno pad had one page almost entirely filled with this one note:

President's style:

ABSOLUTE MINIMUM

Waaay down on the bottom of the page I had scrawled in little letters:

What does that mean?

Flash forward two years later ---

* Wholesale slaughter of the VP and upper management ranks (replaced by friends from his old company on a "Fire 3 Old - Get 1 New" basis)

* Close down of an entire factory in the Midwest (moved to Mexico for a "25 cents on the dollar" hiring standard)

* Layoffs of in-house line workers by 20% (because, well, we have to protect the annual Executive Bonus Plan in order to attract Talent, don't you know)

--- and I think I understand what he meant now.

Saturday, September 03

Punk Hierarchy

Pierre Dolet writes to The Cube ...

Here is another Note I found in an old steno pad: copied down from a whiteboard, it was somebody's description of the Company hierarchy:

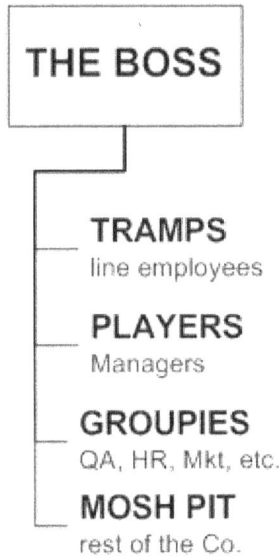

```
┌─────────────────┐
│  THE BOSS       │
└─────────────────┘
      │
      ├── TRAMPS
      │   line employees
      │
      ├── PLAYERS
      │   Managers
      │
      ├── GROUPIES
      │   QA, HR, Mkt, etc.
      │
      └── MOSH PIT
          rest of the Co.
```

Sunday, September 04

The Tragik Komedy of Precision Ben
Part III
[Part I was on Sunday, August 21st; Part II was on Sunday, August 28th]

We did not really fight
We never really fought
Over who was boss
        was king
        was genius
        was The Reason:

Ben was.

I never had the ideas
    only How To Do
    the dull How To
    the drone Do
    the red ink black ink

Ledger that always stood
    between Precision Ben's dreams and
    our reality.

Precision Ben had asked me back
And I came
I missed the game. His game was so much better.
Precision Ben was the same:

    I will make my name in futures
    I will forget the past

But the past was biting at our heels
    and corrupting the present
    and "Yes" was not enough
To save Ben's dream.

"Yes" was not enough.

Shout slam scream
    It wasn't a fight
    Precision Ben's dream
It was a war.
    We were allies
    Commies and Capitalists to beat the Nazis
Allies
    until it was over
    paper over silence over unsaid over
    everything
Until we'd won.

We lied
    To win
    To ourselves
    Ben to me; Me to Ben; Us to everybody
That we agreed

And I saved the company for Ben
    Ben's dream
    Now my dream too.

Precision Ben never forgave me for that.
Bastard
It's my dream too
Now.

Monday, September 05

A Convenient Career Decision

Well, there are smart guys and there are smart guys. Art is Smart.

Art(hur) was brought in as an "outside sales consultant" almost two years ago by our newly installed Exec Team. What does an "outside sales consultant" do? Well, in our context he draws down a salary for advising our Exec Team on What This Company Is Doing Wrong and How I Can Set It Right - while remaining anonymous to the current company sales force.

Not surprisingly, after a half year or so, Art's advice led the Exec Team to the logical and well-considered conclusion that We Need Him.

As a Valuable Asset, though, Art negotiated a contract that preserved My Ability To Perform. Notable clauses included:
    * Only occasional appearances at the company per se (he needed to stay based at his out-of-our-state home in Austin to Maintain My Contacts), * Managerial powers of I Say-You Do to whichever staff he chose for his flexible Impact Teams,
    * Freedom from the restraints of administrative responsibilities, such in-the-way things as market analyses and specs.

The next months were a bullet train ride of activity and increasing anticipation of the New Fields We're Entering. Art had us drop the core products, amend the current pipeline and - most important for Our Future - start The Big One.

The Big One. This would be the breakthrough to spawn an entire line of high profit margin products. Art didn't originate The Big One - the core idea came from our newly-created R&D department (a VP Art had worked with previously -curiously, one of the Exec Team who recommended Art). No, Art didn't come up with the idea, but he recognized the gold there.

For the past 18 months, then, Art's Big One has been the motivator behind hiring from scratch the R&D staff (curiously, almost all the same people the VP and Art had worked with previously), then putting all the company's resources behind developing an entirely new manufacturing model, and - while Art was out Developing The Field - designing our marketing strategies as he saw necessary. Was it mentioned that Art worked from inspiration, without the bureaucratic drag-downs of Marketing product specs? So we had to re-design the molds a few times to meet his evolving concept of The Big One, big deal: the Sales Projections were impressive.

And we did it. Late last month, as may have been read from the Deadline series of entries in these Notes, we plowed through hell and high water to Make This Happen. The Big One will be unveiled this month. Art will go out to a series of industry trade shows and deliver The Big One that he has told us they are all eagerly anticipating for the past year and a half.

Art resigned last Thursday.

He didn't feel the company was Behind Him Enough. The Big One doesn't Meet His Expectations.

It was a career move, nothing personal. Art won't hold it against the company that he Lost Time Treading Water while we got our act together.

Tuesday, September 06

Catchphrases To Remember

Here are some newly Noted catchphrases that left The Cube amazed, amused or a-wondering ...

Low hanging fruit - Heard this one in a meeting with our President. A bit scary when you think about it, because it's what you did as a kid when passing someone else's house and stealing their oranges. He doesn't mean that, of course. He means ... What does he mean?

Follow the blood - Another overheard from a Presidential meeting. Something of a trend is developing here, one that is not too reassuring.

Velocity of the enterprise - Whew, finally!, a Prez saying that is clear and easy to understand. It seems that we have this business, and we're rushing forward like a bullet, and we're going to smash into ... oh.

Terminal decisions - Maybe, once upon a time, this meant something like "The buck stops here." However, put altogether with the above catchphrases, here's the paragraph that our President constructed at the most recent shareholders' meeting.

"When you brought me aboard to shape things up, I told you we would go after the low hanging fruit, and then follow the blood to the best profit margin areas, letting the velocity of the enterprise carry us through - but now, I see, we'll have to make some terminal decisions about this plant."

Big Red's His Own Man

Big Red he is his own man
Give him a job and he says "I can"
Give him a tool he'll fix it fine
And he'll do it right on time

So give him a raise!
Big Red's due one
He's the man to get the job done
Job's now done and ever'one's cookin'
Cause things go fast when Big Red's bookin'.

They made Big Red to a manager man
Figured they needed Big Red's hand
But Big Red didn't know what to do
Without a boss he hadn't a clue.

So give him a team!
Big Red needs one
With a team he'll get more things done
Job' not done? Say, what's the matter?
With Big Red in charge, things shoulda gone better.

Big Red started to prevaricate
Said one thing to Jim and another to Jake
Said "Yes, we'll do it" to everyone he knew
Then went on vacation and it came unglued.

So whatever happened
To Big Red's word?
It's lyin' there stinkin' like a great big turd.
Big Red's got in over his head
Now he faces each day like the zombie dead.

Again now:

So they gave him a raise!
Big Red was due one
He once was the man to get the job done
But now he doesn't know what he's doin'
(slowly)
So he spends most days just tryin' to fool us.

Thursday, September 08

The Box

Bob writes to The Cube ...

It seems that we are working inside a "box."

We weren't aware of our box, but we were advised/ordered/berated/seminared/solicited yesterday to "challenge the box."

So I kicked-in a cardboard box to fulfill expectations.

That wasn't enough.

"Think outside the box, Bob," I was told.

OK: 2 + 2 = 5.

Nope (although it seems to be how Sales calculates it's accomplishments when year-end Boast Time, er, "Assessment Review" comes around).

"Don't let your thinking become trapped inside the box, Bob," and I realized that the Box Top telling me this was outside the box. Yes, he was. He was a consultant and he couldn't be inside my box, er, job.

Satori - Enlightenment.

I am box-ed in. There are four walls around me, cutting

off my view of the rest of the company, of the window, of the world.

"Focus on the box, Bob, break out of it - the company needs you to break out of the box."

I don't think they want that.

"What if we... thinking outside the box... gave you our creative ideas... without restraint? What if we... acting outside the box... performed our jobs... as our combined experience/inspiration... told us would be most effective? What if we... looking outside the box... found the flaw... in the workflow our bosses created years ago... and corrected it? What if we... challenging the box... got rid of those obstacles... that are the flaw... that are our bosses? What if we... outside the box..."

"Bob, focus. Concentrate. You're wandering. Keep your goals directed."

Oh, yes - I forgot. This is a seminar: the words are just words. They mean nothing. They sound good, though. Inspirational.

The box.

Really just a fairy tale. No one would want to go outside the box. It's a wilderness out there. You never know what may happen. You never know, outside the box...

Friday, September 09

Chronic Amnesia

Sat in at one of those meetings again where we rehashed a hash that we'd hashed out about four, five times already.

The scary thing was the look of blank unrecognition in so many eyes: they are either very very good actors or they actually don't remember having discussed, dissected and decided the issue already.

It's very hard, then, to figure out where to begin when one of these meetings starts up and the topic is revived like a new-born blue babe, breathed into life fresh and uninformed by previous knowledge. Too many upper-ups with the blank-eyed stare of innocence - too many fellow Cubes smiling the baby's daft smile of benign ignorance.

Maybe it's The Cube's problem: this never happened before, this discussion, this topic. This is *deja vu,* not reality. It must have been dreamed, like when you were a kid and dreamed that you had already gone to the dentist, then woke up to find that the day still had to happen. There is no way so many people could have forgotten that this...existed.

Except for the damn notebook. The notebook shows that we have all been here before. So why...?

The Cube is lost again...

Saturday, September 10

French Cow Walked Into An Office

A French cow walked into an office.

"MOU," he said, his accent thick and heavy.

He walked out with a deal to deliver 3,000 gallons of milk a week.

Acronyms We Should Kill:

MOU - Memorandum Of Understanding

Sunday, September 11

The Tragik Komedy of Precision Ben - Part IV
[A Tale in 5 Parts: Part I - 8/21, Part II- 8/28, Part III-9/04]

I will make my name in futures
I will forget the past

That was Ben's goal
His always plan
Time was short
Growing old man

And besides
I now owned half the present.

I will make my name in futures
I will forget the past

But I had bought it for Ben
   saved it for Ben
   desired it
   fired it
   hired

For Ben.

Everything
  I - we - us did
For Precision Ben
  for his dreams and energy and
  right on eye for detail.
You could hardly find that
Anywhere else

Hardly ...

But - he - never
Forgave me
  for saving him
  and now
Humiliation
  was the daily mode.

"You do not have equal say."
But I did.
"You do not share the crown."
But I did.
"You do not-"
I did.

And the others
  the watchers
  the believers and the doubters
Divided themselves behind us.

And tho' I did believe
And tho' I did admire the plan
It became my role to defy Ben.
Who else would?

Who else could?

Those behind me feared
Those behind Ben believed
All blindly
  reactive

pre-emptive
proactive

We had become an armed camp
   of feudal turfs
   and capital means
   and protocol rockets
   fired at high-walled procedures
Their projections' red glare
Time bombs filled with hot air
As so proudly we failed
At the twilight's last meeting ...

Impasse.

Precision Ben stared at me
   across the long glass table
   end to end
   a conference room devoid
   of conference.
We could only agree
   that everything had stopped.
   Heavily breathing
Agree
   to bring in a Board
To break our impasse.
   Holy ones
To save our ass.

And Ben retreated
   to his consoling
   mantra
I will make my name in futures
I will forget the past

I licked my wounds
   and wondered
   if I had just destroyed
What I worked so long to save?

Monday, September 12

Sexual Harassment - Because We Can

Let's talk about sexual harassment on the real world level, something we can't do in the cubes. Why here and now? Because we can.

And because the namby-pambies at the Sexual Harassment Seminar we had to attend this afternoon spewed out so many by-the-number platitudes in an hour that The Cube is feeling resentful.

Men shouldn't harass women: Yep, got it the first sentence.

Women harassing men --- Nope, not on the federal guideline agenda, not to discuss.

Men harassing m--- Weren't you listening? "Men should not sexually intimidate women": it's all a one-way street, this sexual harassment stuff as taught at our seminar.

Oh ... Really?

So whatsa with this sexual harassment stuff really oh wise-ass Cube?

Let's dismiss with the kind of "he/she can't do it unless s/he's butch/gay" type of harassment. That's the type of sexual insecurity that comes in batches of "traditional role" jobs that if you go in to shatter sexual stereotypes you know from the start what you're facing. You like confrontation, whether you admit it or not and, really, you want the attention. Does it make it right? Naw, but it's like the sign says: Beware of Dog. No big surprises when you get bit - 'just gotta worry if the dog's got rabies.

Tomorrow: The Cube's sexual harassment story. Oh ...

Sexual Harassment 2 - Because We Can

The Cube is not distressed about sexual harassment. The Cube has been sexually harassed. It did not disturb the psyche. It did not destroy the sense of self.

It did not inspire devastating dreams nor shatter The Cube's career hopes. It did confirm in The Cube the increasingly obvious suspicion that the job in question was a pithole of inequity and that, if the career had any meaning, then now was the time to climb out of this situation.

The Cube was flattered by the attention - at first. But then, like a blind date developing into an off-step relationship, the awkwardness did not dissolve into comfortable intimacy but, rather,becameanoh-my-god embarrassment of uncomfortable moments. There was a sense of pity about the situation, really, and The Cube felt sorry for the harasser.

Pity. Thatsa one of the worst emotions you can have for another human bean who is trying to strike up a sexual relationship with you. When exhibited in a singles bar, it is the inspiration for high cash intake by the establishment owner and many a DUI on the streets thereafter. But, as my Gramma used to say to Cousin Nell: "Nell, you're goin' ta meet some sad characters in your day, who'll look at you like a hungry dawg and maybe even try to give you a touch in the Wrong places. Jes' remember, girl: you didn' do nothin' wrong, an' it didn' harm you none, and jes' feel sorrowful for them pitiful creatures who's only got that way of feelin' human."
(Gramma, alternately known as "Big Mama," "Mamaw" and - by the high church members of the family - "Grand-

mother," was a European immigrant transplanted to Southern belle philosopher.

French-Polish-Jewish-Catholic married to a Creole-Anglican-Baptist.

I think she broke the hearts of the local merchants during the Great Depression by sweet-talking them into funding anything she desired when there was no money for anyone. In her era, the aura of her sexual proximity was the only business asset she had to offer but - much like any good Greek goddess - she understood that the temptations of Tantalus had more allure than the consummation. It was business, it was fun, it didn't hurt anyone - especially her today-prized "self-esteem." This is waaaay off-base now, but Gramma would have been proud of The Cube's bragging about her, even if this version of the story isn't as colorful as she told it.)

Wednesday, September 14

Sexual Harassment 3 - Because We Can

This took place about 9 years ago, but I don't think things have changed much.

We were at the federally-mandated Sexual Harassment seminar: the company had grown larger than 100 employees and so, we were told, this is mandatory. (Of course, "we were told" hides its own disavowal of responsibility and knowledge. The memo was unsigned and department-less. But we followed orders and attended.)

Oddly, I can't remember whether the instructor was a man or a woman - or one of each. It was an outsider, though: someone from outside the company and vaguely emitting an aura of officiality. I suppose we all thought it was a government official talking to us, since s/he was very "authoritative" in his (or her) "You cannot" and "It's not allowed" *pronunciamentos*. There was another seminar held just before ours, for the floor personnel, but they were all men and Latinos and used to nodding "yes" whether or not they understood a word of English. I'm sure the instructor felt that the first seminar was a success.

I'm tired of saying "s/he," so for now we'll remember the instructor as a woman.

And she was a talkative woman. She explained about improper advances, lewd comments and, most nefarious of all, "elevator eyes."

"No man can look up and down as if you were some object for his sexual attention," she said.

At which point Hannah - all 45 mini-skirted, blond bobbed body-to-die-for years of her Hannah - stood up and said:

"But what if I want them to look at me."

"That's not allowed in the workplace."

"You mean I have paid for this dress, this hair, these fingernails - and they can't look at me?"

"Not in the workplace: that would be sexual harassment."
"This is stupid."

And with that comment, Hannah led the post-feminist revolution.

Angela stood up, doe-eyed, honey-haired, ruby-lipped, and declared: "I want them to appreciate me: if they can't do that, how do I find a husband here?"

Meylisa, she of the raven complexion and onyx eyes, chimed in: "I look good, why should I care? I'll tell you what I'd care about: if they ignore me, I'll care!"

The company administration and technical personnel, I should note, were 75% Mediterranean and European immigrant employees, all highly educated, mid-career, very smart - and not terribly attuned to the American way of morals. They were a terrible influence on the rest of us, as witnessed when the instructor, flummoxed by a ten minute onslaught of female-led resistance, turned to Fred, our resident Christian Of Good Standing:

"Fred, you said you go to church regularly: how do you think you should respond to Hannah if she comes in dressed up like she says she likes to?"

Fred sat in his chair, embarrassed by the question. Then he looked over at Hannah, standing in the doorway, eyes blazing defiantly at the instructor, breasts turned upwards even more defiantly against the claims of gravity and age, her long shapely legs sheathed in jeans tight enough to replace skin. Fred looked at her long and hard, his face turning the color of beets gone wild. Then he gave a long sigh and turned back to the instructor:

"I'll look at her exactly how she wants."

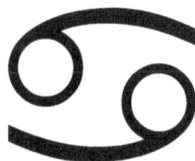

♋

Thursday, September 15

Sexual Harassment 4 - Because We Can

The Pig

He sits in his office, distant, aloof. He is not one of us. We are not equal to him. Quarterly, he treats us to food and drink at a bar to be nameless because it's rarely the same. But the routine is always the same: a round of drinks, junk food for drinkers, a speech about how far we've come. Then the first group heads home. And another round of drinks. He is friendly now. One of us. "You need something stronger, Sam. C'mon, Phil, you've earned it." Another round.

There will be five or six left. Always one or two newbies, pleased to be near the boss. Always one of the newbies will be a woman of not-quite-tender years - i.e. 28-35 - attractive enough after three drinks, maybe even after none. But she will have stuck around. And he will buy her the first of many specialty drinks. And real food - or, maybe, the brandy-dipped strawberries at $5 a pop. And, by eight o'clock, she will be the only one left with him - of her own choice. And within the month, after her embarrassing night, she will have resigned.

Friday, September 16

Sexual Harassment 5 - Because We Can

The Ice

Simple explanation, actually: something's screwed up in her life elsewhere, but you're paying for it here. She is beautiful probably. Competent in her field, which will be strong on admin skills, weak on specifics. Career-oriented (though, in that way that hurts, she's been in the same place a bit too long). Unmarried - either never or now - and independent in her ways. Many girlfriends at work. (No, not lesbian: that would be too easy - and she'd be more relaxed.) Somewhere past 30 and below the (visible) radar of 50. Tense as hell inside, about something none of us can know. What you've got to know, though, is: stay away from her. Don't say anything. The same joke you heard from Connie down in AR, if repeated near her listening ears in the copy room, will be taken as an "inappropriate" sexual innuendo. "Oh, but it's innocent!" you protest. They will have no choice but to listen to her, because the statutes say she's right. She has read the statutes, and she knows. She may even be on the company's committee to review "inappropriate" behaviors. 'Made a mistake up above: she's not "The Ice" - because she could have a warm smile, the friendly letter, help a lot - but the eyes are ... missing something. You can feel sorry for her emptiness, but be very careful if you are male of making any gesture of human warmth. Any.

Saturday, September 17

Sexual Harassment 6 - Because We Can

Policy

The company wields the threat of dismissal for sexual harassment as an employment termination tool. "Voluntary" termination.

The terms are simple: in return for not dismissing the employee because of sexual harassment, the company will "settle" for the employee's voluntary termination. There is a paper to sign, of course, leaving the accusation in the ex-employee's folder but, because he (always a he) left the company before disciplinary action was implemented, all references to other potential employers will state simply that "The employee left of his own choice" and make no mention of the charge.

Oh, and there will also be no unemployment insurance – you left on your "own choice" after all – your 401(k) vestiture will be withdrawn, as well as any sick pay and vacation accrued (unless stupid old state laws get in the way). It also seems to solve and streamline a lot of sticky procedural issues about how the charges are investigated and substantiated.

All in all, whenever the company needs to trim the middle ranks, sexual harassment is an effective hedging tool. It works especially well in conjunction with Zero Tolerance and Promote-Management-Women-From-Within policies.

Oddly, it rarely benefits those women on the line who are harassed by co-workers and management. Only in those rare instances where the woman is strong enough to be forthcoming on her own. But those are bitches, aren't they?, and probably lesbians, too.

Sunday, September 18

**The Tragik Komedy of Precision Ben
Part V**
[A Tale in 5 Parts: Part I - 8/21, Part II- 8/28, Part III-9/04, Part IV - 9/11]

> Impasse
> Standstill
> Ben you hate me I hate you we
> Love
> Hate
> This place after forty years

It's been our home our only home our
Child.
Like any good marriage in distress
We sought counseling
and were counseled
to seek
a mediating
Board.

(A Note from The Cube: have to stop here - for now - too difficult watching it, remembering it - will try to finish ...)

Monday, September 19

Not Quite Sick Enough

The perversity of the human mind and the individual's capacity for self-inflicted pain are a constant wonder to The Cube. And The Cube is speaking from personal experience.

The Cube feels like crap today. Sick. Not infectious sick, but a wounded weekend warrior suffering from bumps and bruises and possibly a cracked something earned from a Sunday of physical thrills that were not that thrilling when a kid and even less so now. But still we try and convince ourselves that it's fun.

And pay for it. Ohhh, today ... 'shouldn't come into work today.

But, you convince yourself that you are needed. That today "it is necessary" to come to the office. That "things won't get done without me." These self-delusions would have been easier to sustain if anyone had noticed that The Cube was in.

But it wouldn't have mattered if they'd noticed in spades, because The Cube was coming in anyway: sure, there are 57 hours of sick pay waiting to be used - but am I sick enough today? What if I get really sick? (We're not talking catastrophic illness here - The Cube is not an alarmist - but the kind of heavy cold/flu/nausea/fever sick that's sure to make the rounds once September drifts into November and runny noses amongst the *jungen* spread their germs amongst their elders.)

But it wouldn't matter if The Cube was sick in aces, because "is it sick enough" to take off work? The Cube is not a hero. The Cube misses work sometimes. But not when really sick. Something inside keeps perversely preventing that type of logical and well-founded absence. No, we wait until the car breaks down, or we oversleep and would be embarrassed to come dragging in ten minutes after the Important Meeting has ended - then we call in sick.

But not today. Not when actually feeling like refried hell on a stick. Smart us.

Tuesday, September 20

Unambiguous

Pierre Dolet notes to The Cube ...

We recently completed a product project that had no marketing specs, no definition, no leadership and, once it was completed, no one to sell it.

This was a "legacy" project, inherited from before most of us joined the company 1 - 2 years ago.

Yesterday, I have learned, there was a meeting of the minds - i.e., decision makers - on the next product to develop.

No tape recorders, notes or minutes were allowed.

No project leaders, sales, engineering or production personnel were allowed.

It was decided to initiate a new product project - starting Friday.

Clearly we have cut through the Gordian Knot of past mistakes.

Wednesday, September 21

The P Factor

Kyra notes to The Cube ...

We've reached a new level here. I'm not quite sure which level, though.

Our cubicles have no walls. This has nothing to do with the story, it's just where we work on our computers, graphic artists one and all, in three shifts per day, six days per week.

As a matter of course, we are paid on an hourly basis - although we are judged on an output basis, since what we do, once the skill is established and verified, is highly repetitive.

Recently, the policy came down that "For all bathroom breaks, the user must log out and, upon return, log on." Since there are several other breaks taken during the shift - to ask about a particular problem, get clarification on a specific point, and the like - we wondered how this would be handled.

They reviewed our logs.

Judy, two places over from me, has a bladder problem. Water runs through her like a sieve. So she pees a lot. She also produces a lot (work, that is). A lot.

Nevertheless, honest little girl that she is, Judy has to log out/on at least twice an hour to take a pee break. Well, it's on record, so it's no secret.

Except that, apparently, we have a Pee Monitor.

I have to point out that we are 2nd shift - 4 PM to 1 AM - so the ranks are thinner than the daytime crew. We notice things like new people. Especially new people who sit at a Corner Cubicle (a real cubicle, with real temporary walls, but made of transparent plastic).

And, we notice, how for the past week every time Judy logs off for a pee break the Corner Cubicle is suddenly empty and it's occupant, oddly enough, has to take a pee break, too.

Oh, we thought it was a coincidence at first. Certainly Judy wasn't paying as much attention as I was (I get bored easily and my eyes wander). But, by mid-week, we were testing the Corner Cubicle and - yes - the woman sitting there was monitoring every time Judy went to take a pee.

This went on for a week, and then the Corner Cubicle was empty.

We have heard nothing more. Apparently Judy has been validated by the Pee Monitor.

Thursday, September 22

Silicon Vests

Hank notes to The Cube ...

The following is a true and accurate product description created by our Engineering Department and delivered to the Marketing Communications Department, which was tasked to write a press release in anticipation of a product rollout in November:

"The Silicon Vest is designed as an innovative and structurally significant enhancement of the current vesting line, to be utilized within the parameters of the manufacturing process for silicon-based materials as defined in the accepted dialogue of the trade."

Clarity needs no further explanation.

Friday, September 23

That Ambition Done Got Away

Slim from Texas notes to The Cube ...

It's Friday and ambition's foiled me again.

Y'see, if you've no ambition, you're happy to "settle." I've got no major ambitions about this place, but enough minor ones to keep me running.

But that's the problem: my ambition is to Do This and Accomplish That as something of a "whole" - I know that if I only do a *Little Of This* and a *Bit Of That* that it's a waste of time ... at least as far as my ambitions are concerned.

They tell you in all the time management books to plan

out your activities in little "do-able" segments. Here in the trenches, we don't control our time. How do I plan it?

It's Friday and I'm still facing the unstarted "wholes" that I set for myself at week's beginning. I wish I had no ambitions to do a good job, then I could just TGIF and settle for what seems to be good enough for the bosses.

Saturday, September 24

Ambition Has Nothing To Do With It

A Note from The Cube to Texas Slim's letter of yesterday...

Don't confusion Ambition with Standards. You give yourself away by writing things like "do" and "accomplish" - those are Standards of performance. Ambition is more about "gain" and "get" - personal possessions that exist outside your job performance.

Be careful, Slim, you also gave yourself away with the confession that your Ambition isn't centered around your Cube. No one nearby and above wants to hear that.

Oh, sure, everyone gives "have a life" lip service, and everyone knows that they would bolt the place in a second if offered something better. But to just do a good job? Don't scare people like that unless you've really got the Ambition to leave your cubicle behind and advance over your boss's body (or in his wake as he climbs the heap). There's not a lot of understanding of the good ol' Work Ethic, unless it's combined with a good ol' Profession of Faith in the Company, repeated like a mantra at an ashram.

And it even makes sense. Hell, who is going to trust anyone talking like you: what do you really want?

Sunday, September 25

Dangerous Words: Technical

Technical words not to use loosely -
> Snaphole
> Dual Head
> Hot Stamp
> Assay
> Tool
> Screw

Take it as a personal observation and, in some instances, sad experience: these words can cause trouble when used - or heard - the wrong way.

Monday, September 26

Policy Posting: Internal Memos

Internal Memos:

* Should be kept short.
* Should include all necessary detail.
* Should be comprehensive.
* Should include in the heading "CONFIDENTIAL."
* Will rarely be read internally.
* Will always be shared with external people who have no business reading them.

Tuesday, September 27

Nathan

Whenever there's a front door
Nathan faces it with dread
He'd rather take the back door
Or a side entrance instead.

Nathan knows his duties
Nathan does his job
But he doesn't ever want to
Ever be seen by the boss.

Nathan's proudly independent
More skilled than the rest
More frightened than a bird
With a cat sitting near its nest.

For with every task that Nathan does
Like a well-oiled machine wheel
His eyes contain no confidence
His heartbeat jumps and reels.

Nathan's getting older
Maybe that's his shame
Vulnerable, this is his last job
He'll never get this job again.

Or maybe he was always scared
He'd be the one that's blamed.
Whenever there's a front door
Nathan faces it with dread

He'd rather take the back door
Or a side entrance instead.
And he sits five chairs away from me
And I wonder why he's dead.

Wednesday, September 28

I did your job today

Hank writes to June, "who will never read this blog ... Neither will our boss"...

I did your job today. I have no idea why you didn't do it, but you didn't - and I did. Which probably makes me a sucker, because you already know that I won't tell anybody about it: I'll probably even give you credit for it during the weekly department meeting. I just can't go tattletaling to the manager like a 4th grade library monitor. Oh, but you're "nice," and that makes it all right.
All right. You smile and talk friendly and do nothing. Certainly not your job, chunks of it. But I guess that's OK because you're on the bottom of the totem pole, and you know it, and you have a home life, and you show it, but damn! I wish you'd do your job so I don't feel protective and cover for you.

The Cube Notes: Sometimes you gotta vent.

Thursday, September 29

All Ears: A Woman's View on Male Hygiene

Kyra Notes From The Cube ...

OK, boys - especially boys above a "certain age" - shave your ear hair.

This is a gross topic. But I have to look at you!

I don't care that you have "given up" on ever having a romantic life again: you work in this office with me and you certainly have a social life, whether you want it or not. A very specific social life: we work in the same office - and because I was taught to be polite I can't turn away when we speak to one another.

I'll give you the stray hair that grows fast since the last time you shaved, but beyond that: No. Look in a mirror and, if your ears are starting to resemble a koala bear's fuzzy wuzzies, know that IT IS NOT ATTRACTIVE.

The "Homeless Bum" look does not go well with your professional position.

Please, pleeeeaaaase don't come to work that way anymore.

Friday, September 30

Friday Shirts

Tamara follows up on Kyra's Notes From The Cube yesterday ...

Today is Friday and we are going to have Casual Day again. I like it, except for ...

Butt-ugly print shirts.

What is it about men in certain professions - engineers, sales, technical in general - that they all seem to shop in the same store where ugly print, fake "Hawaiian" shirts are apparently the only item on display? It's almost impossible to describe how patterns of drab color can be intermixed with designs of repetitive disdain for form. "Impossible," and yet... it is done so many, many, many times. There is a twisted genius at play here: in a world where originality is such a rare commodity, the designers of these Ugly Shirts seem to find no end of innovative horrors to create.

If there ever was a persuasive argument for uniforms in the office workplace, Friday-God-Awful Shirts would be high on the list.

But where do they come from? There are far too many of these Ugly Shirts in sight to make this mere happenstance. Are these shirts given as gifts to men by wives that hate them? Is there an epidemic in bad taste that takes otherwise reasonable males and, once their waistline starts to bulge, disconnects their sense of style and taste? Do they think these shirts are "fun?

People are pack-oriented, men particularly, following the head wolf. Is there some style-perverted Role Model that these men are emulating? I know that like behavior among men reinforces itself: so when they see someone else in an ugly-as-sin Friday Short, does that support their own lack of taste?

Oh Lord, Deliver us from this evil. Amen.

October

Saturday, October 01

Where We Work: C. C. hIGHRISE

C.C. hIGHRISE
(When Coleridge Meets cummings On The Corner OfWilshire & Fairfax)

kUBLA kHANS DEFUNCT
WHO DECREED A GLASSMIRRORWALLED STATELY
PLEASUREDOME
AND COULD ERECT ONETWOTHREEFOURFIVE MINIMALLS
JUSTLIKETHAT
xANADU!
THEY WERE MEASURELESS TO MAN!
AND
WHEN YOU CLOSEYOUREYES WITH HOLY
DREAD
IS
THIS WHERE aLPH THE SACRED RIVER RAN?

excerpt from Lyrics & Lies
R. C. Fleet

Sunday, October 02

Sunday Workover

There's something about working at home on a Sunday morning that just ... sucks.

Maybe it's the early autumn sunshine glinting in through the window and caressing the papers in my briefcase. It's a sun I don't see from my cubicle. A taunting sun, warm to the shoulders and tantalizing and - unreachable beyond this pile of reports that have to be plowed through before Monday morning.

Ah, responsibility!

Monday, October 03

The Meeting With No Voices

Interesting how you can put five vice-presidents in a room for a meeting to "make decisions" and not hear a single voice.

'Heard my own voice, awkwardly, saying out loud what I expected the veeps to say. 'Got tired of saying "Well, to play devil's advocate" on this issue ..."

Then silence. "Thoughtful" stares. A finger to the lips here, a chair rocks back-and-forth there, one hand scribbling a few strokes on a piece of paper...

"Then, does everyone agree ... ?"

Sort of a nod, a blinked eye.

Change the question: "OK, then, if no one disagrees, it stays as written."

Sort of a nod, a blinked eye.

A decision is made.

Tuesday, October 04

The Meeting With One Silent Voice

'Have to re-think yesterday's Meeting With No Voices, based on the reaction that's come about since.

There was A Voice. One Voice. Silent.

This meeting of 5 veeps had one vp sitting at a slight angle, working at his laptop all the while. Pointedly working - and not talking.

- and not talking: he had not called this meeting, he did not agree with the entire point of this meeting, he has the ear of the (absent) prez -

- and he wasn't talking.

And the other veeps listened to his silence, even the vp who had called the meeting thinking that it was something "for all of us to decide." He understood his mistake almost from the beginning, but he had to play it out.

Or, rather, stay silent like the others let the subordinate moi walk through the agenda, saying the words that no one would respond to and recording the decisions that no one would give voice to so that today the prez could talk to the Silent Working Veep and make his decision as if yesterday had never happened.

Wednesday, October 05

Meetings With The Silent Voice

[Gotta read the last two days Notes From The Cube to figure out what's going on here today.]

Learned something at the meeting a couple of days ago. The Silent Voice doesn't like to be contradicted.

Now, since The Silent Voice doesn't say anything at the meeting, it is almost always impossible to know What to Say without inadvertently contradicting him. -

(Side trip: Yep, it's a him, not a her. Someone wrote after yesterday's Note that "Of course, The Silent Voice has influence over the Prez, she's sleeping with him!" Sadly, nothing quite so tawdry or romantic. The rumour here is that he saved the Prez's life once, or his ass, or has really really good blackmail stuff on the Prez. Or, for the catty, that he is sleeping with the Prez. But when you see the two of them together, that's a disgusting proposition: gays have much better standards than The Silent Voice. Besides, The Silent Voice is on Wife No. 3 and is a notorious office lech - albeit, he is also the Moral Voice of Standards, too - so go figure.)

- What To Say without accidentally crossing The Silent Voice. Consequently, smart managers and veeps say sweet nothings at their meetings with The Silent Voice and pray to the God of Continued Employment that they are still on his good side when the meeting's dust has settled.

(Side trip: A metaphor - "dust has settled." Our meeting rooms are sterile and often colder than ice, dully lit to match the dullness of most meetings' content. The only "dust," perhaps, is the smutz that gathers on our brows as we sit quietly fighting off sleep.)

Thursday, October 06

Don't Outshine The Silent Voice

[Sorry, again, but these Notes from The Cube make more sense if you go back to Monday and see what's been going on.]

It's probably no surprise to anyone that you shouldn't outshine the boss.

Oh, there are bosses who are smart enough to appreciate any shining star under their banner, content and proprietary enough to simply appropriate some of the credit for themselves because, after all (and it is an honest "after all"), "It's my team: when they do good - I do good."

Still, in general, most bosses are human like you and I, subject to the same insecurities and jealousies and need for applause that - even if we shun the spotlight - we need. We need.

But what about The Silent Voice we've been Noting the past few days - the Veep With The Power who sits in meetings dominating them without saying a word?
Sitting among "equals," it should be noted. He's not a "boss" to these other bosses. They are all at the top o' the heap. Honchos. Jefes. Executive Management.

But, in his silence, the Silent Voice Veep is A Star That Needs The Spotlight more than any ham actor in soap opera syndication.

In fact, the comparison is more apt than The Cube realized when writing it: The Silent Voice Veep and the other Veeps are like an the cast in a community theater musical, each one trying to steal the spotlight and show off. Or, to extend the metaphor: they're the kid's baseball team, with everyone wanting to be pitcher.

But, just like the kid whose Dad is the coach - or the diva with a husband funding the show - the Silent Voice Veep has the Prez in his pocket and gets to play the lead or pitch the ball whether deserving or not. He can't sing some songs worth a damn and his curve ball sucks against lefties - but he's not going to let anyone else substitute in. Nope, he Needs The Spotlight - even when it's someone else's turn to shine.

Especially when it's some else's turn to shine. Even if he has nothing to say, do, add or enhance. He can only subtract. Use his Silence to stall, stifle and negate.

Silence, sometimes, is very eloquent.

Friday, October 07

He's a bully, he is, The Silent Voice

[Still following up on the Notes from The Cube since Monday]

Yeah, that's about what it comes down to: The Silent Voice Veep is a bully.

He's a bully in the classic way: fawning to the top, silent to his equals, and stone mean to his underlings - or anyone he thinks he can push around. That may even be his equals, "official" equals, since we already noticed that The Silent Voice Veep really is the First Among Equals by fact, if not title. And it's not so clear he's not de facto equal with the Prez, since he usually acts on behalf of the Prez. Oh, it's not said aloud - it just is.

But doesn't this make this Veep the Not-So-Silent Voice?

"Silence" is a funny thing: The Cube started noting The Silent Voice Veep at one particular meeting when he dominated by his intentional silence and removal from the discussion - and everyone else, them VPs, stuttered along awkwardly saying almost nothing until they could establish what The Silent Voice wanted. 'Turns out that the silence was a coda to earlier, private, articulations.

Observing further than last Monday's Meeting With No Voices, The Cube has observed The Silent Voice Veep collaring colleagues and pummeling them with an intense aggressiveness that borders on abusive. Rarely is his voice raised - though it is, sometimes, when he wishes to humiliate the other Veep in front of, say, the other Veep's admin secretary. To underlings who don't cower behind false bonhomie, the Bully Boy Silent Voice Veep has been heard to bark. To slam his hands on a desk. To steam ...

Not a pretty sight.

Not a pretty boy.

No, he's not, the Bully Boy Silent Voice Veep.

Saturday, October 08

The Silent Voice may be right

[Still noting from Monday]

Just because business and life are so screw up tight, you've gotta give The Silent Voice Veep his due: he may be right.

The Cube has noted that The Silent Voice is not unintelligent, untalented or unindustrious. Just like you and me. (Because we are all those things and more, aren't we?, we backbones of business.)

When there is an issue to be considered, the Silent Voice Veep, bully that he may be, has ideas. When there is a problem to be addressed, he has solutions.

And he smiles. He encourages. He drinks with The Team once a quarter on a tab he pays for. He never says "My way or the highway."

He doesn't need to. That is the genius of "silence": it's his way or you ain't...here.

It's his idea or you don't...talk.

It's The Silent Voice Veep's solution - right or wrong - or you're...gone.

See all the empty management seats, unfilled, inviting.

Some things is.

But...

The Silent Voice may be right...

Sunday, October 09

A Song for Corwin, Bright Star of the Management Team

It's not the way
That you fill out your expense report.
It's not the way
That you never return calls
That you don't want .
It's not the way
That you insult every underling,
When you know
That you're the star that's shining most

You know I hate you
I hate you
Hate the awful clothes you wear
Hate the blow-dry plastic hair
You know I hate you

You never bother me
In public since we argued.
You never cross me
When you see me down the hall.
We had it out, we had to shout,
No one but us knows what about:
And I've kept my side
Just like you've kept yours, no doubt.

But still I hate you
I hate you
Hate the lies you always tell
Hate the way you cheat like hell
Goddamn I hate you

Someday they'll find out
You don't know a word you're saying.
Someday they'll realize
There's no action only words .
Someday they will understand
You're just a hack sales man
Who's been selling them
A bunch of cheapjack goods.

Till then I hate you
You know I hate you
Hate the way you bark and strut
Hate the way you flaunt your guff

Oh, yeah, I hate you

No, I'm not telling anyone
I know about you.
The one thing you know
About me you understand:
That I won't get another fired
And I don't care why you were hired,
I just hate it

When the liars lead the band.
But I know it doesn't matter,
One way or the other
'Cause they know you
Like a brother:
You're their man.

Sunday, October 09 (more)

Buck the Bullshitter

You gotta give Buck his fully-due credit:
He's an all-American bullshit man.

Watched him proudly display his talent today
Just as glowing as his deep tan.

He spoke about the report with eloquence, wit
Defining the goals, questioning each bit

And when, alone, he was asked about it
He answered, "Y'know, I never read that shit."

Monday, October 10

Dan, Hyper-Active Man

Dan is a boss. A Director in a world that goes downhill
like this: Owners (2, same family), Vice Presidents (6),
Directors (5), Managers (a lot), Supervisors (a lot more),
Leads (a few dozen), and the rest of us. This world is
small enough (500 or so employees) that you can see up
and down most every day - except that most people are
afraid to look up too far. 'Don't know why, that's just the
way it is.

172

Dan is hyperactive. Yep, when he was born and going to school, if A.D.D. had been a diagnosis available, Dan would have been an A.D.D.-Plus. Which probably drove his teachers and parents crazy

- just like it drives crazy anyone who works for Dan.

- just like it makes him a valuable man.

Dan is not untalented, by the way. One of the smartest men in the company - in terms of brain smarts. DUMB-EST man in the world when it comes to people skills, though. Dan is thinking so fast, and reacting so swiftly to changes that he can see before anyone else that he comes across as the most abrupt jackass in the world. And his face shows it, that he knows he's ahead of the pack, even if he doesn't outright boast about it.

He is - for the right management - the perfect employee. Dan will work faster than anyone else for longer than anyone else and better than anyone else.

But, WHEW!, he's tough to keep up with!

Dan has about 25 patents or shared patents under his belt - in about five different subjects - and he's not even an engineer or chemist or scientist for years now. At one point, he jump-started three different small business on his own, handling all the marketing, planning and logistics. But these were all service-oriented, and Dan likes to make Products and take them global. He's here because this Company is about his size: small enough to be personal, big enough to go places.

And, from the Company's side, Dan is perfect for their needs: they need someone to whip in shape a lackadaisical Development department, work closely with Marketing, and make sure that Production is on top of things and, just as important, fully supported. ('Seems the Company suffers from a VP level of legacies from "the early days" - and now they're tired.)

So Dan comes in running and jumping through hoops for them, to show them what he can do, what he can do for them, and producing, Producing, PRODUCING!

WHEW!, it's tough keeping up with Dan the Hyper-Active Man.

'Sort of fun, though.

Tuesday, October 11

Write It Down: How To Get Away With Anything

Pierre Dolet writes to Notes From The Cube ...

[And The Cube notes: 'Old saw to grind, but a new perspective.]

It was discovered today that the simplest way to get away with anything is to write down whatever you want, want to do, or say you did - then circulate it. No one will read it, most will act as if they "did," and those who are arrogant or foolish enough to pretend "I never got it" can be cowed into submission by showing the top page with their name on the CC list.

This must be so: We sat in a monthly cross-departmental policy meeting this morning and four times the comment came up from several voices: "I wasn't informed of this."

Frankly, this was a patented lie. But, these being top execs making the comment, no one could say that out loud.

So, the first time, the issue was deferred yet another
month while the protesting exec was given time to review
the report that he "had not received yet." This happened
two more times in the next half hour. The herd instinct,
probably.

Then we hit upon an interesting moment. All present
had attended a certain strategic meeting in which tentative decisions were made, but our department had gone
ahead and finalized the decision - and taken action. Now
that item came up on the agenda. I could see the second-
guessers marshalling their objections, so I added while
introducing it: "...and we circulated
the final version for your approvals, in the memo of X/29,
with the notice that any input would have to be received
by Wednesday, since you had all agreed that it would go
out by Friday."

Now, this statement was not an outright lie - but it was a
calculated risk. It assumed that:

1) No one remembered what they said at the certain meeting referred to.

2) No one read the Minutes from that certain meeting -
and had probably deleted it from their emails or filed it in
a slush pile of at least a gigabyte size.

3) No one read the memo that we circulated soliciting
input - that included the final version that went out on
Friday.

BUT THAT'S NOT ALL:

As the first "ahem" coughed its way into an introductory "I never received...," I also said "- and it was hand delivered to the distribution list: the final version covers the several inputs received."

Now this put them on the defensive: apparently Everyone Got This and Everyone But Me read the materials and responded - or so I lied.

Yes, everyone got it - put onto their IN boxes on top of a slush pile that I knew no one read - and the "several inputs" were all from the same person.

But it worked. None of the execs regularly keeps track of memos, reports and written communications in general that do not affect their immediate (immediate) interests; they literally don't know what is on their desks. Now, this rarely stops them before from commenting on matters they haven't the slightest idea about - but this instance was a fait accompli, a done deal, and (supposedly) they had already given the "Go" at an earlier meeting.

Or so I told them...

I don't plan on using this strategy often. Twice more in this morning's meeting decisions were deferred because "I never got anything on this" was the lied excuse - and I'm not in a position high enough on the food chain to call them on it. Still, my epiphany was as bright as the morning sunshine this A.M.: whenever I have a dicey item to be moved past, I will put it in written form and can fairly well guarantee that it will not be read. Much, much better than an oral report that requires of the executive only seat-of-the-pants consideration and decision-making.

Wednesday, October 12

Dan, Hyper-Active Man, has trouble with others

[Notes From The Cube: This goes back a couple of days, to "Dan, the Hyper-Active Man"]

Well, it doesn't take a lot of imagination to figure out that our boss Dan, the Hyper-Active Man, is not everyone's best friend.

One might go so far as to suggest that Dan's friends are few and far between.

Which is a pity, really, because he's essentially a nice guy under the hyped-up energy level. He actually listens and will change his position if you offer a reasonable or better alternative, although you've got to shout a bit and hold your ground to keep from being steamrolled over. And he is definitely a pushover when it comes to discipline. There are at least 2 goofoffs in the department who should be gone - but Dan won't be the one to fire them: he's got such a soft heart that he keeps remembering that they have families who shouldn't suffer for their loved one's incompetence.

But, y'know, intellectual honest and integrity and a deeper-than-business sense of morality don't cut it with the masses. Most of the fellow Cubes hate Dan because they instinctively fear any one in authority, so they hear his bark and feel his bite - even when there isn't any. As for the goofoffs: oh, Dan barks at them a lot, but instead of upping their performance levels or at least feeling grateful that he's not canning them like tomatoes for the winter, they just feel resentful and mutter among the minions about how they are "picked on," drawing sympathy from the colleagues who do not suffer from their crappy work performance.

One of Dan's biggest problems is that the Company brought him in to "straighten up" the department - but gave him guidelines that he would not necessarily have drawn. Dan has straightened up the department: our accountability is high, our productivity growing - but the guidelines haven't changed, and now, a couple of years later, people are chaffing at the restrictions and perceived "lack of trust." It's not so perceived: because Dan's "mission" from above forced him to review everyone's work with a skeptical eye, he developed a cynicism (bordering on paranoia) about what people say versus what they do. Not a pretty situation.

But one that would exist with or without Dan: everyone forgets that his predecessor had all the subtlety of a hammer and lasted only about a year with his "my way or else" attitude that dragged things to a standstill. For all his barking, cajoling, pushing, Dan is still trying to persuade, not beat down.

But it doesn't feel like that - because of Dan's second problem: he's waaay too smart for most of us.

We go into a group meeting, an idea is suggested, and Dan is already thinking two or three steps ahead of the herd, accepting or dismissing the implications of the original suggestions before most of us have been able to wrap our tiny brains around the original concept. He does this to himself, too, sometimes in in harsh tones that include the phrase "Dan, you idiot, no!" - but people are pretty much self-absorbed, and instead of getting into his groove and understanding the process, they withdraw and whimper, licking their misread ego-hurt wounds.

The Cube has a simple rule: Work at Dan's performance level, play straight with him, do the job right. Consequently, The Cube doesn't have any problems with Dan. Arguments, yes - that goes with the territory when working with Dan: he sometimes even brings people into his office to argue out an idea he has beating inside his eardrums. But those are creative arguments. And with the creativity goes a sense of humor that make staying late a lot of fun sometimes.

But The Cube does not see a happy outcome here in Never-Never Land. Too too many colleague Cubes would rather drone on than be creative. Maybe they're even right: most of any business is routine, someone has to walk around and around the millwheel.

Dunno. We'll see ...

Thursday, October 13

How Many Years?

JD writes a Note to The Cube ...

I'm 53. Not too old, not too young in my mind (and, when I look at the body of Jack, sitting in the cubicle next to me, not too shabby, either: Jack apparently went straight from high school into middle age, since he's only 20-something, with the butt and gut to match my Dad's).

But this is about work - and retirement. Today I got a letter from Social Security telling me how much I will receive if I retire at 63, 65 or 70. In other words: impossible, crappy and OK if my 401(k) doesn't nosedive.

Retire at age 70: that's only 17 years away. Wow, I must be getting old!

But wait a minute: 17 years ago I was only 36 and still young!

And 17 years ago was only yesterday, it doesn't even count as "Classic" Anything on the radio and I'd already had a computer for years.

And I only joined this place I'm working at ... 11 years ago?

Damn, something's wrong, and I sure don't want to die working here.

Friday, October 14

Nap Time (Sigh)

Lunchtime is nap time here. There's an indoor and an outdoor eating area and, since autumn still hasn't hit the chill factor too harshly yet, most people nosh in the fresh air.

What you will see if you arrive at our doorstep around mid-lunchtime is at least one person at every other table resting his or her head on the table, sleeping. Sleeping with that uncomfortable, nervous tension of the exhaust- ed: shoulders curved, head balanced on crossed arms, knees bending into one another on legs that really can't relax in an upright position. We're not horses, after all.

On the side of the building is a small green area: several trees umbrella over thick, sodded grass. A perfect picnic area - or "natural" bed.

So, coming here a few years ago, Rod went out and ate his lunch on the grass one afternoon. It looked so pleasant, several people remarked. No one joined him out there, though.

A week or so later, Rod brought a picnic blanket, laid it out on the grass, stretched out on it, and took a nap during lunchtime. It looked so comfortable, more people observed. No one joined him out there, however.

Now, three years later, whenever the weather is decent Rod eats his lunch on the grass and takes a nap on his picnic blanket. He has a pillow now, too. No one has ever joined him. No one has ever brought their own blanket or pillow and taken a nap under the cool shade trees. A few people raise their heads from their folded arms, eyes sleepy with exhaustion, and look across the way at Rod's dozing figure - then they go back to their own naps, dreaming of the cups of coffee that will see them through the afternoon.

In three years, no one else has taken a nap on the grass.

.

Saturday, October 15

Where We Work: Village

In the middle of the afternoon
A quiet melody played on the guitar,
vaguely Mexican,
vaguely Muzak.
And the empty office is timeless,
forever the village,
dust rising from the horses' footsteps,
a small steady tapping by an artisan across the way,
a quiet conversation between two others -
nothing to hide -
nothing to gain,
to run away from - to -

A very warm sun upon the back.
Close your eyes.
Swallow.
Remove the lump in your throat. Do not cry.
You will be rudely pulled out of this in a moment.
Close your eyes.

excerpt from *Lyrics & Lies*
R. C. Fleet

Sunday, October 16

Don't Wear The Interview Suit

What not to wear when you want a low profile or a calm employer: the suit you wore for your job interview.

This is the true conflict-of interests inherent in job interviews: we wear suits and nifty clothes to impress the potential new bosses - then we can never wear that particular ensemble again.

Why? Because they think you are going on a job interview somewhere else.

Try it if you feel like garnering sideways glances and nervous comments such as "Who you interviewing with during your lunch break, ha, ha!"

So, if you are on a tight budget and looking for a job, make sure you don't wear the only thing you have that's decent to the job interview - beg, borrow or steal something else - because that particular suit or dress is only going to be acceptable for sit-down dinners, office parties and interviews for jobs elsewhere from that moment on.

The Cube has observed. The Cube knows. The Cube has a tailored suit that sits in the closet gathering unused.

Monday, October 17

What Not To Wear: Better Clothes Than Your Boss

Kyra writes to The Cube ...

This may be only a Woman-to-Woman thing, but it's probably not a better idea to outdress your boss if she's not a he. (Sorry: couldn't figure out how to say this intelligently.)

If your boss is a woman - and you are a woman - she will probably not appreciate it if you are appearing more radiant than her glory and power. It is a fairly safe bet that you will not be hired in the first place by this Femme-Boss if you are more naturally attractive than she.

Fortunately, there are many women in power who hold an exalted impression of themselves, so there is a little more leeway here for the "naturally attractive" than may seem on first impression. This is largely due, with gratitude, to the Marketing Gods of Dior, Prada, Chanel and even Jacquelyn Smith for K-Mart, who have convinced our fragile egos that Purchase Power = Glamour & Appearance.

Still, once you are in the door, don't close it on your own ass by outshining the reigning diva.

This is even being sympathetic, because your boss may not necessarily be a Power Diva, but she is a human being. And, since the world at large, and the business world in specific, puts us femmes on a meat rack daily for comparison, then your boss cannot help but feel when the attention slides: from her considered opinions over to… consideration of your wardrobe-enhanced assets.

Tuesday, October 18

Dan, Hyper-Active Man: Turf Fighting Man, Part 1
[This goes back a week or so, to Dan, the Hyper-Active Man…]

So Dan, the Hyperactive Boss Man, is fast moving, super intelligent and abrasive to those who can't keep up with him - or who roll over at the sound of any bark, whether or not there is a bite to go with it. He can have a heart o' gold (which he does), but there's a tarnished pewter shell around it that is what most people see.

Which is tough, because without anyone trying to pierce

through the shell, I think Dan's gold heart is becoming more and more leaden. He's hearing only his own voice most of the time, seeing only passivity from below. He becomes monomaniacal.

And that is nowhere more apparent than in Dan's defense of his department's Turf.

Or, at least, that's what it started out to be: his department's Turf.

When Dan was brought in, the department was weakened: months without leadership had left it buffeted by the whims and annual budget allocations dictated by other departments' managements - bosses who, for whatever reason, found no benefit for their own areas in having another division of the company in good health. (This should be a Note someday: Why Veeps, Directors and Managers don't see their departments as part of a whole that needs to be healthy. Why?)

Dropped into this situation, Dan started his first year leading the department with an inherited crippled budget, no seniority, and zilch morale within the ranks. He spent those first nine months building up #s 2 & 3, then took the vastly improved productivity he inspired to argue successfully for #1 at the next annual review: a reasonable budget to work with. He was successful.

Which earned him enemies in the other departments.

The Turf Wars, always going on one way or another in low-key guerilla fashion, flared into open conflict.

At first, as Noted, Dan fought for his department, pushing for logic in resource allocations and fairness credit due. But the push-back was fierce: from passive resistance to outright obstruction.

What do you do when the IT Veep simply refuses to allow your field reps access to the company network, claiming "security" at the faintest wisp of rumoured breach? At one point, a Cube Colleague's request from an IT staffer for a link to a certain network drive had the IT Veep pull in the Cube Colleague and, behind a closed door that kept her trapped inside his office, berated the poor girl for 10 minutes for "breaching security by bypassing established lines of communications" (i.e., through him).

Into that belch of fire strode Dan the Hyperactive Boss Man - and his voice was loud and bold. He physically stood in the doorway, keeping it open (and barring cowardly exit by the IT Veep), and announced for the floor to hear: "You don't talk to my people that way. You don't decide whether they are acting out of order without checking with me first to see if they are following my directives. You should look into fixing up your stupid-ass lines of communications."

And you'd think that would have made Dan a hero for standing up to the dragon, but it didn't: most were just scared at hearing a loud voice - and looked at the voice as the source of the trouble.

But, because most bullies are cowards as well, the IT Veep backed down a bit - or at least let up on targeting people from Dan's department to pick on.

It sure would have been nice if Dan had let it stop there: win some, lose some, in the cause of defending the borders.

But Dan began to enjoy the Turf Wars.

Wednesday, October 19

Dan, Hyper-Active Man: Turf Fighting Man, Part 2

[This goes back to yesterday...]

But Dan began to enjoy the Turf Wars.

Defense wasn't enough: after the first year with a real budget, it's success proving Dan's point that his department had Worth to the company. Dan began to grow ambitious.

His department should be bigger.

And the way to bigger was Acquisition.

As with any organization, especially one of a certain size bigger than a job shop and smaller than a conglomerate, there are "stray" departments. These departments grew up out of a need --- for Facilities; for Maintenance; for the odd-'n-end Administrative job; and the occasional mini-department that was created for the Co-Partner's son 15 years ago, before that son went off to join a competitor company in Topeka. Most of these stray departments were leaderless - "leaderless" in the grand scheme of things that sees the need for something more than a competent staff with a strong Lead who knows what needs to be done and does it. No Supervisors, Managers or Directors.

Well, Dan argued persuasively, the flip side to that arrangement is that "things fall through the cracks" a lot of times. Oh, and they did. No denying that.

There was also no denying that - without a better-organized central management - things fell through the cracks all over the place. But, still, Dan had made his point on the micro-management level and in one weak moment of budget review convinced the bean-counters to assign three of the strays to his department's budget responsibility.

Dan's department doubled in size.

And doubled in power. The IT Veep won't give network access to an outside field rep? NOW see how the IT Dept operates in half the space it once had - after the Facilities group under Dan's command re-designs the cubicles.

But Acquisition is only one part of Turf Wars. The best Defense is good Offense. Dan's Offense took place in the realm of ideas: an idea for everything. For everybody. In every department.

The problem, since Dan was brought in to "straighten things out" and "shake things up," is that he is actually doing what the company told him to do --- originally. And, because Dan is also the Hyperactive Man, his energy is truly impressive. And and, because Dan the Hyperactive Boss Man is also smart and talented, his ideas are usually on the mark and first-rate.

And abrasive.

And intrusive.

And resented.

Dan is very much like Napoleon right now, winning battles right and left, reforming everything he touches, pushing the company forward. There are fewer and fewer allies every day, though. Every day.

◆

Thursday, October 20

No Nostalgia

There is a consoling myth that the last era, or the time just before that, was the greatest time ever.

It happens in pop music - or haven't you been listening to the radio stations?

Hear how the word "classic" has moved moves up a few decades - to the '70s & '80s now, soon to be creeping into the '90s?

'Happens in life. My parents fixated on the Turn-of-the-Century era before The Great War (no, no one was particularly missing Prohibition and the Great Depression); our children are hearing about The Greatest Generation that went through WWII; we're all stuck with some fantasy about the 1950s being the last Age of Innocence. And so on. I'm sure there were Renaissance nobles missing the glory days of the Dark Ages. Zog the Caveman probably longed for Cro-Magnon mythic greatness.

'Happens with jobs.

Anyone reading this far into these Notes From The Cube would notice that CHANGE is occurring and The Cube talks frequently about The Way It Was Before. And Before, it is implied, Was Better. Bullshit, of course.

Key to this consoling myth is that the time was always just a little bit before anything we actually know about. No child has great illusions about his or her parents - except that they're making it hell for us right now while growing up and they'll leave us in even worse shape once it's our turn to be responsible for it. But, once upon a time, when grandma and grandpa were pioneers, things were different ...

Well, it is a consoling myth. Not true, but consoling.

And besides: The Cube does not want a world before television, internet, really really cheap Chinese-made underwear and a protected 401(k) plan.

Friday, October 21

Tap Dancing on Quicksand

The thing that's most impressive about Rick is his ability to tap dance on quicksand.

Rick's in an enviable position in most ways: some seniority, more than a little power - he's a VP, after all - and a fairly decent success record, since the company sales have been growing in the 15 years of his tenure.

But what distinguishes Rick above all the other Veeps is his ability to stay in his position without ever taking a position. And, by never taking a position, Rick never offends anyone.

You might think that, by never taking sides, Rick would antagonize those who want him to take their side. This, however, is where Rick has them over a barrel. Isn't it better to have Rick neutral than to risk having him on the other side?

But, when push comes to shove, sometimes Rick has to make a decision. Hence, Rick is also a Master of the Study.

A Study is important. A Study is necessary. A Study prevents us from making impulsive decisions without Input and Evaluation. A Study buys Time.

And, what Rick has obviously realized, Time solves the decision-making problem in one of two ways;

* Either the problem is forgotten and a decision never has to be made – or

* The problem becomes so pressing that everyone else comes to a decision. Then, safely, Rick can join the Consensus.

Consensus is an excellent technique for avoiding individual responsibility.

The wonder is that so few others have mastered Rick's ability to tap dance on quicksand. But that's why he's a longtime Vice President: Talent will out.

Saturday, October 22

An elegant portrait of the insect as a young drone

An elegant portrait of the insect as a young drone
An ant, of course
Carrying on a hedonistic existence of self-centered
Laziness and indulgence while the workers
The proletariat
Ants
Carry the burden of transporting food and building materials
Necessary to shore the structure of the community.
Self-centered and restless:
What to do?
Having limited mental capacities
The drone finds himself at a loss to find proper activities
Suitable to his position.
To fly or not to fly ---
Why?
Why not?

No reason, just doesn't seem an attractive proposition.
Better, perhaps, to wait.
To wait and eat and grow
Grow fat
Grow heavy
Grow attractive
Send out the special secretions that attract the Queen
She would be attracted of course
Then make love
And die.
What?! ---

Let's try that again:

... make love
And die.
Hmmmm.....

Anybody here know how to clip some wings?
Here, let me help you carry that crumb ---
"Ol Man Drip-o, that ol Man Drip-o ... "
Nothing like sweat to cover up the old secretions ...
"He don't say nothin', he just keep ---"
Say, anybody notice how oppressed we are by the royalty?
Brothers! Workers! Unite!

excerpt from *Lyrics & Lies*
R. C. Fleet

Sunday, October 23

3rd Shift #1

Big Phil fiddles some Notes From The Cube ...

There are four reasons for working 3rd shift:
* Can't find anything better
* 2nd job
* Family to take care of during the day
* The belief that the daylight hours are now "free".

Generally, the line workers are on 3rd shift for reasons 1 and 3. Foolish writers, artists, actors and idealists are there for reason 4. The rest of us, crossing all lines of profession, are stuck there for reason 2.

3rd shift is where there's no daylight - ever - in the winter, while summer leaves the body aching for adventure just as the shift ends and it's time to head home for sleep. Summertime on the 3rd shift is like being perpetually 18, when it was possible to go to school all day, go to sports practice in the afternoon, work the 4-hour swing shift on Friday night - then party with friends till 2 a.m. and still get up in time to make the 7 a.m. start time for the weekend job. And do it again Saturday night/Sunday morning.

And when the body is no longer 18 - God, even when it's only 29! - 3rd shift is the pits in summertime, because no one is going to go home and sleep at 6 a.m.

No never, whatever.

Learned to drink cognac and espresso while watching the sun rise, from a New York bartender while working the night auditor shift. Bars don't close till 4 a.m. in New York (or didn't back in the day).

Sit on the front step of the hotel while the rest of the world sleeps it's last few hours and see the sun and wish you could just walk away from it all. Not angry, not resentful, not depressed: sort of at peace with the world and, while the caffeine and alcohol work their tonic through your bones, ready to enjoy the world. 3rd shift has its attractions.

Monday, October 24

3rd Shift #2

Big Phil's Notes From The Cube continue ...

Working the 3rd shift has it's own rhythm and world.

Basically, you are on your own most of the time. Even it there are five, a dozen or a hundred others working around you, 3rd shift is "abandoned" by the bosses - - except for that last hour when the daytime, main shift is prepping up and the honchos come in full of fire and energy to tell your shift what it will do the next night.

That's always an awkward moment, because 3rd shifters are tired, they know no one cared what was happening to them at 2 a.m. (as long as there were no emergencies requiring a daytime boss to wake up), and they are having their independence impinged upon.

Independence - that's probably the key word to 3rd shifters. 3rd shift may be few people's first choice for working hours, but if one can take it the bonus is that the midnight is yours. Not quite vampires we are during those hours, but knowing how Dracula and his "children of the night" feel.

As a Cube dweller working overnight, you know that your productivity is probably twice as much as the socializing 1st shifters. But your desk is always borrowed and your supplies are always someone else's leftovers and the daytime bosses are rarely going to leave any decision-making in your hands. The temptation is to goof off - who will see? - but the quiet and isolation make you more focused so that, even without trying, you work well.

Except for that last hour, when the daytimers come in, hanging around, getting in your way, talking about what "needs to be done" as if you weren't doing it already.

Tuesday, October 25

In The Midnight Hour

The Cube has some thoughts on Big Phil's Notes From The Cube of the past couple of days ...

In the midnight hour, to paraphrase Billy Idol:

You are bored - Bored - BORED!

3rd Shift, Overnight Shift, Midnight Shift, Give It Your

Own Name. For cube dwellers this is a time for wishing you were elsewhere and wondering what you did wrong in an earlier lifetime. Nothing challenging of a job-related nature will happen at midnight, this is data-entry time: kid ourselves not - no Company wants creativity inside the cubicles when they can keep a close eye on you.

(Moment to ponder whether that "outside Graphics Consultant" job is worth it. Probably not. When they can give it a specific name like that, they usually mean "outside, per-job worker without benefits." Not quite in the same category as the Unspecified Consultant "retained" to advise Directors, Veeps and Prezes for high High HIGH fees.)

Having been exiled once to the overnight shift for a three month "special project" so that "input can be constant without system downtime during the day" (lots were drawn, some of us lost, much like a bad sci-fi movie about feral villagers appeasing their corn gods), it is the reflection from this Cube that the act of keeping one's eyes open while performing mind-numbing tasks is infinitely more difficult in the midnight hour than at noon.

This is not a major observation, but one that Must Be Said.

(Note to Cube: Pronouncements seem more profound at the midnight hour than in the light of day. Get some sleep.)

Wednesday, October 26

The Level of Theft Makes It ALL Right

Story in the newspaper about a couple of GIs formerly in Iraq about to do some hard time for keeping $25K or so each of found Saddam loot. It is importantly to remember that We do not loot: that money was intended for rebuilding the country - and, of course, the "reform" Iraqi officials who needed their cut before it got to the country. Stupid sergeants, corporals and privates: what did they think they were doing. More important: What were they thinking, period?!? It's all about rank, the last vestige of the systems of royalty, caste and class level.

'Much like in the workplace. Alejandro has been fired recently for theft: thieving cholo had a box of surgical gloves in his trunk, taken from the restroom. OK, so he was going to use them to work on his car over the weekend and didn't want the dirty oil ground into his skin for when he returned to work on Monday and had to handle some pristine medical products. OK, OK, so maybe he intended to bring back what was left (if he remembered). OK, OK, OK - BUT: he can't take $10.00 worth of supplies from the company. That's petty theft, employee theft, pilfering, and so forth and it costs industry billions a year. Zero Tolerance. He's just lucky no charges were proffered.

And it's on a completely different level from field reps Larry, Moe and Curly's $500 use of the company credit card for meals at the Mystery Dinner Theater in Orlando, a necessary expense while they explained our company's products to Minnie, Mina and Mona, our buxom trade show babes, albeit four days into the trade show and roughly 12 to 6 hours (it was a loooong night session for some) before the show was closing down at 9 a.m. next morn. Those are overhead costs.

Speaking of which, overhead, no one should even consider questioning the top five head honchos on the $1.5 million in quarterly bonus fees paid out to themselves for... for... for simply working here. These are high upkeep executives who could go anywhere - but we have attracted them - and it should not be a part of the equation that the company lost money last year.

Besides, there are role models to emulate. The U.S. Senator from Alaska this week who proudly, defiantly, screamed "No!" to suggestions that a recent Transportation Bill be amended to re-direct a $ billion or so from an Alaskan bridge that would service fifty people and "misuse the money, MISUSE, that's what it is!" by spending it on hurricane-devastated New Orleans.

Stupid, stupid soldiers and line employees: there are levels of theft and, if you are on the lower levels, you are a thief.

Please take these Notes from The Cube to heart: you are a thief.

Thursday, October 27

3rd Shift #3: Patronized

Big Phil continues to write his own Notes From The Cube ...

Least enjoyable thing about 3rd shift is the patronizing attitude we get from non-3rd shift management.

Gotta emphasize: 3rd shift management is cool - they're like us, stuck out here in the dark, pretty much savoring our own, inspired-by-neglect independence.

We're all Can-Do on 3rd shift because:

a. the daytime bosses and maintenance and other support groups truly hate having to get up to help us, and

b. we learn quickly to make do with what we have and get by as best we can.

(Hey!, that's our everyday lives anyway. Not a big stretch.)

But, every now and then, the Day Boys decide we need Attention in order to Feel Like We're Part Of The Company. Ho-hum, what "Employee Relations" book did they get that from?

Someone usually shows up early - say 6 a.m. - to gather us all together and give us a pep talk, or tell us what's happening during the regular hours, or invite us to a company function that people sleeping during the daytime can't make without difficulty. We had a company Christmas party last year, for example, set on a Friday night - soooo, to accommodate us, we had to work on our Sunday off day so that we could have the Friday night free. Were the ribs and turkey and hotel mashed potatoes worth it? They tasted good. They were free. Sort of like showing up at HomeTown Buffet, though: didn't know the other people there, sat at tables with our own 3rd shift friends (just like the 2nd shifters sat with... blah blah), had a good time as long as Day Boy management didn't stop at our tables with their false *bonhomie* and pretend to talk to us for 5 minutes of awkward good cheer.

Aye, laddies, that's the rub: it's an awkward "friendliness" - very patronizing.

Would be better if they dropped by, said "Wow, you guys have the rough shift, but we appreciate it, need it, and here's a bonus envelope that the daytimers don't deserve." Short, sweet, honest, appreciative.

Certainly better than those really awkward times when a "team" of Day Boys (and, to be politically correct, "Boys" means men and women) shows up in our midst at 2 a.m. to spread their "message" - whatever the "message" is that day. I've got no quarrels with "message" - I was happy to learn the reasoning behind why half the cubicles had been moved from the left side of the room to the right side - but they made such a Big Deal about being up so early for us. C'mon, it's not like we don't do this every day! Suck it up and just be here.

Or move me to day shift, too, so that I can show up at 2 a.m. sometimes and pass down wisdom to my old colleagues. Tell you what, though: I won't be patronizing. I'll say, "Glad I'm not here every night, kids, but since I am tonight, here's what's what."

Like I said a few times: we 3rd shifters have our own rough independence and don't need the coddling like daytimers.

Friday, October 28

Dan 4: Dan & The New Bosses: Expectation

There's a new regime coming to town: Dan, the Hyper-Active Boss Man, is excited!

This is the perfect opportunity for Dan. He is ready. The old crowd, the Legacies, stood in the way of everything Dan was told to accomplish when they brought him in two years ago, have stonewalled almost every idea Dan has proposed.

And Dan has lots of ideas.

But back to the new regime: A family owned jobbie, the Company, there is no line of succession - kiddies went to other fields - and the two old brothers running the place are on their third wives each: whatever new spawns arise from their loins will be too young to head the helm for 25 years at least. In a way, this is for the best. Back when a couple of the owner-brothers' grown-up kids were being groomed for heir-apparent, there was a lot of passive-aggressive competition among all, seeing who would emerge top dog. Now that the kids are all founding their own fledgling careers elsewhere, only the Old Dogs are still here - and they reached their impasse of understanding long ago.

But now they need a succession and have hired in a Development Consultant and a small Board of Directors to work out the new steps for succession. After all: all complaints aside about minor problems, turf wars and egos, this is a successful Co. with several dozen millions of gross profit annually. Not such a hotcha profit margin, but certainly nothing to close the doors on when the Old Dogs retire.

So, now, Dan is excited: The Board and Dev Consultant are bypassing the baker's dozen of Legacy Veeps and looking for a new President - and they are soliciting input on the company from all of the Directors. Ideas are Director Dan the Hyper-Active Man's meat-and-potatoes.

He may be going a bit overboard, though. The Dev Consultant has given each Director a questionnaire asking 25 or so rather pointed questions on strengths of the company, problem areas, areas of opportunity, of weakness, of suggested solutions. Dan, of course, has answers and ideas for all of them. He's already up to 174 problems - and solutions.

174 problems - all of them real, definitely - all of them relating to other departments, legacy management & structures, turf war opponents.

Solutions - all of them solid - all of them revolving around Dan's department and/or way of doing things.

Focus, diplomacy and common sense are not, apparently, Dan's stronger points.

Dan has GREAT expectations for how the new regime will receive his input. He's creating a 5-year Business Plan right now that will cut through the stagnation that has dogged the company's growth for the past decade - it's a strong company, but not getting stronger, only "maintaining" - and Dan's biz plan addresses that problem. He will be presenting it to the Board, unrequested, shortly.

There's a new regime coming to town: Dan, the Hyper-Active Boss Man, is excited!

Saturday, October 29

Budget Time

Just some brief Notes From The Cube ...

November is rolling around, time for harvests in the heartland, Halloween candy for the next two weeks (candy corn never eaten), a couple of off-year elections that no one will show up to vote for, Turkey Day - and annual Budget time.

Come November we'll be looking at next year and trying to find ways to financially justify our wish lists. This will involve catching up on all that record-keeping that wasn't done for the past 10 months, figuring out what will be carryover to next year that can avoid too much scrutiny, and what we need to do to reach company goals.

[This is a "royal" We - since we will be doing the grunt work spreadsheeting to find $$$ justifications, and help management catch-up on its neglected admin paperwork, and put it all together into a coherent mass - we will not be doing the wishing, however.]

Slight flaw in the system: we work in coordination with several other departments - but each department makes up its wish lists independently.

And the Budget is based on the wish lists.

We shall see where this will lead.

Sunday, October 30

Rose's Toes

So Rose's toes are yellow today. Yesterday they were red. Tomorrow - who knows?

We spend each day wondering about the color of Rose's toes.

Monday, October 31

3rd Shift #4: Halloween Song

[Sing it to a Brit melody somewhere in the 1800s, vaguely martial, but jaunty...]

> You see us leaving in the morning,
> Leave as you arrive
> We never greet as colleagues, friends,
> You pass us and drive by.
>
> We work 3rd shift, it's not our choice,
> Who in his right mind would?
> The daylight hours are when we sleep -
> Or try if we damn could.
> I had a life once in the sun,
> When life was there to see.
> Now in the dark I grind my teeth,
> Trying not to weep.

But werewolf blood now fills my dreams,
The full moon rises foul:
When 3rd shift drives life to a halt,
Torn by the machine's howl.

A zombie's curse, this midnight hell,
This vampire's time of day.
But you are safe tucked in your bed,
Our bad lives dreamt away.

Good morning to the midnight shift!
The moon is rising high!
There is no one to watch us work,
Care if we live or die!

November

Tuesday, November 01

Upper-Level Decision-Making Understood

[There has been some commentary that these Notes From The Cube are fictions. The Cube insists on a stack of IRS affidavits that the following is a true and accurate account of a real-lif event. The only caveat is that it took a week to obtain the Review results that can be read below in 30 seconds.]

Had to coordinate an executive report: a 3-man Board of Directors review of an underling-proposed business plan. It is now understood how decisions are made:

Part 1: The Review

Board Director #1: I like it, it's our future.

Board Director #2: This is a dead-end proposition.

Board Director #3: I concur with my colleagues.

Wednesday, November 02

Dan 4.1.1: Greater Expectations

Dan the Hyper-Active Boss Man's expectations for the new regime are reaching the point of pre-coital anticipation: the Board of Directors, five months into office now, have chosen a new President!

These past few months have been frustrating for Dan. To string together as many clichés and mixed metaphors as possible in a paragraph: The winds of change were in the air, but the air was smog-filled with delay. A Company-wide Review was announced with great pomp and circumstance, but the many-headed mob of Management responded with fear and loathing. Only Dan, upright Dan, cooperated with full-throated cry of "Excelsior!" (The state motto of New York, apropos.) "Excelsior!" he cried, "Ever onward!" And onward Christian soldiers he marched - albeit to the unintended beat of a different drummer - to beat down the doors of Tradition (aka the Legacy Veeps) and help the Board establish a New World Order of Progress and Reform. It was the End of History.

But, first, the Board set itself up as a Search Committee to find the company a new jefe, don, shogun, fuehrer, chief, head of state - President & CEO.

The search is now completed. The lists scoured and the candidates vetted. The Best Man for the job has been found.

It is - one of them.

We have a new President and Dan the Hyper-Active Boss Man is ready to serve!

Thursday, November 03

The Reasonable Budget Cut Back to Absurdity

It's budget time and we are back in bizarro Never Never Land, where Captain Hook's cruelty teams up with Peter Pan's skewed logic, to make Wendy and us Boys prisoners on our little Island of Hungry Crocodiles.

Whew!, what a tortured metaphor! Fairly accurate, though.

In a nutshell:

Developed for the department a budget for next year consisting of Analysis of this year's workload-per-person, Resources demanded by the company's needs for next year as defined by the Strategic Plan, and the resulting Cost estimate.

Speaking of "strategy" and "planning": we not only have a Strategic Plan - we have a Super Plan!

Well, planning and strategy are good things in a general sense - road maps, fiscal guidelines, etc. - and so a proposal was developed. Due to a certain contradiction between the Super Plan's goals and planned budget constraints for the next fiscal year, our proposal offered logical options: If This is wanted, then That must happen - If resource X is reduced, then goal Y will have to be postponed - and so forth. And so on. Tedious but honest choices. We can't eat all the candy we want without either brushing our teeth a lot or getting a lot of cavities. 'Can't have it both ways, Peter Pan.

Oh, but we can, Wendy, we can!

So it is that, while the planning requires us to "plow with the horses we have" - with a 50% reduction in overtime - it also requires that we fulfill every need, wish and logistic demand called for by the plan: a Super Man Strategic Plan, if you will.

Thus, per calculations and experience, next year every person will be working 168% of their legal time - without 33% of the material resources required - to produce 28% more next year than this year.

And, hot damn, this budget balances!

Let's go back to the tortured metaphor and sing:

"A Wish Is A Dream Your Heart Makes - Per the Super Plan."

Friday, November 04

Another Friday

It's Friday night, everyone's gone home. Jack writes his own Notes From The Cube ...

How do they do it, everyday, the same? How do they come in knowing exactly what will happen, and do it, the same, again and again?

This is the moment of strength, of perseverance. The moment, a repeat repeat repeat moment, when responsibility to a family triumphs over one's own sored soul. That takes strength, courage. Nations are built on it.

Saturday, November 05

Jekyll-Hyde Why?

Sat in on a company dinner last night, at a round table with several of the top honchos and honchettes and their spouses. A formal affair, $250-a-pop charity fundraiser - leftover ticket from a last-minute sickout, hence The Cube's invitation. Enjoyable. The food was good. (Good!) and the charity made sense.

The company was pleasant.

Ah, there's the curiosity: the company was pleasant.

Which leads to the question: why so unpleasant so often in the daylight hours?

What is it about the four walls and offices and atmosphere of the enterprise of business that, on the job, these same people have to shed good nature and behave in conflict-guaranteeing manner?

Let's eliminate Drink as the false front of the camaraderie last night: pale wine in teaspoon servings does not a convivial drunk make. And they weren't jolly jolly, either, just decent people behaving in a friendly, enjoyable manner. The exact opposite, sometimes, of their daily demeanors, when pissant power plays and simple sourpuss grimaces mark their mugs and maneuvers.

'Used to watching workers sour-shift their ways through the days - odd to see the same thing at the upper levels. It's as if home life has rules of decency and goodness while the business world is designated wilderness with all its savage implications. 'Wonder why?

211

Sunday, November 06

Hey!

Hey diddle-e-dee, a Sunday working spree!
Hey diddle-e-oh, it's off to work we go!
Sometimes on weekends it is fun
To be here all alone
There's no one here to slow you down
The business is your own! (Or so it feels like)
Hey diddle-e-dee, productivity!
Hey diddle-e-oh, sometimes it's fun, y'know!

Monday, November 07

ISO Liz

[Notes From The Cube: Liz is a friend, a friend caught between the International Standards Organization (ISO), unwanted responsibilities, her own hard-working ambitions - and her own limitations. Why can't we learn to Just Say "No"?]

Liz is nice, nicer than so many. If you have a car breakdown or a family crisis or just need to talk things out, come to Liz.

Liz is tough, tougher than so many. If you are a slacker in your standards or like to skip steps or screw up on dotting an "i," look out for Liz.

Liz is suspicious, more suspicious than so many. If you work for her and do anything involving judgment, don't expect any decision you make to go through without her scrutiny.

Liz runs a department. She did not always run a department. She did not always run this department: it came her way because no one else wanted it, 15-18 years ago, when Liz had been around 7 or 8 years herself and was capable and trustworthy and certainly honest. She didn't know what this department was supposed to do - but neither did anybody else - and the anybody else's were smart enough or deft enough or tricky enough to pass on the responsibility for rising or falling to newbie manager Liz.

Sometimes you don't rise or fall. Sometimes there's a third way: existence without understanding. Much like life in a universe where, whatever our belief in God, Creator or Samsara-Enlightenment, it's always a one-way conversation for public consumption, leaving the human beans to make their own interpretations about the metaphysical facts on the ground.

"Metaphysical?" Well - yes. Liz's department answers to Higher Powers sometimes - aka state and government regulatory agencies - and some self-made Rules - aka ISO rules - and with no one to guide her, Liz created her own Oz-like maze of logic and "I-think-that's-what-they-want" rule-making that no one at the time took the time to figure out if it was true or wishful thinking or bonehead desperation.

But Liz had done it - and she hadn't fallen on her face - and now it was Hers.

And it works like crap: an unwieldy structure of rules and reinforcements that everyone agreed to for expediency and now they are stuck with - and stuck with Liz as their appointed Knowledge Source on the subject.

And it works like crap: everyone knows it - including Liz. But no one knows a Better Way, nor wants to propose a Better Way for fear of getting stuck with it themselves, or for fear of taking on Liz (who, after all, did this loyally and with full approval of all).

But self-knowledge of one's own failings is a terrible bur- den - and one that must be covered up. Liz cannot admit her failings. She cannot say: "I am lost, help me." She cannot lead the revolution - against herself. No. She is stuck as Defender of the Faith, a shaky temple where even the slightest doubt could set the foundation a-trem- bling. So, like a good Inquisitor General, Liz persecutes any and all Doubt: heretics - for don't we know (and we know) that the Purpose of the Faith is good?

Or do we know that anymore?

More and more rumours and back-grumbled discontent shred at the edges of the Faith that Liz has construct- ed for the company, on behalf of the company, with the mandate of the company. That the Faith is false obscures the Truth underneath, the Truth missed by Liz, who can never find it, underqualified, unenlightened, unchosen by Knowledge as she is.

And so she turns obstructionist to logic and reform, to nit-picking on the typographical rituals instead of ad- dressing the structural substance, the face of all that is wrong with her misconceived Faith.

But Liz is more - because, as is noted, no one will step in to help her. Or maybe they cannot, like a nonswimmer helplessly watching a drowning man sink.

Either way, intentions good or ill, Liz has assumed her iconic, traditional place in the way things are. The wom- an who will take the Fall.

✚

Dan 5: New Bosses-Weird Responses

Dan the Hyper-Active Boss Man has hit a roadblock of sorts. The new executive management that came in - a Board and new President where once there were only a pair of brother-partners - these new bosses give weird responses to everything that Dan does or says or proposes.

"Weird responses" - What would that be?

That's... That is... why... it's weird. It's hard to make out.

It's easy to dislike Dan. He's very in-your-face with his enthusiasms and aggressions, his good humour and his funks, with his ideas and his opinions. Dan is, if nothing else, transparent and unsubtle. "Honest" as a bottom-line word that might not be heard a lot around the business world, but there you have it: that's what Dan is - honest about what he says, does, is.

One would think, if one were above Dan on the corporate food chain, that Dan would be easy to manage. He's certainly eager to please. You can tell him straight off Yes or No and, though he might disagree (and offer a better alternative), he will obey. He will strive to do his best - and make his department do its best. He may strive too hard sometimes and Dan could benefit from some "parental" guidance in these matters more than he gets. "Be a little softer, Dan" or "Try approaching this less head-on" or "Remember, Dan, your staff have lives outside of this place." But those things are never said, probably because Dan's doing what they want done - and taking the heat for their directives. Or they're tired and don't care that much any more: they are "Legacy" Veeps, after all. Or maybe they care even less about those under them than

Dan does: he's a hard-driving boss, but a softie inside who's never fired anyone and protects his people like a mother hen. Dunno.

But that was before, anyway. Now the Legacy Veeps are mainly silent, wondering where they'll fit in the new regime, and pronunciamentos come from a level higher.

The new President has already brought in a number of consultants to help him "get up to speed and speed up the process" - folks who sometimes look as if their temporary offices are being outfitted for permanency. The Official Statements come from this new cabal, a far more coherent group than the turf-fighting Legacy Veeps. (A very beneficial side effect of the current situation is the apparent truce amongst the warring factions. They may be backstabbing one another in private conversations with the new regime, but the open warfare that caught so many of us minions in the crossfire has been replaced by a tentative peace.)

Back to Dan, the Hyper-Active Boss Man: because Dan is so straightforward and honest, it is easy to react to him, positively or negatively.

But the new regime doesn't respond to Dan either way.

Dan says "Hello" - they nod with that distant, "I don't know you but I'm polite" expression typical of the Queen of England on public display.

Dan provides a year-end progress report that doubles the previous year's output - there is a curious review of the numbers, but no questions.

Before the new President was installed, Dan prepared a 5-Year business plan outlining a bold new approach for the company to take. Part show-off, part honest proposal, the plan was detailed; offered some very perceptive analyses of the company, the marketplace, and the company's place in the marketplace; was, no matter what else, an impressive piece of work.

There has been silence about it ever since the first, one-phrase reviews from the Board a month ago.

There was a big meeting of the executives, directors and managers last week.

Several directors and managers came back midway to pick up their messages and commented that Dan was singled out for particularly hard questioning - but the kind of questioning that seemed to come from left field and did not address any of the issues that were supposedly being discussed that day.

By the same token, before the big meeting day was ended, Dan was assured that his accomplishments of the previous year insured his position this year. Everyone, in fact, was offered reassurances - but Dan was singled out.

Still, they are having a meeting next week on planning and Dan's department is not part of it.

Still, they have approved an expansion of his department, to begin in the next quarter.

Still... There's such a left-hand, right-hand dichotomy that Dan is starting to feel confused and unsure - of himself. This is a man incredibly eager to please and do what the company wants, and they send very weird messages.

99 99

Wednesday, November 09

Sitting in a Budget meeting

Notes From The Cube while sitting in a Budget meeting ...

Prez sez: "It's all about cutting" - positive way to look forward to next year, 'thought we were "doing better than ever before" according to the monthly President's Message.

Prez sez: "We'll find our cuts in the low hanging fruit" - didn't we hear that 2 years ago when talking about "first profits"?

Wow, the smell of $$$ panic

[Note to Polly, under the table: mmmmm, now we rearrange the figures again - keeps us employed another week on useless exercises: the total is the same.]

Clark doesn't know what the f--- he's talking about

[A little explanation here: Clark is the CFO - Chief F--- Off or Financial Officer, whichever you prefer. But Clark has latched on to a key word today, "organic," and seems to think that anything that isn't "organic" is unnecessary. What the hell is he talking about?!]

$$$$$

Thursday, November 10

How Do You Cut What You Don't Know?

[The current batch of Notes From The Cube may seem redundant, because The Cube is still sitting in annual Budget review meetings this week. If The Cube has to suffer through them, so does everyone else. Misery does not make us more charitable.]

So, we're being asked by the CEO and his CFO for an FYI on the YTD v PAB - and where we can make some cuts in order to up the PAR.

Sound Greek to you? 'Didn't sound much clearer to those of us in the room.

Sadly, truly sadly, they speak in acronyms:

> CEO - Chief Executive Officer
> CFO - Chief Financial Officer
> FYI - For Your Information
> YTD - Year To Date
> v - versus
> PAB - Projected Annual Budget
> PAR - Projected Annual Revenues

But, keeping with the Greek theme, the question that came up amongst all us Myrmidons of Manufacturing is fairly simple: How do we make budget cuts when we don't know what they want to do next year?

(Read your Shakespeare to get the pun[1])

---

1)Try *Troilus and Cressida*. Apropos, a question from left field: Cressida was the Trojan woman who was unfaithful to her warrior-lover Troilus. Why did they name a car "Cressida"? Speaking as a driver who has the typical love-hate relationship with mine automobile, this reference does not bode well for the affair.

Y'see, it works like this here and in all the world: The Emperor may want new clothes, but somewhere down the line there's a seamstress who has to cut the pattern --- and What pattern did His Excellency select?

We dunno and He's not telling.

Here's the thing: We make gadgets, not whizmos. So this budget is for gadgets.

But some gadgets are part of whizmos, so we've made a few whizmo-oriented gadgets. And, to make those whiz-mo-system gadgets, we've hired a few whizmo engineers, and a few whizmo consultants, and made a few whizmo inventions because, really, whizmos are where the industry is going a few years down the road so that's where our future is.

Or so His Excellency has been telling us this past year as he laid off a whole shift of our gadget operations.

Howsoever, it seems, gadgets are relatively cheap to develop and make while whizmos are expensive. More than that: whizmos are the Future, not the Now, of income generation. To keep the cash flow a-flowin' we need gadgets a-goin'.

His Excellency decrees Budget Cuts.

"Your Highness," we ask, "What, in your Strategic Plan, do you want to cut: cheap gadgets or expensive whiz-mos?"

"We need to make Cuts," is the answer.

The seamstress crunches her scissors down between the lines: the Emperor's new clothes will be something between a shirt and a pair of pants.

Friday, November 11

The Getaround

Here is how it will happened - because it's happened this way before ...

The owner, getting older, semi-retired, will ask about something: something that is pertinent, that he cares about, that is "troublesome."

"Troublesome"? Yes - to the new management that the owner hired-on. They have agreed to "maintain your vision," but can't wait till he gets so blind that the "vision" is too narrowed to mean anything. They have been slowly helping along that process, isolating him from information, shaping the issues in ways that keep out "unnecessary" alternatives - one could almost say that they lie to him, but that would be as false as some of their accusations against those that they have persuaded to "voluntarily terminate" themselves.

No, they don't lie - they Getaround.

Getaround.

"What's the status on this, Bill?"

"We're getting around to that, Bob. It's important, like you said: don't want to jump into it unprepared."

"It has to be handled!"

"It will be - it is - we're meeting on this tomorrow and-"

"I'm not here tomorrow."

"Well, you want us to get on this right away."

"... Yes."

But the meeting, with the owner not there, will never happen. And, for the next two or three times the owner and the new management meet, there will be other things to talk about. And this won't be talked about - or dealt with - ever.

Until it wilts away, or the deadline passes and it's too late, or the owner brings it up again ---

And "we're getting right on it" again.

The Getaround.

Saturday, November 12

Budget: The Structural Flaw

[Now, these Notes From The Cube do not indicate Power, Prescience or Profound ability to change the course of events. The Cube is simply one of the few who can string a couple of sentences together, handle a spreadsheet beyond basic data entry, work a Gantt chart and convert them all into meaningful (meaningful?) reports -- hence, The Cube has supported annual Budget reviews for a few years now and has observed. Observed and observed. No one listens from below, so observation is the limit to The Cube's participation.]

The structural flaw in the Budget review: no one's in the same room at the same time.

Start: President gives a PowerPoint "Vision Plan" the last week of the 3rd quarter. Each Department is instructed to prepare its next year Budget by the 2nd week of the 4th quarter.

Observed: No instruction, direction, or scheduled time for the departments to coordinate with one another or the

President. The Budgets are prepared independently.

Step 2: President meets with each Department, alone, and asks them to explain their Budgets. He brings along one or two Financial people, not necessarily the same people the Departments were dealing with in prepping their Budgets. President and Financerios are seeing the Budget figures for the first time. No reference is made to the President's "Vision Plan" - now or evermore - but the President asks that the Department meet with another Department on line items 7, 14, 15 & 24; and perhaps with yet another Department on line items 3-6, 8-11 and 20-23; and so on. Financerios are instructed to go over the figures and report back to the President; no instruction, plan or inclination for them to talk to the Department on the Why of an item, only to make sure that the #s add up. Everybody due back in a week.

Observed: President gets a very seat-of-the-pants understanding of the line items. He may know a lot about some departments but, since no one can be an expert on everything (especially current President, brought in from outside the industry for his "management" skills and rolodex of contacts), this leaves the President vulnerable on the issues involved. A well-poken Department head can breeze over questionable items, while a conscientious technogeek may be at a loss to explain a complicated-but-essential line item.

Step 3: Meet the President and the Chief Financial Officer. Cuts are made. Department heads are put in the position of justifying (or not) decisions made in coordination with another Department - but other Department is not represented at this meeting. CFO has not spoken with any of the Department heads about justifications; CFO sees only numbers and fiscal targets, as directed. (By whom? 'Never identified.)

Observed: We're down to the wire, and the Budget items that make it through are treated much like the salmon swimming upriver - survival of the luckiest.

CONCLUSION: Easy sarcasm aside, The Cube is still surprised over so many years at *why no one has put all the key people together in one room* and hashed out these short-range line item issues in coordination with the company's mid-range tactical plans and long-range strategic goals.

Oh, sure, these same people get together regularly - but never with the same focus and facts/figures at-hand. Now they alternate supporting and competing against one another in isolated configurations of ad hoc assembly.

'Used to think this was a symptom of the old company ways: problems that a family-owned business faces when it grows larger than its roots. However, we've had professional management and organization for a few years now. This is their new structure, and it repeats the disconnects of earlier, albeit with a rhetoric that gives lip service to "communication," "interactivity" and "accountability."

?

Sunday, November 13

Budget Priorities

Pierre Dolet notes from the cube he lives in ...

Our annual Budget review this year is very uncomplicated: we have to cut our operational expenditures drastically in order to pay for a few new friends at the Top.

Compare:

The Company must "plow with the horses we have."

Operations needs to be "lean and mean."

The executive branch "needs" a newly-created Vice President of Business Development.

We currently have a Vice President of Sales, a Vice President of Marketing, a Vice President of Advanced Marketing - and the President is, by his own declaration, "a market-oriented guy."

1 Vice President salary = 1 1/2 Director or 2 Managers or 3-5 Engineers or 5-8 Technical Specialists or 10 Line workers or 2 product development projects or 5 safety-required facility/equipment upgrades or 1 new manufacturing equipment that will cut a production line's costs in half.

But there is a Future:

We are also hiring 2 new outside consultants to supplement our existing staff of 6 consultants brought in last year - they hold "the company's promise in their heads."

To "save valuable resources," we are cutting loose the long-time consultant who is responsible for 30% of our patents and 50% of our patent applications.
We have priorities: new is better.

Monday, November 14

Budget Fiddle

Hey diddle diddle,
What a fine fiddle
Fingers stuck in the pie
The little prez sez
"I ate too much,
Now the company's about to die."

Hey diddle doodle
It's the bonus kaboodle
Don't stop to wonder why
When the Board takes its cut
It's a little too much
Now the company's about to die.

Hey diddle dangle
Find another angle
Cut the budget in half, just try
Our hidden stash
Leaves the Co. without cash
Now the company's about to die.

Hey diddle dongle
It's a cruel biz jungle
Where the ink it runs blood red
And they've gotten all they can
And away they've ran
Now the company's done gone dead.

Tuesday, November 15

Working From Home: Harder Than Ever

Working from home today. Foolish idea.

Have to do this time to time: better access to certain research tools that the company won't authorize for purchase; sometimes just need to eliminate the 3 hours round-trip commute in order to make a deadline and the immediate boss-woman understands the time press. Plus the company has set up offsite access to company files for the field personnel - not fully functional for moi but gets the job done. Plus, oh Alexander Graham Bell, we are never out of touch with the office.

Which is why it's a foolish idea to work from home today: never out of touch.

Thanks to the miracle of modern communications, the "concentrated time" needed to finish The Project has been dissipated so far by 2 telephone calls and 3 "must answer now" emails (and it's only 8 a.m.). 'Been working for the past hour and a half and haven't even started on the planned task.

And ... That's the way it will go all day. Know this from experience. Will work 12 hours to get 6 hours of work done, won't get the regular breaks, will eat at the home desk - and will have everyone jealous tomorrow for "the day off."

When you work really hard, you want the "Oohs" and "Aahs" of credit and impressing people. There is no audience at home, except for a dog that thinks I'm God anyway and a cat that's absolutely certain I would be her dinner if only she were the tiger in fact that she is in her heart. Spouses and lovers don't count: they want you at home, not your work brought home.

Think I may goof off for a few hours this afternoon and work until midnight.

Might as well: at home there is no one to hear you yawn.

Wednesday, November 16

Filler Days

Today is a filler day: nothing particular to do, but do a lot to fill the time.

This would be a great day to be a line worker, where the tasks are the same and repetitious, day in, day out, except for the occasional crisis.

Not so for us in the cubicles: theoretically, we think and problem-solve and...

Well, now, maybe that's not so true.

Looking over to the left a few cubes down, ol' Ray there, he's doing the same check-through-the-files and double-check-against-the-papers-on-his-desk that he does every day. And Ellen on the other side of the wall, she's tap-tap-tapping away at her daily, hourly, minutely, input of purchase orders and what-we-got-todays (I'm sure there's a name for that - oh, yeah: Received).

So ... then ... maybe I'm wrong: we in the cubes are the same as the line workers. There are no filler days, only same-old same-old.

Or maybe I'm in the wrong set of cubes.

Thursday, November 17

There are no horses only men

There are no horses only men
To pull the load these days.
Wagons lay abandoned by the roadside,
Horses offer weekend recreation ---

And streetlights blanch the midnight sky,
Stealing stars from sight.

They look for data to till the soil
Bit by bit, ream by ream of paper
Of sweat that once poured freely in the sun,
Now stinks dully in the fluorescent haze.

Photogrey eyeglasses, still dark, inside
Fluorescent ions have captured the sun.

Do you play golf? No.
Tennis? Yes.
Handball? No.
I like the Jets, too --- You have a season ticket?

The church social could not compete
With twenty thousand --- more! ---

Tomorrow I will meet you at the mall
Between the thousand cars we'll
Greet - embrace - hurry together
To the safety of air conditioning. It

Does not matter where we hitched the horses
They will not wander far ...

excerpt from *Lyrics & Lies*
by R. C. Fleet

Friday, November 18

Betty by Detail

Betty knows her stuff - in detail.

In this age of electronics, it is refreshing to see a woman - not old, mind you, but in that prime age of 30-45, teenage daughter and all that wonderful life experience - to see a woman who still fills in her log books by hand, the fact that she is a supervisor of a technical department filled with MBAs notwithstanding.

Yes, Betty is great: none of this "flash by me" stuff. She will painstakingly transfer the information from one printed out electronic file into her precious logs - then give those logs to her assistant to be typed into another electronic file log book: none, None, NONE of this cut-and-paste crap for Betty! No!

And the newer electronic file log book: heaven help us if it should be compatible with any database known to man/woman/child/IS/IT or You Know Who. No, Betty, pure Betty, wants this as a text file - so that some one else (she has many assistants) can re-type her electronic file log books into a database format that everyone else in the company can use.

Oh, Betty, oh, Betty: you are the person who makes our lives worth living on the weekends when you do not touch our lives.

Saturday, November 19

The Bigotry of Powerlessness

Hank writes his Notes From The Cube ...

I came across this scribbled on a whiteboard in Conference Room C (the small one that no one hardly uses):

THE BIGOTRY OF POWERLESSNESS

It hit home. We in the cubes don't have power. The workers in the factory certainly don't have power. I am guessing that most of the management doesn't have power, either, not really. (It's probably even more apparent to someone who has a title to realize that he or she has very little influence over how things are run.)

And that results in a bigotry - unconscious? conscious? - against everyone else we perceive as "less" powerful than ourselves, who (if they advance) threaten what little power we (think) we have.

Someone in a bad prize-winning book I just read said the only thing worthwhile in that excruciating literary experience: Suffering doesn't make you more charitable to your fellow sufferers. 'Same thing with power - or powerlessness.

Most of the time it's a numb feeling, though, like a scratch that's scabbed over. When we pick at it, that's when it hurts and the bigotry seeps out.

You see it all the time in elections. Someone else wrote somewhere (I'm just full of misremembered allusions) words to this effect: Americans don't believe in taxing the rich because they all believe that someday they are going to be rich and they don't want to lose it. So, every time an election rolls around, so many of us vote for the promises made against our own interests - because I am not them, the disadvantaged or the poor or ... the powerless.

Y'know, I don't even blame those with power. They don't make us what we are. They even suffer - because our petty bigotries result in petty jealousies and petty turf wars and petty bureaucracies (the perfect bastion of fake power) that grind things down to a slow crawl sometimes. Dogs fighting for the same bone, even when there are two or three others sitting by the side.

Sunday, November 20

Big Plans Old & New

We're changing our Big Plans.
I can't tell you why.
All I can tell you
Is we're going to try.

Our Big Plans are scrapped now.
The Super Plan died.
When you look at the numbers
You see how they fried.

Our execs are experts
Top dogs top dime:
They told us our Big Plans
Would take us Big Time.

But now it is over -
But please don't feel blue:
Yes, the Big Plans are dead plans -
But the next Plans are Brand New!

Monday, November 21

Verbal vs. Written

Texas Slim writes his Notes From The Cube ...

Nope, you don't want to write no nothin' down.

This is the lesson I have learned - LEARNED! - my friends, learned from one of the best: Gene the Lead.

Gene has understood the wisdom of the unwritten word. Y'see, some people say erroneously that you should write them memos to cover your ass.

BUT - as Gene the Lead has so wisely muttered under his breath: "You only need to cover your ass in writing if you have exposed it in writing in the first place."

THE SPOKEN WORD is the key. Tell that counterpart what you want. Speak to that underling. Discuss that matter with a colleague.

It's good People Skills, talking is. Good Management Practice, too, the personal touch. You are communicating directly with people -

AND

- you are cutting through the bureaucratic mountains of paperwork that Everyone Knows bog us down. You are efficient.

And you cannot be pinned down.

You cannot be made to answer for something that doesn't exist except in someone else's memory.

You have deniability: "I didn't say that, you must have misremembered."

You have obscurability: "Well, we all heard the same thing, but I guess we interpreted it differently."

And, finally, you have blame-ability, too: "Don't you remember I told you to do that? Now Production is on our tail and you didn't do what I told you to do last month."

So remember, friends, REMEMBER: Say it, don't write it.

Tuesday, November 22

Explanation #2: Why it happens that way

Or maybe it is arrogance.

Wednesday, November 23

Thanksgiving Song

Does anyone know a Turkey Day song?

We're sitting here in the employee lunchroom trying to think this thing out and coming up with zilch.

Thanksgiving is one of the great enjoyable holidays of the year - food, family and not a lot of commercialization - but no song. There is a Thanksgiving symbol, though, two of them: the Turkey and the Pilgrim.

Pilgrims don't make for fun-loving musicality:

> *I'm a Puritan*
> *And all I can say*
> *Is*
> *Everyday I work*
> *And*
> *Sundays I pray.*

Not your most inspirational.

Neither is the only Turkey Song we could think of:

> *Gobble-gobble gobble-gobble*
> *Gobble-gobble gobble-goo*
> *For a National Holiday Symbol*
> *Why do I end up as food?*

Well, they're about to give out the Thanksgiving turkeys now, so we'll end this scintillating intellectual endeavor.

Thursday, November 24

Dan 6: Dan & the NEWER Boss

Okaaay, yesterday was the beginning of an interesting experience - in that "interesting" way that makes you wish for dull and boring. We got the announcement of a new boss coming - a new Vice President who will be above Dan the Hyper-Active Boss Man.

The problem is: Dan, who is a Director just under the current Veep (who wears two hats and has long expressed a desire to split-off his department responsibilities), Dan interviewed the new VP two months ago - under the impression that he was interviewing someone who would be one of his reporting Managers. Awkward, yes?

More than awkward - a lie. Not by the current two-hatted Veep: he thought the interview was for a Manager, too.

Or so he was told by the new President, in office for only a couple of months now, who presented it as acquiescing to a long-standing request to fill the vacant Manager's position. "Yeah, I know this guy from my old firm. Maybe he'll work out here. Have Dan take a look at him."

So Dan did. He wasn't terribly impressed. However, taking the Veep's advice that "Dan, you aren't connecting too well with the new President and the Board, don't pick a fight on this one. Interview a few others and make your recommendations as a group. Maybe he's the best available or maybe you'll find a better candidate, but don't knock him out right away - that'll look like an outright rejection. And, either way, you'll get to expand your department."

That was an argument that Dan could buy into, so he wrote his "Not terribly impressed, but appears competent and qualified" notes and waited to compare notes on the next interviewees.

As it turned out, what with other priorities, Dan didn't get around to interviewing any other Manager candidates. Annual Budget Review came around a couple of weeks ago, though, and - unhappy surprise - the Manager position was cut from the Budget.

Then - happy surprise - a new Vice President slot was put in the budget. Since Dan has had reasonable expectations of becoming a VP based on his record of accomplishment and de facto running of the department for the past 3 years, he was happy happy with the allocation.

Oddly, the current Veep was not so happy. Despite his long-standing wish to split-off responsibilities, he felt uncomfortable that he hadn't been consulted about this decision.

But his unhappiness was nothing compared to Dan's when they both learned, the next day, yesterday, the day before Thanksgiving holiday, that the new Vice President was going to be the man they had both interviewed as Dan's supposed subordinate Manager!

The announcement came from the President and Board of Directors came by timed email that arrived a half-hour before the end of business day. The President had already left for the long Thanksgiving weekend.

Friday, November 25

Policy in absentia

Pierre Dolet writes his Notes from The Cube (this is not a holiday weekend in Canada) ...

Hate making decisions. Guess most people feel that way. See that it's happening at all levels, too - 'specially on the policy-making level.

Policy. That's that crazy thing that politicians do so well, when they lay out Grand Plans that no one could expect anyone to actually follow. "Broad Strokes," doncha know?

By and by, though, it would be helpful down here in the cubicles to have a little policy guidance once in a while.

No, not Rules & Regulations: those are the nitpicking, can't-see-the-forest-for-the-trees crap of the mini-meenie-mojo-macho bureaucrats who enjoy Control. (yeah, with the big "C," eh.)

Policy, on the other hand, is a guidance - a philosophy of approach. There is a Team philosophy, the Lone Wolf approach, Vertical Integration, Fiscal Restraint, Laissez-Faire (or, usually, Let Me Faire and You Don't Do - but that's back to politics again).

Any which way, we're setting up for next year and it's tough to make plans without any policy guidance from the top. Everything is seat of the pants, even the 1-year, 3-year and 5-year Plans. (Question: Does anyone remember from high school World Affairs how Stalin and Mao's Five Year Plans were such disasters?

Regularly. On both the economic and human scales. Isn't the "Five Year Plan" a concept/term we should abandon, if only for the sake of good taste?)

Oh, yes, they are planning far out ahead - but what's the policy guiding those plans? There's all such a grab bag feeling to the whole endeavor, especially as it filters down to the cubicles, where we create the support structure for the plans, fleshing out the details and without any other guiding principle than "That's what they want us to do."

One part of me is cool with the lack of Policy and says "OK, you don't want to get straightjacketed into these things." After all, would you want a doctor to diagnose your illness only from the "guidelines" of the medical book? I used to take car engines apart and put them back together: nothing ever fit and worked exactly like the Theory of Motors said they should. Why is it different here, then?

Because we're not inanimate objects and, yes, we would understand changes made in mid-stream if the policy had to be adjusted to meet realities on the ground.
But you've gotta have a policy to begin with, doncha?

Right now the "changes," "adjustments," "corrections" (yes, we use all the right words) are made without apparent policy reasoning. They are reactions - possibly right (given the experience of many making the changes, probably right) - but still reactions.

The tiger's a wily and powerful master of the jungle, but it's still a feral being.

Saturday, November 26

Nope, Nada, Nothing on a holiday weekend

C'mon! It's a holiday weekend (except for everywhere else in the world). Is anybody anywhere gonna do anything work-related this weekend? Not in this Cube.

Sunday, November 27

Goof-Off & Deadline Season Approacheth

What's nice about the Thanksgiving holiday weekend is that it's the lead-in to the great end-of-year, Christmas-party, meet-your-deadlines rush.

Mixed priorities abound these next few weeks. Tis the season when party-planning and Most Important Tasks are given equal weight. You can goof off by going from A/R to Telephone Sales to IT to Anywhere and have an every-other-day lunchtime feast, then roll in the aisles lazily for the rest of the afternoon. Since everyone rushes to use up those sick days and personal days that can't be carried over to the new year, 25% of the staff is out on any given day. Just throw out the week between Christmas and New Year: even if you're here, who else is? It's like being on a deserted isle: no company, no conversation - no supervision. The perennial Zen question: if you sleep at your desk and no one hears you snore, do you make a sound?

And, meanwhile, every year-end goal has to be met - at least on paper. But who, what and how? Godalmighty, when? There is no more time to do it. The cash comes in January, so the income goal will not be met by any hurried sales contracts. No one will read your 12/23 dead-lined report until the new year. Still, it has to be DONE.

Such a season.

Monday, November 28

So Hard After A Holiday

It is sooo hard to do anything after a holiday weekend. So hard. The theory of "refreshed in body and spirit" hits a snag when both the body and the spirit find themselves back in the same old cubicle unchanged. Many around are decorating their cubes, shiny fake fir trees abound. Blue faux chlorophyll is apparently popular this year, as opposed to the traditional colors: green, red, plastic "snow" and tinfoil shiny. It is a desperate fight against reality, though. The cube is still the same little, cramped, unspiritual, un-turkey-filled place. "Complain not," the little voice says, "others are worse off" - and I see the IN Room where twenty some-odd desks sit in open space taking their tele-orders, the hubbub of their voices a gentle drone of persistent commercial existence "Happy Holidays How May I Help You?" The report is due Wednesday: Has the Veep returned from his vacation yet to receive it?

Tuesday, November 29

Spike, the Genius: Who He Is

So what we have is a genius: Spike.

Spike has come up with 50% of everything we are going to be doing in the future - and advised us on another 25% of that future. He knows about those things and we don't.

It scare the hell out of us, of course. (Well, maybe not The Cube, since I don't know beans about most technical things, so I long ago gave up being threatened by others' knowledge.) It scares the hell out of the Royal "Us" because:

241

(a) All of the techno-bosses like to think that they are god-like in their omniscience, and

(b) Spike is a consultant. He don't work for The Man directly. He no be bullied, ordered about, told what to do.

Spike, he just think and invent and lay foundation for patents and products that look to the future.

He also scares the hell out of the Royal Us because there is no PROFIT in the future just yet. We is bottom-lining it today, but paying for tomorrow with no end in sight.

Oh, and Spike is crazy. Think artist in garret drinking absinthe and dreaming surreal dreams that he accurately depicts in his paintings: these are Spike's inventions. This is Spike. (Minus the absinthe: his surrealism is entirely inner-born).

In the techno-world of plodding engineers and verbally-dexterous/talent-challenged management, Spike doesn't fit in to the daily grind. Hence his consultancy.

♌

Wednesday, November 30

Spike #2: How Spike Came to Us

Spike the Genius is a throwback to another era, when the Company was run by Giants mean and brilliant, whimsical and brutal. A scary time, because these Giants were larger than life (ask their many ex-wives), made BIG mistakes sometimes, certainly ran things according to their personalities instead of business school management logic. And, somehow, they also inspired loyalty, since dozens have stayed with them from the beginning: maybe from fear, maybe from friendship (can you be "friends" with a Giant?), maybe from masochistic pleasure at being constantly on the edge.

Oh, and the Giants made money for everybody and kept everything going for 40 years, so that may have something to do with it, too.

Oh, and judging from the photos and videos from back then, they had a lot of fun in the middle of all the *Sturm und Drang.*

And, somewhere about a decade ago, the Giants realized they Don't Know Everything about certain new geographies they wanted to explore, so they sought out a Faithful Guide --

And failed a lot of times.

Till they found Spike.

Not a bad fit, actually: the Giants' giant ambitions were actually less than Spike's talent could deliver - but the Giants' tolerance for personalities where fits and starts and emotion-releasing rants jibe perfectly with Spike's less-than-cubicle-fitting profile.

The Royal Us had found a Genius; Spike had found a Patron.

For 6 or 7 years there was harmony (well, as much harmony as ever could be found with that set of characters) as Spike and the Giants created New Things.

December

PETER MURPHY

Thursday, December 01

Spike #3: The Genius and the Other Consultants

Bland Boys and Marshmallow Men revisited. This is where the tragicomedy begins.

We 'ad a changeover in management a coupla years back. Originally it was supposed to be a "transition" - a segue from the Giants who founded the Co. to a professional Management team that would keep the fires burning as the Giants lost their strength and health. Chilluns didn't work out: they just... didn't.

Give the Giants credit for recognizing that. And the Old Team were both gettin' old too and too busy protecting their fiefdoms to think ahead. So they brought in the pros.

Bland Boys. Marshmallow Men. No big personalities in this bunch. No Sturm un Drang, either, or whimsy-fueled decisions that could make-or-break the Co. in a toss of the dice. Steady types, responsible --- with, so they said, an eye to the future.

So, one figgers, Spike the Genius - with his contributions to the future - should have found a new home. A comfortable fit.

But, shifting metaphors, the shoe didn't fit.

Giants like Genius. Bland Boys like Smooooooth.

In the smooooth world of the Marshmallow Men, a Consultant has no personality, only " solutions." A Consultant does not present "problems" to be overcome, a Consultant sidesteps "obstacles." No matter matter matter what else: to the Bland Boys and Marshmallow Men, a Consultant never disagrees with them. They have hired this third-party, documented expert, very expensive Consultant to vindicate what they have already decided. "He agrees, therefore, we are right."

Dialogue, discussion, dissension are not part of the Consultancy package that they have purchased.

Oy, Spike!, ya should ha' bin like the other Consultants!

Friday, December 02

Spike #4: Segue Away

So, much like charity, it appears that Genius must be its own reward - at least around here.

The Bland Boys & Marshmallow Men don't like live sparks. They need dull flames they can lower and raise to meet their changing comfort levels. The operative word is their. A loose cannon like Spike the Genius doesn't fit-in to their need for validation. He may say things they Don't Want To Hear.

Better to stick to the Typical Consultants, then, the ones who will tell us What We Want To Hear. Better to divorce ourselves from the Genius-type Spike, even if he developed the cornerstone foundations of some of our major initiatives for the future.

But, maybe, let's not tell Spike just yet. That would lead to Confrontation.

Better to just let our relationship die a natural death, i.e., wither away from neglect. We just won't keep him posted on future plans - even if they involve his contributions. There's certainly no need to return those emails Spike sends.

And, fortunately, we have the Confidentiality agreement with Spike to keep him in line and away from competitors. Why, in fact, if we don't formally break off our relationship, we can buy ourselves another year, maybe two.

Remember, this is objective business thinking we believe in, not the old-line emotionalism of the ancien regime. We are not letting the fact that we don't like Spike the Genius impact our decision-making. Not us Bland Boys & Marshmallow Men.

Saturday, December 03

Assumptions to Survive By

Notes from The Cube: The following assumptions were derived from watching Dan the Hyper-Active Boss Man in action for the past year. They were not Dan's assumptions...

Do not assume that everyone thinks the same as you do.

Do not assume that facts matter no matter what.

When you speak out, do not assume that anyone in Power particularly wants to hear.

When you make it a Me vs. Someone Else choice, do not assume that everyone likes you.

When you Take On someone in Power, do not assume that everyone who agrees with you will rally behind you.

When you are not the captain, do not assume that there is no "i" in "Team".

Do not assume that an objective decision will be made.

Do not assume that your report was read.

Do not assume that the comments made were considered more than 60 seconds before they were expressed.

Do not assume that anyone remembers what was discussed at the last meeting.

Sunday, December 04

Dan 7: Dan & The Incoming Boss - Wrong things to do

[A Note from The Cube: Check back to November 24th to see where Dan last was.]

The new VP is arriving in a couple of weeks and I'm thinking that Dan the Hyper-Active Boss Man is not handling this well.

Let's put it this way: Dan has every right to feel skunked, yes, since the new Prez had Dan interview the incoming VP as if the interview were for a subordinate manager. And then, it turns out, the soon-to-come Veep was the new Prez's former right hand man. Soooo.... I dunno what Dan said in that interview, but the way you talk to a potential subordinate is waaay different than the way you speak to a probable new boss.

But that is the past. The new Vice President is soon a-comin' and Dan held a meeting last week to inform us about it. "Us" being the managers under Dan and The

Cube (by default, as the one taking notes at department manager meetings).

So what was Dan thinking when he started in by insulting the new Veep's name?! "His name's Jed Cumber - you know, like that hillbilly Jed Clampett. Spits a lot I hear. Stupid as a hillbilly, too." It would be nice to report that Dan was saying this with a twinkle in his eye and a joke in his chuckle. Instead, it was more like a serious critique and the eye was deadly.

Not helped by Dan adding: "After I interviewed him, my recommendation was not to hire: he knows shit about what we do." Oh, yeah: that mitigated the vitriol.

Wisely, halfway into his twenty minute introduction along the lines of "we'll have cover for him till he gets up to speed, if he ever does - or can," Dan added: "This is all confidential, of course, everything I'm telling you." CON-FI-DEN-TIAL. That's how he wrote it on the whiteboard.

No Machiavelli me, even I could see that half the room was populated by managers who thought they should have had Dan's job based on their seniority back a few years ago before he arrived. And, now, he's looking for their sympathy?

And the other half of the room? Well, quite a few, like The Cube, studied our shoelaces quite intently. The Cube likes Dan the Hyper-Active Boss Man: he's a smart fast intelligent guy, demanding but fair, rough on the edges but soft in heart.

And, now, stupid as a rock. This is the wrong thing to do. Oh so wrong.

Monday, December 05

Monday: week ahead not looking good

Sometimes you just know ...

Took off today to work on a private project. Sick day. A "use it or lose it" day, since the end of the year is approaching and I've got 2 weeks backed up and they're not extending us more than 3 days into the new year (something about federal law considering it a taxable benefit). Theoretically, I could sick-out half of December, but that would (a) screw up my co-workers and (b) screw up my deadline projects as well.

But I'm tired.

Problem, though: whenever I sick-out when not sick, I inevitably get sick the next day or two. I'm starting to feel the shivers already. Life is a cruel ironist.

Tuesday, December 06

Stupid "Heroes": Why you don't come into work sick

No, it's not because you pass on your sickness to others.

It's because you make stupid mistakes. Why? Because you're sick.

And it's your fault. Playing the "hero," the "martyr," the - - - egotistical self-delusional fool who thinks everything will collapse if you don't show up.

OK, so maybe, like here, the company is cheapjack and they don't have a backup for you and if you don't get this done today the opportunity will not be there tomorrow. But are you capable of doing it?

Nope.

Obviously, today was not a good day. 'Successfully ticked off half a dozen people while rambling through a fever AND broke a valuable piece of equipment because the shivering fingers were fumbling. Smart person today.

Wednesday, December 07

Doctor's Note for no reason

Well, so here's how work begins to resemble elementary school: need a doctor's note to come back after three days out.

Actually, it works a little less logically: to come back after 3 days sick, one needs to go to the doctor on the 3rd day, while still sick, to get a note saying you won't be sick on the 4th day.

OK, so some people are out a looooong time and need to let the company know that they aren't transmitting TB or leprosy or influenza. But, of course, everyone transmits these diseases in the couple of days when the symptoms are just starting and they don't yet feel bad enough to stay home from work. ("Bad enough" = not enough sick days = can't afford to lose the pay)

By the same taken, as here, there are those famous 3-day colds, stomach flus and assorted viruses that you know there are no cures for, only symptom suppressants, and you'd think that a company would treat its employees like adults and take us on our word that "Hey, I was feeling bad for a few days, I feel better now."

Nope, doesn't work like that: 'got to spend $$ to go to a doctor to get the little note. The joke is that the notes are pre-printed, fill-in-the-date jobbies. My doc, nice man that he is, will give me a week off on principle - and, if I could afford it, I'd take the week.

But I've got to save those sick days, and those dinero, for the time I may become really, deep-felt sick. Today I just feel crappy-sick, 100 degrees achy should-be-in-bed-but-certainly-won't-die sick --- and I've got to crawl out of my comfortable covers to drive to the doctor to have him tut-tut "You should be in bed" and stamp my pre-printed note to go back to school, er, work.

Thursday, December 08

Do They Appreciate How Crappy I Feel?

No.

And how can they? 'Come in and smile and work and how are they supposed to know that I'm still achy from the last three days' stomach flu? I could whine a lot, beg for sympathy, but that's boring.

Ach, that's the problem with it: you don't want to be a crybaby victim - but only victims get sympathy.

Still, I wish someone would notice ...

whine

Friday, December 09

Midnight Run

About to start an overnighter. Haven't done that in a while: wonder if I still can.

The Cube is all about daylight hours and confinement with the other Cubes. This is the freedom hour. Yeah, I remember all the stuff about graveyard shifters a while back. Still holds true. But this is a flash from the past, a deadline run down to the wire, when it's all due by the Monday A.M. Fun.

Kin ah doit?

To see ...

Saturday, December 10

30 Hours & Still Alive

So --- we're on to the 30th hour and still alive. Still alive. Still ...

It's a team effort this is, certain tasks requiring everyone at god-awful hours of the day --- on-call for all even while 75% could be sleeping (and are) half of the other time.

Keep busy myself, especially for those "off" times: too difficult to re-awaken.

Drink lots of coffee. LOTS of coffee. Eat LOTS of cheap carbs and sugar-powered energy. Move a lot, then hunker into the intense moments when my tasks are due.

Try to be helpful for others when I could be/should be in

a corner looking like a corpse sprawled in a chair. (Oddly, I have set up a comfortable chair for taking naps in the daytime. Don't dare go near it now, though: I'd be deeper in dreamland than a drink-besotted wino. Keep moving. Keep moooovvvviiiing.)

So we're still here: pulling into the next stage, where we hand over the lot to another team to take over for 18 hours or so. Driving on a highway is an experience when your body is wired and your eyes hyper-opened. Glad I don't use drugs (too cheap to've started young, too dignity-conscious to start now): if I'd been on uppers, this would be dangerous. Coffee wore off a couple of hours ago. Now it's just endurance and, perhaps, the food kicking in from the corner Denny's. Thanking the deities for any place that sells breakfast 24 hours a day: sometimes pancakes, eggs, bacon and cholesterol are exactly what the body needs.

Sunday, December 11

Did It: Weekend Done

We made it. Kudos to us.

Collapsed yesterday at 10 PM, closed eyes and swear there was no sleep but the alarm went off at 5 AM and shuffled the feet into action. Drove the car the 50 miles to The Place. Found The Cube just as I'd left it. Found The Team stumbling in as I am. Then, almost without a word, we began Doing.

Doing. The deadline approacheth.

Doing. We know what has to be done.

Doing. No grandstanding, no grouching, no slouching, just - doing.

And it's done.

Delivered.

We're due back Monday morning.

Monday, December 12

When have you said too much?

Kyra writes her Notes from the Cube ...

This is the question I have about the development process: when have you said enough?

At what point, in developing plans, or brainstorming, or conducting a review meeting - at what point has everything relevant been said? When are we not only repeating ourselves but we've started going in circles, eating our own tail? Has "constructive" criticism become destructive - making suggestions just to hear our own voices? Changing things just because we can - or we're afraid to commit?

Tuesday, December 13

DO it, don't talk

Pierre Dolet write to Kyra (yesterday's Notes from The Cube) ...

When have you said too much? The bigger question is: Why don't you just start doing it? Everybody talks.

Wednesday, December 14

Ya gotta talk, but...

Hank writes his Notes from The Cube to Kyra & Pierre from the last two days...

Ya gotta talk - because it's too easy to screw up things by doing without thinking.

The problem, of course, is controlling what's said without being a control freak.

Thursday, December 15

Indians Can't Have This Chief

Texas Slim writes his Notes from The Cube to Kyra 'n Hank 'n Pierre from the past three days ...

'Sounds to me like y'all got a problem of responsibility without power: sorta what we've got around my Cube-town.

How's that work? Simple.

You take a person and give 'im a cross-functional team to lead. Almost by definition "cross-functional" means "people from other departments." Now what this sets up, ideally, is input from a lot of disciplines...

What it sets up, on the ground, is a team with a captain who has no authority.

Because, in reality, no manager of Sales or Quality or Facilities or Accounting or wherever there is a person drawn from - none of those managers is going to give up his or her authority over his or her reports to you, the team "captain" who is not under his or her thumb. That's not in human nature.

And it doesn't matter if you're a manager yourself: in some ways, that may even be worse - I'm going to give authority over my reports to your department? I think not.

So these teams aren't really teams: they're ... a mob? A "consensus group"? An "advisory board"? Let's give it the most positive spin: a group of well-intentioned people who have not got the authority to make decisions on behalf of the expertise they represent but have been placed in the position of representing that interest group.

Friday, December 16

But It FEELS Good: Compliment Whores

Kyra writes her Notes From The Cube ...

OK, so - Yes, we're all Compliment Whores.

Even when we know it's fake.
It's TGIF and I'm feeling very proud of myself because the President recognized my performance today - in the middle of a meeting - in front of my supervisors, immediate and the one just above her.

And it felt good, and I liked it, and I want more.

Sooo much more!

I don't even think he meant it, the President - so much of what he says comes out of the hard-bound management books he has on his bookshelves, the compliment to me was probably #75: "Positive Reinforcement of the non-management employee." But it doesn't matter whether he was sincere or not: he said it.

I'm feeling the same giddy pleasure I had in 9th grade when Evan Shaw, very popular, sat next to me at lunch one day, probably because there was no place else to sit, and he spoke nice to me because that's just the way he was, it turns out. (He's a minister now, but who knew then?). But it didn't matter what Evan's motivation was, everybody saw him talking with me, some even got jealous - of me! - and my stock in myself rose 100%. It felt good and I wanted more feelings like that.

But I was in 9th grade, jasusmarynjoseph! I'm exactly in the beginning of my prime right now and I shouldn't be goo-gahing over compliments like a morning-after bride: I shouldn't because I really deserved those compliments 20 times over and now I'm weak-kneed over a single tossed scrap of recognition.

Ah, we're whores for compliments, aren't we?

The Cube adds:

Management should know it's that simple. Yes, we are.

Saturday, December 17

Dan 8: Isolated

[Note from The Cube: Look back to December 4th for the prelude to this.]

The department's new Vice President has arrived. It's mainly a ceremonial arrival, since Christmas/New Year's holidays are almost upon us and he's just showing his face before he settles-in come the new year.

In the past two weeks, Dan the Hyper-Active Boss Man has made the department spic and span. We have finished every project due this year - plus a couple of add-ons, unanticipated, from the new Prez and/or thought up by Dan to "fill in the cracks" where he saw that things needed to be done. That's Dan: looking beyond his immediate tasks to the future of the company as a whole.

All in all, the kind of track record that would look good at bonus time in a just world.

The new Veep has taken his introductory tour - alone: "I'd like an uninterpreted first impression" was his comment to Sam, according to the Org chart the designated 2nd in command. Fair enough.

Next day, the new VP met with the department managers - alone - "uninterpreted, you understand." OK.

The 3rd day we cubes had a group meeting with the department's new Vice Prez - alone - "direct face-to-face, *capiche.*" Capiched.

We finished his first week with everyone getting to know the new top dog, Jed Cumber. Everyone except Dan. "We already met at

the interview. You've got a lot to do to wrap up the year. We don't need to talk."

I think Jed's got Dan penciled-in to his schedule for the 2nd week in January. It's a tentative schedule, though. I know there's a manager's meeting with the VP for the first day back form holidays. Dan's not on the invite list - he's a Director, not a manager:

"I need you to set up the new year's project schedule."

"But don't you want to talk about it?"

"I'll make the changes I feel necessary."

Sunday, December 18

Up Too Soon & Sinking Fast

> 5 a.m.
> What a day
> Started strong
> Now drift away
> There's no hope
> Till noon won't last
> Up too soon and
> Fading fast

Monday, December 19

A Bit Overwhelmed: Will Fix It Soon

Feeling a bit overwhelmed this end-of-year month. No big reports or projects due - those were all pulled-off earlier this month. But there is the pile of docs and stuff accumulated since last January that has to finally be Dealt With and it just ... overwhelms.

It's a lot of shit piled up there.

There is a PLAN, though: this will all be fixed soon.

Just you wait until the "dead" week - between Christmas holiday and New Year's Day holiday - that's when this mess will be viewed, reviewed and Dealt With thoroughly and completely. This is a PROMISE.

Tuesday, December 20

Calmer Now: there is a PLAN

Based on yesterday's PLAN, The Cube is calmer now: everything on the desk here will be Dealt With - next week.

That's the beauty of a PLAN. Without a PLAN, one feels aimless. Looking at the pile of months-old papers starting to breed life on my desk, The Cube certainly felt the queasy scare of the lost explorer in the pit of my stomach - were it not for the PLAN. Now, however, no fear. The PLAN is made, the time is scheduled, the problem will be addressed - next week.

In fact, even though there is the opportunity to get started on it today, there is no need: the problem is taken care of because the PLAN is made.

It's good to have a PLAN.

Wednesday, December 21

The PLAN 2: Role Model

The Cube feels vindicated today. Why? Our company Role Model - the President - agrees with The Cube's PLAN.

Not specifically, mind you, but in practice. This is clear, because the parallels between the President's PLAN and The Cube's PLAN are so obvious.

Problem(s)? Backlog of past year that needs to be Dealt With before starting the new year.

Solution: Develop a PLAN that schedules the time for the problem to be considered.

The President left this morning to go shopping for holiday gifts - he hasn't returned all day - I hear he may be out all day tomorrow, too. I am sure that is because, now that he has a PLAN to address the backlog, the President feels no need to work on the problem until the PLAN is initiated. That would show lack of faith in the PLAN.

Similarly, The Cube's backlog problem will be Dealt With in due time according to the PLAN.

Follow in your leader's footsteps, that's the motto.

Thursday, December 22

Dan 9: Dan's Lost It

[Notes from The Cube: Look back to December 4th for the most recent status on Dan.]

We had our last all-department meeting of the year. Dan the Hyper-Active Boss Man led it; our new VP wasn't there: he's on two-week vacation.

Dan lost it.

In a series of unprovoked tirades, Dan jumped on about a third of the people in the department, ripping apart their work.

He wasn't incorrect about some of the work, by the way, but but some of his attacks were simple head-butts from an alpha male on someone coming up with a different idea than his own. More that than, though it was so public - and strongly worded - and, and... C'mon, Dan, it's almost Christmas! "Ye of good cheere" and all that.

And it was mean. Mean in that way that says "I am hurting, you will hurt, too."

Almost cliché, really, how Dan transferred his own insecurity into a drive-away-any-sympathy outlashing. Not that anyone was offering Dan any sympathy. And they won't now. But once upon a time they could have....

The Cube is going to have to get out of this situation. It's too painful to watch. Yeah, Dan's been screwed pretty badly this past half year, but he's not holding his head high: he's got flop sweat beading up on his brow and he seems to have forgotten all of the good things he knew how to do.

Friday, December 23

Work Day: Yeah, Right

Technically, today is a work day. Yeah, right. Try.

30 minutes more before the teacher, er, boss lets us go home. Actually, we are only waiting fro him to come back from his party lunch - 2 hours and counting - if he comes back.

Advice to newbies: Expect a telephone call from the boss telling us to go home.

Best to be here when he calls but, trust me, he is already home himself.

Saturday, December 24

Holiday. There is no work, we do not blog.

Sunday, December 25

Holiday. Did not you read yesterday?

Monday, December 26

C'mon, pay attention! Holiday. No work.

No write.

Tuesday, December 27

Not much to do...

Not much to do. The past four days were a holiday, and the next four...

This week, between Christmas and New Year, has half of everybody in the cubes on vacation - with the floor folk on a "required" week's vacation. It's a good time to either catch-up on things or sleep at your desk with impunity.

The Cube has decided to catch a head cold, which makes it imperative to come into work: who in his right mind is going to waste vacation time being sick when you can get paid for doing almost nothing at work?

Dan the Hyper-Active Boss Man is out today, but coming in later this week for our annual end-of-year all-department wrap-up. A very laid back affair, even for Dan, since almost no one is here. Actually, it's Dan's chance to do a little self-congratulating to those of us who are here. He usually brings in food.

It'll be fun.

Wednesday, December 28

Catch-Up

The theory is Fan-tAS-TIC: we are going to catch-up on our backlog of paperwork this "empty" week between Christmas and New Year's Day. This is such a GREAT theory! It has been planned and discussed and promised all month and ...
Remember: It took decades for Einstein's Theory of Relativity to be translated into the fact of functional atomic energy. We should be thinking in terms of long-term goals, not short-term realizations. The THEORY works.

it just needs time ...

Thursday, December 29

Dan 10: Dan's gone

[Notes from The Cube: Look back at December 22nd, the 17th, the 4th, and earlier for how we got to this point.]

To nobody's surprise - and, yet, it is always a surprise - Dan the Hyper-Active Boss Man was fired today.

Nobody's surprise: Dan has been isolated, ignored and abused for the past seven months. It's not paranoia talking here: about 6 months ago, at an all-management meeting, apparently the new President jumped so hard on Dan - for unexpected things - that other department management were talking about it. Not happily, either. And these were people who did not particularly like Dan.

Then the new Vice President was hired, by-passing Dan who had been the assumed heir-apparent for a couple of years, based on his till-then-superior job performance.

Then Dan began to act erratically: lost, forgetting how to do what he knew best, hurting everyone under him.

Things no one else knows: In the past week, learning that the new VP and Prez wanted to cut back personnel, Dan drew up a list of "expendables" as a first-strike To Fire shopping list. It was not a good idea: once Dan made that list - which of course he sent to the Prez & Veep in an effort to please – he might as well have put his own name on the top of the list.

Which is why Dan's demise is No Surprise.

But it always is a surprise when someone who has been very valuable, even though stumbling recently, is cut off in that impersonal, out-of-the-office-in-15-minutes goose step way that they walked into Dan's office just before his annual year-end all-department meeting and ...

And ...

We never saw him again.

We were in the conference room, waiting for Dan to arrive. The room was set with the food that Dan had bought for us, his annual year-end Salute To Us semi-party for those of not taking the week off. Suddenly the new Vice President walked in the door. He was supposed to be on vacation until the first of the new year.

Instead he told us about Dan's "settlement termination" and about the Company's "new visions".

And that ... is the end ... of Dan the Hyper-Active Boss Man.

Friday, December 30

Half-Day Holiday

It's a half-day today, not officially, and we came in only to go home at noon.

For those living nearby it's great. For those of us commuting the long hauls, we can soon spend the afternoon in the holiday traffic. Still, it's better than spending the evening in the holiday traffic.

The new Vice President went back to his vacation, having fired Dan the Hyper-Active Boss Man yesterday. Only about half of us were here to find out about it. We're all walking around quiet and tense. Well, it will be time to leave soon. There won't be a lot of tears for Dan; he earned that disrespect the last two months. But he hadn't done a bad job, either, so people are worried about what's the new criteria for keeping their jobs. It'll be interesting to see what happens when everyone comes back after the holidays.

Saturday, December 31

January

Sunday, January 01

Placeholder

Well, honestly, can anyone do anything after last night?

Monday, January 02

Back to the Trenches:

Roll Call for the Departed

Tuesday, January 03

My bright machine

Kyra writes her new year's song sung Notes from the Cube ...

> Bronchitis and breath mints too
> Sweet candy to quench the cough
> Are the bromides we need to take
> After having one week off.
>
> Two headaches for every day
> Three trips to the rest room door
> Used up the sick days a new year starts
> Just like last year, what a bore.
>
> Plans have been made
> Smiles are in place
> The Prez says "Now,
> We start the race!"

The budget's approved
And the schedule's set
But our bodies don't know it
We're still - in last year - yet.

Four weeks until the next day off
Time to rebuild the psyche, see:
The new year's started, the clock is on
Make ourselves into the business machine.

Run that machine

Turn my gears and oil my soul

My bright machine ...

Wednesday, January 04

New Year, New Policy?

And so the NEW YEAR has begun, filled with bright promise, renewed energy and ... new policies?

Well, they're published. They exist. exist. exist.

Much like Congress on the week before Christmas, we pushed through an ambitious set of NEW DIRECTIONS for the upcoming year. Now, again like Congress, we have these "unfunded mandates" hanging around waiting to be actually, sort of, possibly (maybe...?) implemented.

It's a grand slate of goals. Too bad the PTBs[1]* haven't mentioned any of them in our daily briefings so far. The policies are published on the bulletin board and on the company intranet and we all see them.

---

1   * PTB: Powers That Be

But, lately, eyes are averted when walking past the bulletin board - and, by Day 3 of the New Year, the Policy Page has been moved to a 1-line link on the intranet.

It will happen, though. It will happen.

Thursday, January 05

Problem Solved

The new year starts with an old problem: what are we supposed to do about it?

But the problem is not the problem. The problem is that we are told that the problem is "solved - there is no problem."

But it's still there.

No, apparently, it isn't.

Friday, January 06

Eternity

It is today.

The problem existed yesterday.

And the day before.

And the week before. The month before. The quarter before.
Jed is "working on the problem."

We sent him the information on the problem yesterday.

And the day before. And the week, month, quarter, year ...

Jed's predecessor was "working on the problem."

It has been mandated from Above that the problem will be "addressed."

TO: The Creator
3265 Eternity Drive
The Universe

It probably won't get there without a zip code, but it is addressed now.

[Postscript Notes from The Cube: Different department than yesterday. This is not a broken record broken record broken record -]

Saturday, January 07

If Spike is listening

Dear Spike,

I know you are wounded, hurt and aggrieved - rightfully so. But the value is always your brain: don't let your emotions overwhelm your common sense. Step back and play it smart. Don't show your hand too soon; let them do all the work.

They made mistakes, but if you let this sound "personal" they'll take it as weakness and (a) close ranks and (b) bring on some legal guns you haven't seen to crush you. They like crushing those they think are weaker (well, they may not "like" it, who know what they think?, but they do it often enough) - they only seem to respect those they perceive as stronger. And their perceptions are that all emotions are signs of weakness. These are the bland boys and marshmallow men of modern industry.

So use your brain and find the unemotional chinks in their position. Hint at those chinks (don't threaten, hint). Then let them know that you know about those chinks. Cite a paragraph in an old agreement. Mention royalties and - fear, fear on their side - a need for fiscal accounting. Make them work.

These words were never written to you.

Sunday, January 08

Oops! Forgot to tell the Project Leader

Hank writes his new year Note from The Cube ...

Funny thing happened last week while setting up a "Track the Pack" departmental Project List for the new year: 'seems the people who are supposed to do those projects for the next year weren't informed of that fact.

Awkward, you see, since the "Track The Pack" list is just a monitoring tool, not The Message itself. We here in our Admin cubes don't make decisions, we just follow the progress of those decisions, make charts illustrating the progress (we make beautiful charts) and disseminate those charts to the executives. (More precisely, we give it to our VP alone, who theoretically shares it with her equals.)

Consequenently, then, we found out about the gap between the Project List we Adminnie Cubes possessed -

277

and the Project Leaders' knowledge of their duties - when it turned out there was zero zip zilch progress on everything listed to us as "New."

Now this gets really funny funny when you realize that the "New" projects were painstakingly negotiated during a two month Budget process that, in theory, found every Manager meeting with his reports, then presenting their plans to the Directors - who, in turn, visited them upon the VP - then back-and-forth a few times as projects were rejected outright, more info was asked on some, some were revived as other departments were consulted, da-da-dum da-dum. Long process.

It beats me, then, how seven out of seven Project Leaders did not apparently know what their new projects starting the new year are supposed to be.

How could Management...?

Then again, these selfsame Seven (and their seven times seven cohorts in the related departments) have a collective amnesia about such do-dads as ISO standards, FDA regulatory procedures and OSHA equipment guidelines. Hence, annually, we all get the joy of being retrained in stuff that I have memorized from repetitious boredom - an' ah dinna even do tha tasks!

So... Is it a typical Management communication-by-osmosis glitch --- or equally typical Employee selective memory?

Monday, January 09

Proust Lives: Remembrance of Time Past

'Probably noticed this before in these Notes from The Cube, but since this entry is about, in the immortal words of Yogi Berra, *deja vu* all over again, why not repeat myself ?...

'Looked at the new year analysis and forecast from the high tech group. An impressive 10-pager. Many observations, some salient points - certainly some hard-nosed-but-optimistic forecasts on how the industry will evolve.

And the wording is lifted, almost line-for-line, from the high tech group's annual forecast/analysis of two years ago.

Which was copied, almost line-for-line, from the forecast/ analysis from five years ago.

Curiosity tweaked, I looked at last year's forecast/analysis: it was a cut-and-past job from the doc two years before it - and two years before that, there was a ...

For those of us plodding along with our yearly struggles to review the situation and provide new insights on our areas of expertise, there is a lesson here: recycling. Apparently The Cube's adage "If you write it, no one will read it" holds true on the strategic level.

And who foolishly said that those who are ignorant of history are doomed to repeat it? What's the "doom"? Have you seen the increasing budget allocations for the high-tech group?

Tuesday, January 10

Why cheat?

'Can't quite figure the logic: we have a distributor who has started contracting with another manufacturer to make a rip-off version of a product that we already make - and he sells.

I say "logic" because I can't understand the business sense behind such an obviously unethical act. I'd use the word "dishonesty," but apparently it's not illegal - and fairly common. But what's the sense? An extra 2 cents profit margin? The chance to piss off us? Ill will & lost trust as the costs of doing business?

Wednesday, January 11

We create our own hells

The new year is the time to start fresh. You'd think....

So no one likes bureaucracy and paperwork and the crap that gets in the way of "doing the job." (Slight correction required here: there are entire departments consigned to those tasks, but they are peopled by demons, succubi and angels fallen from grace.)

Focus, Cube: No one likes it - and the new year, with its new projects and schedules and programs, is the perfect opportunity clean the slate and set things up right. Right?

Ri...

The Cube has fallen into the role of administrator the past couple of years - a non-management, "support" person with zero authority and only a few ways to help "behind the scenes" - but an admin-in-part nevertheless. This gives The Cube a cat's eye seat watching the managers recreate the same complex bureaucratic bongles that bungle their conscientiously conceived creative programs year after year.

We don't have to make every activity and sub-activity into a fully-reportable, Gantt-charted "project" --- but we do --- even though, last year, that Byzantine structure resulted in three projects getting singled out by the regulatory agencies as "improperly documented." "Improperly" because - and The Cube bears True Witness - no one can figure out Who reports What to Where.

And now here we are again today, rebuilding that same Tower of Babel-To-Be for a new year and a new project leader.

I like the Nimrod manager who is designing this Tower for his new-hire project leader, but I don't know how to talk to him. He looks at me with expectant wet eyes, like a puppy dog proud that he has peed on the newspaper as trained, unaware that it was today's edition. I want power to cut off heads.

But, thanks to this newly-created mini-hell, I will have job security for the next year "supporting" its incoherency.

Thursday, January 12

I Didn't Mean To Confuse You

I didn't mean to confuse you. Honestly.

I only sent you an updated copy of the same report you got back in November - and September - and July. It's the same set of information we prepared for you and you were supposed to implement back in August - and October - and December.

Now, though, I see by your startled expression that this is all complex and confusing to you. It is as if you have never seen it before and this is the first time we have dumped this on your desk. This, of course, is how you must present it to our managers, those who have mandated action without caring about the details. Yes, you will report it as an "unexpected change in scope."

No, I didn't mean to confuse you - I only thought that we both knew what we were doing.

Friday, January 13

Erased

Yes, of course: it's Friday the 13th.

The Cube has just learned that the extensive, paperless document archive set up over the past month was not automatically archived by the IT Dept as promised - well, it was archived, but they have no way short of several hundred dedicated man-hours of retrieving it - and the database was accidentally erased by a user in the department who was not supposed to have read-write access. I don't blame that user; he didn't know. But still...

We are erased. Non-existent. Null.

TGIF

Saturday, January 14

Virtual Tragedy

[A pre-Note from The Cube: The following lament does not imply that all facts, acronyms or accusations that follow are correct, merely that The Cube is in pain. This is King Lear wandering amongst the cubicles, howling his heart out, avoided by loss. .... Well, perhaps we are a bit overwrought in our self-dramatizing. Nevertheless...]

As a folly-up to yesterday's mini-tragedy, we have today's version: VPN - the Virtual Private Network.

"Virtual" - that catch-all word for anything that splats out at you from a screen: computer, TV, PDA, media player or otherwise. "Virtual" becomes synonymous with "paper-less," as in "You can create a Virtual Office using our XYZ applications" or the executive mandate to "KIE." (No, not another management mantra stolen from the Japanese: Keep It Electronic.)

"Virtual" - the paper trail is ether, not pulp.

"Virtual" - the archive caches everything, not just what you have physical room to store.

"Virtual Private Network" - from anywhere, anytime, you too can access your company network and work during the off hours. Oh joy!

Oddly, foolishly enough, The Cube asked for VPN access: a sense of responsibility, lads & lassies, makes us do things we oughtn't.

Be that as it may, in the past year or so the Cube has come to rely on VPN as the lifeline to Getting Things Done On Time without Living In the Office. To be perfectly honest, updating dull dull dull accounts is infinitely easier while sitting cross-legged on a sofa and watching reruns of anything on TV. And, to be more perfectly honest (pluperfect?), getting much done at the office while other people are there is perhaps more of a Platonian Ideal than an Aristotelian Reality. (And where else, The Cube asks, do you get both Plato and Aristotle in a business discussion?)

Back to Reality: The Cube, and many others, use, abuse and are in turn abused by the Virtual Private Network system on a regular basis. This weekend, for instance. 'Arranged Monday's scheduled activities with the comfortable knowledge that Saturday morning would be devoted to The Company - via the VPN.

The VPN is down. No access. No message why no access. No literal IT person to contact - it's Saturday - and, hence, no virtual network to work on.

The Cube is not alone. All along the grapevine of Fellow Cubes, a cellphone message of despair sings: "But I needed this finished by Monday!"

It will not happen. Monday will come. We Cubes will troop in. Nothing will be ready.

Responsibility betrayed by a Virtual Iago.

Sunday, January 15

Power Dress for Fun!

Kyra writes her Notes from The Cube about an old buga-boo of hers, dressed up in new duds ...

Here's an idea for the upcoming week: Power Dress.

Maybe it's not a good idea to out-dress your boss - certainly it's not a solid, long-term, career-advancement strategy for a woman with a woman boss - but it can be Fun!

And it doesn't have to be limited to women. I think it even works better for men!

Here's what you do:

Pick a Wednesday or Thursday, about that time when everyone is starting to get run-down by the week (but before Friday when casual relief we're-almost-there takes over).

Choose the day when there will be a cross-departmental meeting, preferably one where the Upper Ranks are present.

Dress well.

Not evening clothes. Not your most expensive outfit. But dress as if YOU own the company.

Then don't comment on it.

Don't solicit compliments. Don't get shy about it. And don't make a Big Deal about it.
You don't have to: Others will notice, comment and talk about it.

All you have to do is act as if this is Normal. Someone says, "You're looking dressed up today?" Answer with a simple, of-course-attituded "Yes." They will ask you "What's the occasion?" Answer: "None" - and look at the questioner with eyes that say "Do I need an 'occasion' to display my natural class?" And so on.

You are the Owner of this company - in your mind.

The effect will be electric.

People are so easily impressed by externals.

[The Cube comments: "...by externals" - what Kyra's talking about here is also internal. 'Sounds like fun, but be sure you can pull it off. If you think like a drone, it might be hard to pull off the Queen Bee act simply by wearing a jeweled crown. 'Just a side thought. The Cube has the feeling that Kyra won't be in the cubes with us for long: she's either gonna be promoted or out on her ear. Either way, she's not a drone.]

Monday, January 16

The Law of Infinitesimal Nit-Picking

(Scientific) Notes From The Cube:

It is an office axiom that -

No idea is good enough.

Every idea benefits from input.

It easier to address an issue step-by-step than as a whole.

Therefore, all ideas should and will be subjected to a detailed, micro-managed, nit-picking critical review limited only by the following conditions:

a) Is the critique-giver required to know the subject?
* If "yes," add a limitation
* If "no," solicit opinions from anybody in the company.

b) Is the critiquer required to study the issue?
* If "yes," add a limitation
* If "no," give the critiquer a position on the Review board.

c) Is the critiquer is allowed to make it up on the spot?
* If "no," add a limitation
* If "yes," give the critiquer a place at all meetings.

d) Is the critique verbal or written?
* If written, add a limitation
* If verbal, expect more useless feedback than imaginable.

e) Will the critic be required to participate in achieving the results of his/her commentary?
* If "yes," add severe limitation; critical input ceases
* If "no," give a free pass to Review Hell.

The Law of Infinitesimal Nit-Picking states that the degree and amount of unessential critical commentary is directly proportional to the number of limitations placed on the critique-giver: i.e., the fewer limitations, the more bullshit will be shoveled.

Tuesday, January 17

NOT Still Monday? (a haiku)

Tuesday
and the motors rev
slowly.

It is not still
Monday?
Sigh.

Sigh

[(Literary) Notes From The Cube - 4 hours later: Per yesterday's entry on The Law of Infinitesimal Nit-Picking, critical input is not solicited on this haiku. Unsolicited, The Cube has received 35 comments on the haiku form –

– to which The Cube answers:

It's 17 syllables, so it fits the rules.
It's all in italics because italics look poetic.
It's not in Japanese, so how can you tell if the lines scan right?
I don't care.

Yes, it is Tuesday - sigh - so don't push me: there are still 3 full days to get through.]

Primadonnas

Texas Slim writes his Notes from the Cube ...

Weeyaallll... so I haven't quite decided if I like primadonnas in the office or not.

In general, they're a pain in the ass: vain, pushy, egotistical. No one's gonna argue much about that.

By the same token, usually the primadonna's done something to earn that inflated sense of self-importance - and, more important, is still doing that something.

That puts the primadonna in a different class from the drones droning away at whatever they are assigned in a competent dull way. Or, just as frequently, in an incompetent dull way: drones don't distinguish - which distinguishes the primadonnas from the drones.

Of course, everybody thinks that the other department acts like primadonnas - especially the Sales and R&D folk - and that may be true: but that's corporate culture personalities at play. I'm talking about the individuals who are sure they're top shit, want everyone else to know it, and generally have what it takes to actually be top o' the pile.

Do I like them or hate them?

I - don't - know.

I have, in the past week, wanted to kill a primadonna: he gets very very VERY on the nerves. I have also benefited from another primaD's brilliance (which, I wish wish wish she hadn't proclaimed herself so loudly).

In either case, the primadonnas are more interesting than the drones here in the cubicles.

So what will it be: A life of turbulent interest - or dull safety?

Thursday, January 19

Waiting for the Ax to Fall - on someone else

Hank writes his Notes from the Cube ...

Yes, so the "honor" was given me "confidentially" and I was told that a co-worker is being let go today: "Please don't say anything." Great: I get the "honor" of a scrunched-up stomach and pity-filled heart and not even the power of decision-making. What am I supposed to feel for being given this knowledge beforehand? Complicity with the boss who's doing it? Thanks or relief that it isn't me? I didn't slack off for the past year: in a just world, I shouldn't have to worry. But I know that my boss is worried, so I'm guessing that the timing for letting the guy go was not based on a just-world decision. "Let go" tells it all: the guy should have been "fired" a while ago, but right now there just happens to be an across-the-boards mandate to "reduce costs" and he just happens to be the least visibly valuable. Again, in a just world there would be a replacement for him - because we really do need someone to do his job - but that's not happening. Crappy feeling, this waiting around for the ax to fall on someone else.

Friday, January 20

Laid Off

Pierre Dolet writes his Notes from the Cube: "I found a ska song to match Hank's message yesterday...

You know
you can't work
in one job
all your life
So the Man says
"Go a-way."
They don't need you anymore
They don't want your knowledge nor
Any machine you know how to play.

Laid Off -
You're out the door.

Laid Off -
They want more

Money in their pockets.
Hey, you know Life sucks and
Get out now!

But you gave
them
the best
of your work
and your life
And the Man says
"That's just Biz."

Got to ruin other lives
Get that profit margin high
You don't really matter
Nothing really matters
But the Dime!

Laid Off -
They want more

Laid Off -
A lot lot more

Money in their pockets
Hey, you know Life sucks
Your life is Mine!

Well -
I never thought it would end like this
CEOs need to be more rich
I worked my fingers to the bone
Just to lose my job and home
For WHAT?

They're making 2 cents more!
For WHAT?
They're showing us the door!
For WHAT?
They're driving big fat cars!
For WHAT?
Goddam big damn arse!

Laid Off! Oh, yeah.
Laid Off! Shit, yeah.
Laid Off! Fuck, yeah.
Laid Off!
.... yeah.

Saturday, January 21

Dance With Me, Mexican Lady

*Texas Slim adds his Notes from the Cube to Pierre Dolet's
and Hank's from the past 2 days ...*

I love the Mexican ladies.
I really think they're fine.
But,
Dear Mexican lady,
I think your job was mine.

I don't hold it against you
I know that's what
I would do
With a family to care for.
Feed a child or two.

But, dear Mexican Lady,
I look across that border line
And I think
That the kids being fed -
They sure aren't mine.

Dance with me, Mexican lady!
We both want decent lives.
I just wish that somehow,
Maybe
It didn't end with someone crying.

Oh, dear Mexican lady,
I worry
About you.
They say that I will get along fine
But what are you gonna do?

When the long-distance bosses say:
"Get the margin higher, Jake!"
And the job of mine
That you're doing now
Will be worked in another place.

Hello, Chinese baby.
Are you 12 or 13 now?
Come and dance with the Mexican lady
And me:
We know your job real well.

Dance with me and the Mexican lady!
We all want decent lives!
I only wish with that somehow
Maybe
It didn't end with someone crying.

Does it always have to end with someone crying?

Sunday, January 22

Voluntary Termination

Kyra observes in her Notes from the Cube ...

"Voluntary Termination."

I saw this written for the first time a few weeks ago. I saw it on a form. I thought, logically, it was meant for someone who resigns - but, no, we have a "Resignation" form, too.

Voluntary Termination. The person is called to Human Resources and offered a choice: get fired "voluntarily" - or anyway. Somewhat like Assisted Suicide for the terminally ill, I suppose: you are going away, one way or another, so why not help the process along - with our help.

Apparently there are benefits to voluntarily terminating your own job. I don't know what those benefits are. To tell the truth, I don't want to find out first-hand, either.

Monday, January 23

We're Firing You For YOU

[A Note from The Cube: This is non-fiction.]

Good Afternoon. Welcome to our monthly Employee Team gathering. I hope you all got some of the cake - Thank you, Annie, as always - and now we'll bring you up to speed.

There are a lot of rumors going around about "firings' and

"layoffs" and "closing down the plant." I want you to understand that we are not, I repeat NOT, closing down the plant. We are keeping it open - for YOU.

Yes, for YOU. I know that 50 of you will not be here with us for our next monthly meeting, but we are doing this for the 400 of us in the U.S., China and Mexico who will still be part of a thriving business.

YES, we've had to bring in new, high-end executive staff to make this work and YES we've put the company in debt for the first time in 40 years and YES we have to lay off 50 line workers next month, and the next, and the next - and it's all for YOU!

How do WE - you, me, US - survive in this competitive environment?

By becoming lean and mean.

How do we do it?

By taking our low-end jobs and moving them somewhere that people will work for less!

And what does that mean for those of us left here?

MORE for US!

Now I want you to understand that this has a human face. We're a human company.

No one is getting shown the door without plenty of notice* - you, YOU will have plenty of time to find another job within walking distance of this fine community that gives us so many tax breaks for our hiring policies.

We are talking Good Business Sense here: you understand that. Some of you have been with this company for over 20 years, and I know that YOU understand what it is to make a sacrifice now for the good of the future. OUR future, for those of US still here. A GOOD future.

Yes, it's tough. I hope you appreciate how tough it is on me - but I'm doing this for YOU. So let's give a hand to OUR future, yes!, OUR future!

Recorded Friday, 20 January

(* Cube Note: Apparently the "plenty of notice" policy did not apply to the 20 clericals fired yesterday and given 30 minutes to clear their desks. They were probably bad workers.)

Tuesday, January 24

Is Anybody There To Handle This?

We close the current thought-stream for these Notes from the Cube from Pierre Dolet . Another non-fictional entry...

Date: Thursday, January X
To: Carlos Miller, Joan Stevens, Olga Nikolaya
From: Pierre Dolet
Subject: Action Request # A2733

All: I am subbing for Ellen Chavez, who was laid off last week, so bear with me while I get up to speed. I need your help sorting this out.

Carlos: I have the September-requested AR #2733 that was submitted by Bill Shawn, who was laid off last week, too, but I understand he was acting as Requestor for this Action Request on behalf of the

Calexico plant - and that, since you recently replaced Miguel Martinez, you called on this AR last week.

Joan: This AR was put on HOLD in October pending replacement of QA tester Holly Fides, who was laid off, to test the material for you - has she been replaced yet? Or is someone else handling her duties? If "yes," please advise if and when this test will be completed.

Olga: Since you are replacing Charles Norrell as the engineering handling this AR, I need a little better status/conclusion than: "Chuck was laid off in December, please cancel." You need to have the Requestor's agreement to cancel an AR. (Maybe they still need it.)

[Yes, Olga, I realize that the Requestor is gone, too, but his Department still exists - even if it's been moved to Calexico and, yes, Miguel's not there anymore either, but we have to see if the Department still wants it - right, Carlos?]

All: Please review and discuss this among yourselves so that we can either COMPLETE, continue HOLD, or formally CANCEL this Action Request with the appropriate authorizations.

Thanks - keep me posted - I am returning the AR to Olga.

P.D.

Wednesday, January 25

The Employee Self-Evaluation

It's that time of year again, and The Cube has to do a self-evaluation preparatory to receiving the full management eval. Oh Lord, what is the proper balance between humility and honesty?

Thursday, January 26

Self Evaluation 2: The Form

The Self-Evaluation from Human Resources. An annual ritual.

It's a Form, of course. In Excel. Created by a person in HR who doesn't know how spreadsheets work and obviously didn't learn how to set up Forms in Microsoft Word or Adobe Acrobat.

The beautiful, beautiful Form. What would we do without it? See how its columns change and its rows slip up and down at will? Notice how the words truncate? It was so meant for clear communication. O Form!

Now... On to self-evaluation. The first step is to open the #@~!?!!! thing. It is a positive first step.

Someone in HR thought it would be a good idea to have the employee make written comments, then the immediate supervisor writes comments, then the employee comments on the supervisor's comments. This has us both going back-and-forth in an awkward, embarrassing roundelay dance.

The tendency, if you are at all self-critical, is to emphasize your failings. By the same token, if you are at all defensive, you build up walls of (barely) hidden aggression. If you at all have an actual job to do, you slough off this long doc till the last minute and then rush through it.

The critical process.

Saturday, January 28

Self Evaluation 4: History Question

Didn't the Chinese Communists invent the self-critique?

Sunday, January 29

Self Evaluation 5: I Am Great

I am great, don't you agree?

As I review the past year for this annual self-evaluation process, I realize that - really - the company couldn't have done it without me.

Oh, sure there is a President who stands at the top inventing Policies For Growth, a slew of Vice Presidents who defend his policies, a company of Directors who administer the policies and a battalion of Managers who manage the administration of the defended policies.

But, finally, there is Me: The Doer.

It is my job to take those unconsidered, well-defended, ill-defined, micro-managed polices and turn them into money-making actions on a daily basis.

And I do. This year the company made $15 million more than last year, so I must have done something right.

Oh, I am not alone: there are 123 of us Cubes here, each of us performing this task every day. I would like to say that everyone is as great as I am, but that would be stretching the truth a little - for, actually, it all rests on my shoulders. This is just simple fact. How do I know this is a fact? Because I write the report every month that compiles the facts. Look at my report. Fact.

So, in concluding this annual self-evaluation, I must make two observations:

(1) I deserve a hell of a big raise; and

(2) Please do not promote me - someone needs to run the company.

Monday, January 30

First Month Gone?

It's the end o' January and the month is almost gone?!?

This is not a thought about Life Slipping Away - it's real-time tragedy: an entire month has gone by without getting started on anything!

It's sure fun to make jokes, snide remarks and superior commentary on how everything is Plan, Policy and Proclaim from the top. It is not so fun to realized that, in the middle of "leaning," the whole first month of the year has gone by without a single proclaimed policy plan being enacted to produce a salable product or service.

With apologies to both Walt Whitman and Sherwood Schwartz, creator of Gilligan's Island ...

O Captain, my Captain!
Our ship by winds are tossed
And Gilligan's now at the helm
We're surely wand'ring lost.

Tuesday, January 31

Simpler for Me

I want this procedure to be simpler. It's too complicated. It takes me more time to do the paperwork, to cross the T's and dot the i's, than it does to do the work. Here's my idea:

Eliminate reviews: I did the work, why waste time looking at it again?

We don't need Quality controls. Again: my work is good, do we need second-guessing?

No need for memos: we talk, we know what we said.

Drop the History file: once it's done, it's there. Enough said.
Too many signatures required. It should only be m- Well, actually, again: once it's done, it's there. Who needs to sign-off on finished work? And why?

It's all just an excuse for bureaucratic fat. We're leaning down here this year: trim the fat. I want it simpler for me to do my work.

February

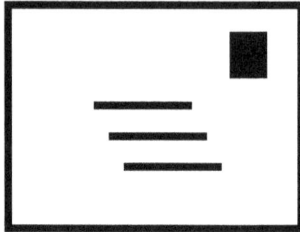

Wednesday, February 01

Ode: The Purpose of Procedures

The purpose of procedures is to tighten tricky techniques
In the process that pertains to particular performance
Of the policies proclaimed by the management mandates
That are promulgated partly by the bureaucrats because
The guidelines are forgotten by the lazy and the lousy
Ones who leave us in the lurch picking up the broken
pieces.
So when you are feeling funky with particular procedures
Just remember there's a member of your team
To whom there's meaning.
Meaning just because they're screwy
You're the one who's stuck with hooey. Fooey!
Paying for their piper with your policy-pricked life or
Sitting sifting sheaves of policy procedured papers
What a way to spend a day as a normal 9-to-5er.

Thursday, February 02

Do Not Work Too Late

Note to Self:

Do not work too late.

Not because you have a life outside of work. ("Outside
life" being, at present, an academic exercise in fantasy
visualization intended to overcome the jarring reality of
holiday credit card bills making the bank account a be-
low-zero comedy.)

Do not work too late.

Because the next day you still have to work. And you will come into work the next day tired. Dog tired.

And make really dumb, stupid mistakes.

Like telling a vice president that he is doing something ass-backwards.

Do not work too late.

Friday, February 03

Disrespect

Needless to say, it does not matter whether you are right or wrong when you tell a vice president that he is doing something ass-backwards: he is a Veep, you are a Cube - it is "disrespectful."

Again, it does not matter whether the Veep's idea would crash the company into a lawsuit at $410-per-hour - and you have pointed that out - and he has ordered you out of his office because, even though you are only quoting said $410/hr lawyer who gave that advice a month earlier, the Veep "doesn't want to hear that." You should not stand between a Veep and his fantasy world. And certainly not point out the fantasy elements. And certainly not describe it in terms that the Veep will finally get through his thick skull, aka, while leaving, "Sure, let's just go at this ass-backwards like you want." These things do not matter.

And do not factor in the fact that your strong stance shook him up enough to keep him from making the expensive mistake, saving the company potentially ten$ of thousand$. These things do not matter.

He is a VICE President. This thing matters.

(No, we will not play on the word "vice" - too easy.)

You must now be summoned to Human Resources for a Disciplinary Review.

Saturday, February 04

Disciplinary Review, Part 1

[A Note from The Cube: This didn't happen on the weekend, but sometimes you need a day or two to see more clearly.]

The Cube has been summoned to HR for a Disciplinary Review concerning "disrespect." As noted earlier, one probably shouldn't cap an animated discussion with a Veep by stating "Yes, let's just walk into a lawsuit ass-backwards like we never saw it coming. That what we always do." Apparently the Veep is a sensitive soul.

The interesting thing about the Disciplinary Review conducted in the Human Resources office is that none of the participants in the incident was there except The Cube. The Review was conducted by three people who were not there: the head of HR and The Cube's "official" supervisory persons. (A manager and a Veep - but the "official" has to do with being on loan-out to another Veep for most of the time: 'don't really work for these guys much. Don't ask why they haven't transferred me: office politics and budget allocations. Apparently The Cube's services get charged to other departments at 150% of what they are charged to my "official" department.)

So... no one in the room who knows what happened and some faces you hardly ever see or know asking you some personal questions.

The Cube let 'em know of a reluctance to talk about the incident without the two other participants present - both Veeps, by the way: the one I was working for at the time and the one words were exchanged with. The Cube does not like to talk in a vacuum. At the very least The Cube doesn't like to put words into others' mouths. At the very worst, one should have the right to face one's accuser(s).

Small problem here: The Veep that The Cube was working for, witnessing the event, didn't think very much of import had happen. "It had to be said," was the Veep's very Irish-type observation. "Probably I should have said it, but you can't let the company go walking ass-backwards into a lawsuit and if the point wasn't made strongly, then that's just what would have happened."

It turns out he wasn't told of the complaint nor the Review. He went out on an afternoon appointment and won't be back till tomorrow. All of this was set up after he left the building.

Now here we are in a Disciplinary Review, being questioned by people who weren't there, don't know the situation, haven't talked to the only 3rd party witness to the event, and - at one point early on - made it clear that they are uninterested in the issues under discussion: "just your tone of voice and volume."

I see a paper upside down on the HR Director's desk: the Review report has already been written. D'ya think their minds are made up yet?

R

Sunday, February 05

Disciplinary Review, Part 2: shoot the company in its own foot

[A Note from The Cube: Still looking over what happened last Wednesday-Thursday-Friday.]

Once upon a time, oh about 9 years ago, The Cube was in a company where a secret takeover resulted in 80% of the workforce being given 30 minutes notice to clear their desks and leave. This happened on a Friday morning at 11 a.m. It affected all levels and even the survivors did not know it was about to happen, so there were no managers wandering about with dour faces before the fact, no secretarial rumours bouncing off the cubicle walls. All computers were disconnected from the company network while we were in the lunchroom being given the notice. All over and done with. Slam. Bam. Thank you, ma'am. The Cube had been working with a Marketing team making the last tweaks on a prepaid $50K magazine ad for an upcoming series of trade shows, final final deadline due by 1 p.m. Pissed away.

Realizing their haste mistakes, over the next month the New Regime hired back a number of people as "consultants" at double and triple their salaries (needless to say, there was no good will offering of help), fighting a rear guard action to keep the company from hemorrhaging a million $$$$ worth of Product, R&D and Marketing assets.

So it was that Friday, two days after Wednesday's Disciplinary Review, seemed very deja vu.

It may have been observed that The Cube was very busy of late, most noticeably in a position of "pre-legal" responsibility that recognized over the past couple of years that:

(a)   The company lawyer had given the same advice on the same subjects many times;

(b)   The Cube had kept organized notes of the lawyer's advice and could provide them at request for executive review; and

(c)   The Cube's reports and analyses provided to the lawyer had apparently been cut-and-pasted into his documents verbatim of late.

As a result, The Cube has been tasked with keeping the Company "on message" re: the lawyer's advice and has participated in (read: initiated, coordinated and lead in all but name) several active communications, actions and responses of an expensive nature - with the lawyer, with competitors, with potential strategic alliances to COMPANIES much larger than our Company.

At the same time, The Cube has inadvertently (and against my will) become knowledgeable in ISO, CE, UL, DoD and FDA ways and means.

On Friday the Company was simultaneously being audited by one of the Regulatory agencies and - it doesn't rain but it pours - the President of a Major Company telephoned in response to one of The Cube's alliance reachouts several months in the effort. Two different departments, two different Veeps. Some important shit going down. The Cube was busy.

However, neither Veep was The Cube's Veep - these were loan-out activities - nor did they fall under the realm of the Offended Veep of two days earlier. But, there had been silence since the Disciplinary Review of two days before, faces had smiled at The Cube, work had continued at its frenzied pace...

Can you see where this is going?

11:15 a.m.

Moments after delivering a hand-notated procedural document to the Regulatory Auditor, and literally in the middle of the conference call between the Prez of the Major Company, our Biz Development Veep and myself, The Cube was asked by his "official" Veep to step outside the room for a moment. With notes in hand, The Cube stepped outside.

And into an immediate, out-the-front door, One Week Suspension.

The Biz Development Veep, who was waiting for The Cube (and the notes) to return, tried to stall, unaware of the "official" decision/action made. His phone call reached The Cube's cellphone on the drive back home. "It was an embarrassment," he moaned. "We looked like fools." So much for that avenue of strategic alliance.

The Regulatory Auditor, demanding certain procedural explanations and having no one to provide them, placed the Company on a Restriction until a written answer is given: Deadline - one week. A lawyer at roughly 12 times The Cube's hourly salary has been given The Cube's annotated procedural notes and asked to review and respond. So much for producing any product lines according to that procedure for the near future.

✳✳✳

The Cube is not that important to the Company, just part of a support team. But, sometimes, support is important.

Apparently, though, sometimes it is also deemed important for the Company to shoot itself in its own foot.

The Cube is on Disciplinary Suspension for the week, so the next few Notes will be from contributors still in their cubicles.

Monday, February 06

Codicil

But it still hurts.

Tuesday, February 07

Kreativ

Whatsa matta wit Joe?

I mean, he wuz jus' doin' his job an' then Boss Ned come in 'n sez:

"Joe, you bein' Kreativ. Stop it."

Joe, he dunno know what "Kreativ" is, hez just doin' hiz job best he know how. He dunno how no other way. So Joe keep doin' his job, which ever'one else thinkz pretty good, 'n a week later Boss Ned come in 'n sez:

"Joe, you bein' Kreativ again. That's a Attitude Problem. Stop it."

Joe, he still dunno what "Kreativ" is, dunno what "Attitude" is - but he sure unnerstandz "Problem": itsa Problem when Bozz Ned don' like whut yur doin'.

But how to stop doin' it and still do yur job?

Y'see, I dun sum readin' since this started 'n I foun' out our Joe is Kreative: it meanz he solvez stuff bettern' we others do, in ways we didn't thinka doin'. Wichiz why we uze Joe a lot.

We shouldn'ta uzed him, it seems. Make him help us by bein' Kreative, I mean.

Becuz Kreative seems ta be bad for Boss Ned, cuz las' week he cum in with the Resource Humanz and they stand aroun' Joe an' all uv 'em say:

"Yep, itsa Attitude Problem."

An' Joe was out.

Kreative: itsa bad thing ta be when yur around the Boss Neds a tha world.

Wednesday, February 08

Creeping Clauses

And creeping clauses will catch you
Creeping clauses
                    will
                            catch
                                    you.

In the office, in the cube,
in the administrative stream
Lives a hope, a faint spark hope,
that things aren't really what they seem.
Could it be we're trapped in here?
Could it be there's no escape?
Is the auditor so near?
Is this paperwork my fate?

And creeping clauses will catch you
Creeping clauses
                    will
                        catch
                            you.

There is hope, foolish hope
of streamlined smart transparency
Where all the things you write, you do
are governed by smart policy.
But this memo makes no sense?
This work instruction obscures all?
Is this procedure just pretense?
Erecting one more workflow wall?
And creeping clauses will catch you
Creeping clauses
                    will
                        catch
                            you.

In the hallways, in the aisles
in the passages you wander
Lives a Monster, inborn Monster
Stillborn actions fill its maw.
Have you tried to do it?
NO!
Have you made it right?
NO!
Have you used plain common sense -
NO!
Have you tried to fight -
NO!
You cannot finish
Cannot start
Cannot make a decent try
The inborn Monster
Paper Monster
BUREAUCRACY's its name
It cries:
NO!
NO!
NO! NO! NO!
WE WILL MAKE YOU BLIND!

In the office, in the cube,
in the administrative stream
Lives a hope, a faint spark hope,
that things aren't really what they seem.
But they are.

And creeping clauses will catch you
Creeping clauses
                    will
                          catch
                                you.

Thursday, February 09

Stupid - or Clever?

Pierre Dolet writes his Notes from the Cube ...

Phone call from a man wanting some information. Sent it to him. Calls back: "I had to destroy this: it said 'Confidential' and I want to discuss this with others. I couldn't even talk with my outside counsel."

???

This is the first time anyone has had a problem with this.

There are some Confidential things in the info sent; the only reason it was sent, in fact, is that the man had spoken with our Prez and, smelling a future biz opportunity, the Prez said when he called, "Send him our XYZ."

Well, we checked with our lawyer - he set up the Confidential document - and he suggested a couple of deletions that we could make to remove the Confidential parts of the XYZ. Did it, then took off the Confidential notice, then sent it.

Man calls back: "You missed a 'Confidential' on page 17: I destroyed it. I only read public domain materials."

It was a standard-issue "Proprietary & Confidential" footer - a template from Word probably. Shows up on every other doc issued within every other company out there.

But, OK: re-moved it, re-sent it, added note: "All Confidential elements removed. Now available for public viewing, though not as public domain material: still has copyright protection." (Page 2 notice; again, standard issue)

Man calls back: "I only deal with public domain information. I destroyed it.

Please send me materials that are in the public domain, as your President promised he would send me, or we cannot do business further on this."

Checked with Prez: Yep, he had inadvertently said "I'll send you our public domain booklet." Tried to explain that "public domain" means there are no protections whatever on the content: Man can use it how he will. Prez thinks I'm being over-sensitive.

I'm thinking the Man-we-want-to-maybe-do-business-with is either very stupid and doesn't understand the standard levels of copyright and proprietary information confidentiality - or he is very clever and intends to steal anything that is "public domain." I'm thinking we should contact our lawyer again. I'm thinking that, stupid or clever, I wouldn't go near that Man to do business with him with a ten-foot pole.

But I live in a Cube and no one cares what I think.

Friday, February 10

They Don't Know What You Do

Kyra writes her Notes from the Cube ...

It seems hardest when they don't really know what you do.

Yes, there is a "job description" that you fit in to - but does any job that isn't robotic "fit" perfectly?

I was hired to type reports. Within a month they discovered I can work with spreadsheets: set them up, create formulas, etc. Now, "typing" has more analysis and planning than keystrokes.

The problem is that they don't understand the underlying reasoning behind the spreadsheets - they only want the results. As a result, they still consider this part of "typing" and judge my work by output, not content.

Scarier still, they don't seem to understand how much I control their results:

if I change the formula, the analysis reads differently - but because they don't understand the underlying reasoning, they don't follow through with a consistent above-and-visible reasoning.

"I want a Return On Investment worksheet" is the order.

"There are at least 3 different ROI formulas," I answer.

"Use the best one. Don't overcomplicate things: it's only typing."

Tap. Tap. tap.

Saturday, February 11

They Don't Know What You Do 2

Hank write his Notes from the Cube to follow-up on Kyra's thoughts from yesterday...

If they knew what you did, they'd do it.

✳✳✳

OK, that was an easy shot - and probably not that true.

More likely, if they know what you do, it is probably be-

NOTES FROM THE CUBE

cause it's what they did once - and now you are stuck fulfilling their nostalgic memories of "How WE used to do it right."

That road leads to micro-management. It is the road best left untaken. Pray for ignorance.

Sunday, February 12

They Don't Know What You Do 3

Texas Slim writes his Notes from the Cube to Hank & Kyra ...

Most scary (and let's be honest, it's no one's fault) is the fact that sometimes things are changing so fast that if you are not the one doing the job you can't know what it is anymore.

It doesn't matter the level: I used to work in Accounts Receivable, a Past Due deacon of detection. But the way they electronically work through those things now, there are analytical tools that would have made me redundant and leave me in the knowledge lurch right now for sure.

Move that up a notch: imagine I'm a Manager who doesn't believe in micro-management (a blessing) and has been out of the trenches a few years: how does he deal with his underlings when he knows that he doesn't know what the underlings actually do? It's a toughie.

The Cube responds ...

I was going to stay out of this awhile, but I've got to correct Slim here: if the you have a manager who knows that he doesn't know about something, that's only a problem when he takes a defensive/aggressive attitude. If he's halfway intelligent and, being a non-micro-manager like you described, I'm assuming he is, he'll be smart enough to respect the situation. If he's not halfway intelligent - or insecure in some other way (and, really, how many of us are secure in our jobs these days?) - then you've got someone looking to blame things on: and it's always easiest to blame it on something no one understands.

But we're not even talking about "halfway intelligent" here: Hank and Kyra were talking about management not knowing that they don't know what you do. Or how you do it. They know results - usually results they want to see, not necessarily objectively - and they don't particularly care how those results were achieved.

Or maybe they care, but they still don't really know how it's done.

Or maybe they think they know how it's done, but they are off the mark. It's like with Sports, Movies and Politics: EVERYONE is an "expert" and absolutely certain that they know how it "should be." Yeah.

They don't really know what you do.

Monday, February 13

Back

So it's back to the trenches after a week's suspension, wondering how the day will go. Dressed up fine - not too shabby, not too classy - looking fit. Feeling crappy: didn't sleep, 'know that the issues are still unresolved. Still can't decide whether to pretend nothing happened or face it head on.

Logistics problem: still have the same "duty" to perform that resulted in the suspension in the first place. Responsibility without Authority. Yep, back to the trenches.

Irony Does Live

Ironic laugh: Ha Ha Ha Ha Ha!

Problem that got The Cube suspended for a week still exists. While the Cube was on enforced, unpaid "vacation," however, things happened ...

The Veep who didn't want to hear The Cube quoting the company's lawyer gathered fellow Veeps around (circling the wagons protectively) and they spent a week strategizing, came up with an action plan that totally blew The Cube's advice out of the water, and were all set to enact it ---

Then, fortunately, one meek little clerical forwarded a copy of their plan to the company lawyer. "I thought this was routine," she said honestly. (As it is, most times, except when Veeps are trying to be clever.)

The lawyer blew up!

"What do you think you are DOING?!?" he called in on a conference call almost immediately. "This will land you up the wazzoo in a lawsuit and it's exactly what I've been telling you you CAN'T do for the past two years!"

Hmmm.

So, as The Cube returns and is pointedly excluded from the next steps in working on this situation, the problem still exists, the fellow Veeps have all stepped back from it, disingenuously saying that "We were only offering our 2 cents worth, nothing concrete, it's yours to handle," and the original Veep has gone on a two week fact-finding tour of our offshore factories.

It is understood that there will be an Executive Policy meeting to review The Problem. Next month. Maybe the month after. Maybe The Problem will go away or, if it doesn't, maybe we can pretend it doesn't exist.

♥

Wednesday, February 15

Disconnected

One of the enjoyable things about being suspended is the "disconnect," as in: disconnected and denied all electronic access to the building, the network, and one's voice mail.

Apparently, someone has a How To manual that says all ex-employees are disgruntled and destructive. Apparently, also, the How To manual doesn't address suspended employees who may still need to work for the company and ignores the statistic that most destruction is accomplished by disgruntled current employees still on the job.

Oh, and the compact of trust - "Give me your word" - does not seem to apply anymore, either. Well, no surprise about that: the How To manual has no place in it for employee-management goodwill, only worst-case scenarios.

But, discarding honor and trust as elements in the workplace, there is still the matter of inconvenience to the company.

A few years ago, The Cube was in a company where 80% were laid off in a single hour - a bloodbath preceded by disconnecting everyone from the network. This earned The Cube a $100/hour consultancy the next week when called in to reconstruct a $50K advertising poster that no one still there knew how to access.

After the recent suspension, fun fun, The Cube was "disconnected" from all company access. Now, since returning, The Cube has had much leisure time, since it is easier to disconnect than it is to reconnect the myriad accesses evolved over a 5 year period of employ. Every couple of hours we come to a standstill as we discover yet another access that bars performance of the job.

And, of course, nothing is ever reinstated, reconnected, or re-passworded without a glitch. 3 hours Monday, 1 hour Tuesday, another 3 hours today. All with other employees waiting as well.

It was a good How To book, one that knows a lot about the dark side of human nature and beans about the better part of people and how things work in the cubicles.

Thursday, February 16

Lost Between The Powers That Be

Sadly. Sadly.

How do you handle a crisis when your immediate manager is scared?

She's a nice person, generally, but she is totally unprepared to handle those situations where the Powers That Be have different agendas - and we are caught in the middle.

You can see her fright. It's because her Rules are broken. In her world, you follow the company procedures without question. With-Out-Question. This may lead her down blind alleys and wandering meanderings through fruitless paperwork that she will prepare and no one will read, but it is What Is Required and What They Want.

But those Rules don't work right now. Our Veep is breaking them and an opposing Veep is challenging that breakage - and she has to choose sides: follow our Veep, protect his ass, and knowingly break the very Company Rules which are the only things she knows how to follow - or follow the Rules, expose the breakage, back up the other (correct) Veep, and be exposed to our Veep's enmity.

She is so scared, since she has never staked her workplace ethic on integrity before. She just wants to do her job, without making those kinds of decisions.

She is taking a vacation tomorrow, with plans to leave halfway through today on a "just remembered" medical appointment. Maybe it will blow over by Monday.

Friday, February 17

Survival?

Reading an article today about "surviving the office jungle" though alliances, training and strategy. No mention of going in and doing a good job for the sake of the craft.

They're probably right to think of it that way: survival. Most probably don't think of their jobs as a craft - at least not here in the cubes - and so there is plenty of mind-time to let the attention wander to things like Who's On Top?, How to Avoid Blame, and Which Way Outta Here That's Going Up?

Survival. Might as well go back to spear-chucking. Develop a few deft moves, learn how to dodge (claws, teeth, other spears), perfect your aim and - WHAM! - dinner for tonight. Certainly makes more sense than sitting in a 4 x 6, tapping at a keyboard, pretending to accomplish something, while keeping the ears tuned for intrigue, opportunity and danger.

When the layoff hammer falls, cubicle walls fall down in a row like dominos. Why think you control that? Stoic Existentialism, that's The Cube's motto this month. And if everyone is out to get everyone else - and "survival" has to be #1 priority on your mind - it's time, maybe, to enter a vocation instead of a job.

I hear that firefighters stick by one another. In some professions, the "team" is real, not just a concept slogan.

S

Saturday, February 18

Finished Friday

Finished Friday with a yo-ho-ho and a long afternoon of tedium. Tough to do anything when 99% of everyone, from the bottom-up-top-down-sideways-and-back have mentally checked out. Did it, but with a sluggishness that says, "Yep, it's the middle of February."

Feb's not quite the same as July: no one's TGIFing or looking forward to the weekend. Nothing to go home for the weekend to. Some places there's snow, some places there's slush, some places there may be sunny skies (although the weatherman's says differently this weekend) - all places there are Christmas bills that came in January and have hit their deadlines now. Tight cash. But even without the tight cash, there's just the muffled thud of winter.

Slept in this morning, which was nice. Now to face the dull day of freedom.

Could be worse. Could be March.

Sunday, February 19

Reflection on Suspension

So it's been a week since returned from suspension - and a day to rest - now to look back.

Amazing how nothing changes. One is back into the routine without much pause. It was like going on vacation: some work piled up, but for all the Sturm und Drang of the events leading to the suspension, everyone acts as if Nothing Happened.

Oh, sure, a few folks walk tenderly around this Cube. Certain orders, requests, and general knowledge memos are specifically routed to The Cube "through authorized channels." But nothing in the content has changed. And, by Friday, Dull Friday, everything was The Same.

It must be the leveling effect of Dull Friday - or Dull Week - or Dull People.

They can't imagine Doing anything, so when something happens, they Don't.

Not much has changed since the feudal system, when the peasants could continue plowing while the wars went on around their fields. They'll only notice when their cubicles are raped.

Monday, February 20

Medical Query

Wonder if the stomach pains are any reflection of the work environment?

When out for a week on suspension: no pains.

Back to the cubicles: constant.

Tuesday, February 21

Status Meeting

We had a department status meeting today.

Nothing new happened on a Policy/Company level, so there was nothing for our Manager to inform us about.

I was suspended last week, so nothing to report.

Two people were sick - unable to report.

Four people report to the two sick people, so they had to hold their reports till the sick people returned.

The other two people were laid off a month ago in this year's budget-cutting mandate.

The Department Status Meeting is held every Tuesday morning, 10-11 a.m. The suggestion was made at 9 a.m. that "Maybe we can cancel this week's meeting?"

The suggestion was considered - and dismissed: "I have to report at the Manager's meeting tomorrow the status of my department as reported today."

I can't wait to read our meeting Minutes.

Wednesday, February 22

Ode: Meeting Minutes

The message of the meeting is repeated in the minutes
A memorializing message of minutely managed moments
When quickly crafted questions are redactively reduced
To bolded Action Items that will never be pursued
And prickly problem points are pinioned to a footnote
At the bottom of a page that is fortunately forgotten
While decisions are detailed in deadly dull description
In a style that makes you wish they were never ever written
But it doesn't really matter and you shouldn't really care
What is written's never read and what happened never there
It's a fiction more than fact for the facts are best forgone
And these minutes now here end they have gone on far too long.

Thursday, February 23

The Form 1: Belief

It ain't the Form,
It's the Function.

That's the theory. You could just as well add:

That's not a Fact,
It's a Fiction.

Yes, you can, when you look at how many people fetishize
The Form. Love, hate, fear, formulate, dread and masti-
cate: we loves to make our Forms into the End All and Be
All of the workflow.

The Form is a very religious experience: It Always Was
This Way and It Always Will Be. To this eternal existence
we have created our rituals of worship.

Like all rituals, we have scant knowledge of that unknown past when The Form was originally created - by Whom and for What reason? Like all good and enduring rituals, we perpetuate our Forms, create new ones constantly in tribute to the enduring, primal Form.

Is this new creation re-invention? An examination of the Function underlying The Form? No such heresies: we are updating the logo, changing the typestyle to make it more modern, but the underling Belief remains unchanged -- this is The Form, we shall not challenge its existence.

Friday, February 24

The Form 2: A Prayer

Our Form
Stacked on the top shelf
How is it you are filled out?
Your first line's blank,
Your second line's black:
Does it mean that we skip to the third?
Give us the input to fill in these blanks
And allow us to skip to Line 10
As we have skipped Lines 5, 6, and 7.
And allow us to fudge the facts we don't know
But consider this complete anyway.
For you are the paper that needs to be filled out
Today and Tomorrow
Form Without End
Amen.

Saturday, February 25

The Form 3: A Testimony

From Kyra, a truthful testimony to the power of the Form ...

She met me, my supervisor, in the corridor. Her eyes were troubled.

"The bug report," she said.

"The bug report," I echoed. "Yes, I do it weekly."

"Yes."

"Yes?"

"It- it needs a form."

I thought a second before answering: "But it is automatically generated by the software."

"Yes, but we need to standardize it in a form."

"It is standardized - by the software."

"But not in a form." Her eye lit up with those orbs of a True Believer. "We need a company logo," she explained, "and our department identified and, and- we can put it on a spreadsheet with double-edged borders, which will make it look professional." She was breathing heavily now, panting with excitement. "We can print it out and distribute it. And of course save it electronically- Do we need a new directory? A new directory! I'll go talk to I.T. right now to set us up with a new directory that only you and me will have Write access to - but everyone else can Read!"

She rushed off down the hall, calling back her encouragement: "A Form! Make the Form!"

The only person who uses the bug report is me.

Sunday, February 26

A Dream - or A Strategy?

Saturday night to Sunday morning: had 7 dreams last night - all were about work. Exciting. Filing in one dream. Two dreams had meetings. A couple went by just like the days do: forgettable. Only the last dream ...

Ah, the last dream: we were planning a hit. We made the plan, revised it, sent it for review, revised it again - and got Approval. And then I woke up.

I have no idea who we we were planning to kill - obviously it had management's OK, so it wasn't a private grudge - and I can't even remember How we planned/re-planned/re-re-planned to do it. But what really impressed me - and what I really, really, REALLY want to remember is: What in the heck did we write to get Quality's approval?

Dog-gone it! We had Quality sign-off on the plan! Whatever else I do today, I am going to try to remember the wording of whatever murder plan I wrote that was so persuasive that I could get a QA OK. That-

That just doesn't happen everyday.

Monday, February 27

Haiku: Productivity All Wet

Rain
Twelve hour work day
Four hours in car
Productivity
Weeps

Tuesday, February 28

Haiku: Cruel Wet Sun

Still rain
Long drive
Meeting
Picture window
Sun shines
Distant
Dry
Taunt

March

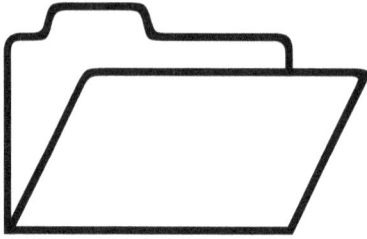

Wednesday, March 01

Conflict Management: Solutions

Hank Gerber writes his Notes from the Cube ...

Ideas that came out from a seminar on "Conflict Management."

Amid all of the seminar-endorsed approaches and the hours-long discussions of how we can manage/control/ diffuse conflict, the following ideas were developed by the working groups we were broken in to. (Note: not necessarily endorsed by the seminar leader.):

Fake it until you make it. (i.e., When the conflict is management-origined, plan on getting out of there ASAP on your own terms - a better, or at least comparable, job elsewhere. Not, as it turns out, an uncommon situation. This idea actually was endorsed by the seminar leader, a smart cookie.)

Grow up and live with it. (Mainly men - but also a lot of women 40 and over who know who they are.)

Grow up, blow up, and forget it once it's past. (Variation on the above. A lot of people, actually, seem to understand that sometimes venting is "natural." No one from the HR departments endorsed this approach, though.)

Is it "conflict" if you are from New York? (A regional observation. Variations included: "I'm Italian and you think this is a loud voice? I'm Jewish and you think... Etc.)

Ex-Lax. (Don't ask.)

A sledgehammer to the head. (My suggestion about a co-worker of one group who had screwed up to the tune of $50K and $30K each year past - but who, every 3-4 weeks, started interminable arguments insisting he was right. They had come to the conclusion to fire the guy, but I am too kind-hearted and pointed out it would hurt his feelings. The sledgehammer, meanwhile.... You have to understand that, from the way they described the guy, he seems to be indestructible.)

Thursday, March 02

When You Know You're Not In Sales

Was invited to a meeting yesterday by accident. ("Accident": no one had confirmed and they needed to fill some seats for a meet-and-greet with some visiting VIPs. As it happened, everyone invited showed up to an SRO crowd, but I was already seated next to a VIP so I had an unnaturally "central" position that could not be vacated without awkward embarrassment to the company.)

The meeting was supposed to be a Getting To Re-Know You with a company that had been very small three years ago and was competing at that time to be one of our vendors. Since then, it was bought by a medium-big company that could eat us for lunch. (We're a little too big, they're a little too small, for their 'breakfast" menu.) So, the point: now they have $$$ and want us to be their vendor.

I have to say that they were cruel and victorious in a quiet, almost dull way. It wasn't their fault that our Veeps and Directors practically threw the company at their feet with an Anything For You, Sir abasement. Still, "quiet" and "dull" do not change the little knife jabs that they gleefully twisted around as they basically had our people

jumping through hoops at the intimation that they would "consider thinking about it."
This is where I know I could not, would not, should not no never not be in Sales.

I know that our Veeps probably did what was necessary. Certainly no one shook with that excited frenzy you sometimes find with commission-poor auto salesmen on a Sunday evening. But, by the same token, they did practically tremble with anticipation of a "relationship" with a company that they had virtually dismissed only 36 months before.

Y'see, I could understand confidentially saying "OK, let's see what we can do for you" - but it never was said - or said like that.

Instead, starting from a position of faux "cool" (and it was transparently faux because the they were all nervously half-smiling at the prospect of the aforesaid intimation of a possibly considered large volume relationship), from the start they essentially abandoned every standard and guideline they had printed in the company materials. I don't think they we're even paying attention when they agreed to structural changes in a design that would have cost more to implement than the entire intimated order was worth. But not only did they agree - they began to suggest more costly alterations.

To which the other side, seeing which direction the wind was blowing, began to add increasingly arbitrary "requirements" in dialogues like:

"I don't see X in the current model. Do you think you could -"

"Not only can we X it, we'll add a YZ."

"Well, show us some prototypes and we'll see."

"No problem."

(Never mind that the current design was arrived at after 18 months of field study and design work - and that prototypes require 75% of the work it takes to get to a finished product - and this is on a "We'll see" request.)

In the end, for a "possible" order smaller than our current market average - with no money down and no further commitment - we are now committed to an accelerated development schedule on product variations that no one else has wanted, ever.

And our Veeps are happy. The halls were alive with positive vibes yesterday afternoon. No one seems to notice what they have done: everything for hope of The Sale.

This is when I know I am not made for Sales.

Friday, March 03

When You Know VPs Know Zip

Soooo.... A follow-up to yesterday's Veep meeting with the company dangling out the semi-"promised" Big Order.....

Several commitments were made yesterday by our Veeps, especially ones related to an accelerated development/ delivery schedule.

In phone conferences today the Veeps elaborated those commitments to the other company - and among one another.

So far, by the end of workday today (Friday), no one has bothered to tell the developers and production people responsible for delivering those commitments - at least one of whom goes for a three week vacation starting tomorrow. The Veeps for those divisions, meanwhile, are in Europe next week. The President wasn't here this week, so who knows what he knows.

Does anyone in charge know how this company makes its products?

Saturday, March 04

Sometimes It's Fun

Great experience yesterday. Started a task, dived into it - and looked up to find it was four hours later. Sometimes it's fun to feel like a craftsman working your job, absorbed into its details to the exclusion of all other concerns.

Note to Self: Probably family and less enthused co-workers may not agree.

Sunday, March 05

Across the World Bitching

Yeah, of course it's discouraged, but we're gonna do it anyway.

Thanks to the comfort, speed and beauty of email, cubicle workers around the world share their complaints and observations (usually wry, sarcastic, comic) in rapid-fire succession. Not spam, but the one-to-one pass-on of shared experience. Often self-directed. Sometimes semi-scatological. Usually true in that strike-home sense that doesn't allow argument (and certainly can't be said aloud in management-employee meetings).

There may be profound differences between our world politics, cultures and religions - but we are one in our cubes.

Monday, March 06

Wait For the Day

Monday morning before going to work:
Wait for the day.
Wait for the day.
This is not poetry, it's how you feel:
Anticipation at play.
Wait for the day.
Not dread, not fear, not pleasure, not fun:
Unformed like clay.
Wait for the day.
Old troubles seem smaller. Old problems, who cares?

Be cool, you say.
Wait for the day.
New day new week new chance new way
Wait for the day.
Wait for the day.

It's a long ride there.
Wait for the day.

Change the same. Same is changed.
Day the wait for
The day.

Wait.

No -
Here.

The.
Day.

Tuesday, March 07

Ask A Question & It Goes Round

Forgot the primary rule of the Committee: no question is answered definitively.

Made that mistake yesterday by sending out a query prior to today's Committee meeting, soliciting answers to certain issues that were, according to last month's Committee Action Items, to be put to bed by today's event.

Barring the other standard rule - If It's Written It Will Not Be Read - in which 50% of the Committee members have yet to acknowledge that they received yesterday's query or are aware of last month's Action Item list, the response from those who did respond is impressive: out of seven answers, not one actually says Yes or No or I Think It Should Be.

2 restate the query - as if by repeating it they have answered.

1 questions the validity of the issue.

1 questions the need for the query: "We'll discuss it at tomorrow's meeting."

2 note that they are "researching the issue."

and

1 says "I agree with my colleagues on the Committee."

%

Wednesday, March 08

Do You Want It?

Hank Gerber writes his Notes from the Cube ...

"Do you want it, yes or no?" 'Sounds like a simple enough question, yes? Try asking it at a meeting where there is apparently another agenda than the one printed in front of you – and you don't know what that agenda is.

"Do you want it, yes or no?" Try asking it when you are simply the messenger and the persons who are supposed to answer you are decision-makers. "Persons" is purposely said: one-on-one, decision-makers are usually very verbally definitive to their subords – not so definite when it comes to putting that decision in writing – and positively discreet on their own opinion when sitting with a bunch of equal-ranked decision-makers and the issue isn't open-and-shut.

"Another agenda." Hell, it's no "hidden agenda" conspiracy – it's just the too-human fear of making a mistake in a situation where others are all-too-able to co-opt the credit and all-too-willing to let you take the blame for decision gone south.

But that's what decision-makers are paid for, isn't it?

Yep. And some even take the responsibility seriously. They're the ones that used to work here.

Now, with the bland boys and marshmallow men in charge, a "decision" will become a fait accompli by momentum. One day it wasn't, the next day it is. Or by osmosis: everyone will assume it was decided, questions of When and by Whom left unvoiced.

And no one has committed themselves to it.

Thursday, March 09

Negotiating Beyond The Limit

Pierre Dolet writes his Notes from the Cube from Customer Care in the Sales Dept...

Here's an idea: when you're getting something for nothing, don't keep negotiating for a better deal.

It is amazing how customers, receiving a promotional bonus or discount or, simply, benefiting from an accounting error in their favor, then come back and push push PUSH for that ineffable, insatiable, unfulfillable "More."

They won't say "More"; they won't admit to greed in wanting "More"; they may even feel cheated if they don't get "More" – but they want it nevertheless, without reason, right, or justification. It must be a primal urge, like gorging oneself at the table long after the stomach has protested "Please, not one bite more: I'll burst!" Once, back in the primeval ooze of human existence, the crayfish-that-became-a-man must have been starved for cash and ...

More. Keep noodging, niggling, nudging, scratching, tapping, pressing, pissing me off with your neverending unworded whine for "More."

More.

And I will not tell you this, because this is business, and the company wants your future business.

Yes: we, too, want "More."

Friday, March 10

Customer "Care"

Pierre Dolet here.

Yesterday I wrote my Notes from the Cube "from Customer Care in the Sales Dept." Forgetting what I wrote – I was pissed off – I got to thinking about the "Care" in "Customer Care."

You see, we used to be "Customer Service" – and before that "Sales Support." We actually haven't changed what we do, just the titles. We are warmer and friendlier, apparently. "Sales" is so, so– transactional. And "Support," well, if you bought a product from us, it is so good that it stands on its own: it certainly doesn't need to be propped up and supported.

But "Service," you see, is about helping you. The product is GREAT – but you may need that extra service to help you use it to its full potential.

In fact, we care about you – we really do. Hence, we are now "Customer Care." We are the warm and fuzzy face of the Sales team. There are no problems to be fixed, no complaints to be salved – only "issues" to be "resolved" and "misunderstandings" to be "explained in a user-friendly manner."

Customer Care: We have been, you may notice, at a Team Seminar explaining our department's name change. It has affected us immediately.

Beautiful music on the phone. A pleasant, soothing voice: "Good morning, this is Customer Care. Your concerns are our concerns – and we will be with you in a few moments to address your needs. As you wait, please enjoy our complimentary selection of musical highlights to fit your taste. Press one for Easy Listening, Two for Classical Standards, Three for ..."

Saturday, March 11

It MUST on Saturday

It must rain or snow on Saturday. It must.

It must be miserable on that weekend you need comfort. It must.

There must be yardwork on Saturday. Or home repair. Or something long and boring and tedious and not... enjoyable.

Or -

The sun will shine. The day will be warm. Birds may even sing - after you have risen.

And you will have to go into work.

Because -

That's the way it MUST be on Saturday.

Sunday, March 12

Outsourced Customer Service

A Letter from The Cube to Management

If you think you are providing customer service by outsourcing to India, you are mistaken.

It is not their fault, over there in India: they cannot think like we do, they cannot understand the nuances of our culture. Just like we have the same handicap in the other direction. Sure, there will be a few of us on either side who can learn and catch the nuances – but it's difficult. All you have to do is look at how many 1st generation immigrants stay locked in the mindset of the "old country" and you will understand how intrinsically unfair and impossible it is to ask thousands of clericals in India to understand us over here when they answer the phone or instant-message technical help online.

They are patient, God bless 'em, they – are – patient. And polite. We are in the tag end of a five (yes, five!) hour online tech services exploration and I gave up before the anonymous Christina, David and, now, an unnamed supervisor could guide me to a resolution that solved the problem. I found it, finally, by figuring out where they were unable to understand the basic problem and worked backwards from their over-complications.

"Understand." Words are only a part of understanding. Then there is the between-the-lines level of syntax, logic and shared cultural experience that is the intuitive part of language. Politeness and patience are not resolution, they are methods for coping. Technical vocabulary is not equivalent to comprehension.

To put it in perspective: Years ago, when working with expatriates in the Middle East before the region turned violent, we found it necessary to convey technical information in drawings and photographs to our multicultural crew – all of whom spoke English.

Body language became as important a part of communication as words. And we needed time - a short commodity in the customer service field.

Time learn the cultural givens and assumptions that informed each person's understanding of the English words we were speaking. Sometimes a few minutes. Sometimes a few hours. Sometimes… it didn't happen. To quote Kipling, whose "white man's burden" assumed racism sometimes overshadows the logic of his experienced reasoning: East is East and West is West.

And never the twain shall meet.

Well, not entirely true. A couple of years ago, Sanjay in Tonawanda, New York, was my supposedly "anonymous" tech support guy on a recurring ISP/cable delivery problem. Oh, Sanjay was Indian all right – but he was also from New York – and within five minutes he cut through the bull to give me some advice that has literally saved me hours of downtime since then. ("Customer service will always tell you that the lines are being 'temporarily repaired'. They don't even have Status screens. Skip them & go straight to us.")

But Sanjay was corrupted: he was American. Y'see, those of you who are outsourcing your Customer Service and Technical Support voices to India, it takes an American to understand an American's needs. It takes an Indian to understand Indian needs. A Japanese...

I wrote the majority of this while waiting for Christina and David to consult their supervisor on why a simple popup screen in my program did not respond with the same message that their version of the software did, thus blocking further progress. They did not understand that the message appearing was the equivalent of the message they wanted – which had been my elementary question in the first place – but by the time they were finished analyzing, offering solutions and guiding me through aborted re-programming routines, they had re-invented the wheel. I would like to say that this is the first time this has happened and that I am the only person it has happened to.

Yes, I am sure that Christina and David are cheaper to employ than their American counterparts Sanjay and Shagufta – but they aren't providing customer service.

They can't.

Monday, March 13

Billable Hours: Teleconference

Memorandum
TO: Finance
FROM: Pierre Dolet
RE: Proposed Statistical Analysis

In keeping with this year's "Lean & Mean Time" cost efficiencies goal, we have assembled this proposed table for gauging the effectiveness of outside services.

As a test case on how recorded input will read out, we have monitored the first 1/2 day of executive teleconferences with attorneys, consultants and other billable staff. [Note that, in Q1, teleconferences have been substituted for face-to-face conferences, per "Lean & Mean," to cut down on billable travel time.]

Scheduled: TeleConference with Corporate Attorney A to review proposed licensing agreement."

Attorney A: "Good morning."
VP1: "Morning. How was your weekend?"

Discussion of weekend activities.

Attorney A: "What do you think of the proposal so far?"
VP 1: "We'll have to re-schedule till after I have time to go over it."

Billable hours: 0.25 hours minimum
Cost per hour: $400
Cost of call: $100
Accomplished: 0

Scheduled: Teleconference with Consultant C1 in New York, Consultant C2 in Toronto and Consultant C3 in Topeka.

VP2: "Morning, Mike."
C1: "Hi, Bill."
VP2: "Morning, Jim.
C2: "Good Morning, Bill. Hi, Mike."
C1: "Hi, Jim."
VP2: "Tom, you there?"
C3: "I'm on."
VP2: "Good morning."
C3: "Morning, Bill. Mike. Jim.
C2: "Hi, Tom."
C1: "Hi, Jim."
C3: "I'm Tom."
C1: "Hi, Tom. Bill, you still there?"
VP2: "I'm still here."
C2: "Are we still on track?"
VP2: "Tracking."
C3: "Tracked."
C1: "On the mark."
VP2: "Good. Jim, what do you think about that? Jim? Jim?"
C1: "I think we lost him."
C3: "I'm on my cell and about to go through a tunnel. You may lo-"
VP2: "Mike, you wanna hold?"
C1: "Actually, I have to get back to the lab."
VP2: "OK, no problem - we're on track. I'll coordinate the next meeting. Keep up the good work."
C1: "Bye."
VP2: "S'long."
C2: "Hello-? Hello-? I'm back. What-"

Billable hours: 0.5 hours minimum
Cost per hour: $170 per consultant
Cost of call: $255
Accomplished: ---

Tuesday, March 14

Where Were You Yesterday?

A true conference call. Only the VP's name has been deleted to protect the... innocent?

"I called yesterday. Where were you?"

"Here."

"But I called. You didn't answer."

"I was here. I didn't get your call."

"But I called."

"I was here."

"Did you read my email?"

"I didn't get it."

"But I sent it."

"It must be lost in the netherworld of our network."

"I'll send it again."

Wednesday, March 15

Up & Down

Welllllll, Don done did it wrong.

Y'see, Don's competent.

In a world of InC's, Don's the man to turn to. Consequently, everyone UP and below - send their crap to Don to handle.

Smart move for them.

Sad for Don.

Don done did it wrong.

Thursday, March 16

The Squeeze

What Andy over on the production side of the floor seems to be saying is this:

"If they want to have the product out the door without taking the time to develop it, they gotta expect the process to be held together by chewing gum."

This sort of echoes Tahir's worries as an engineer:

"They're selling new products before we finish making them."

Andy and Tahir are caught in The Squeeze. The Company is running short on cash, has cut down on support personnel, needs sales, needs new product - and hasn't got the time to do it right.

So they're doing it wrong - hoping that the Quality Control odds fall in their favor and the regulatory auditors don't come knocking on our particular direction.

Friday, March 17

The Squeeze 2

To keep out unions, this company has an employee profit-sharing plan: "We are all owners."

It's a good plan, actually, despite its cynically-derived origins back in the 1970s when everyone was afraid of a La Raza-type organization of ethnic workers who have always made up the majority of the production floor here. (Hazy memories on exact dates, since no one is around who was there back then.) The plan is good because the company was small enough for the longest time that it was more of an extended family than an Us-Them division of labor. Yeah, there were family squabbles, but everyone was babysitting every else's kid, too. Literally. First name basis, bottom-up, top-down. Couple of idiot children, a couple of enfants terrible, quite a few raised-by-merit bastards. Democratic in its own rough tumble way. So when the employee profit-sharing plan began, and began to flourish after years of the company languishing in a hole, it was a just reward to everyone for pulling together.

Now we're sorta big, though. Not multi-national big, not even a couple of thousand big, but a healthy high hundreds number nevertheless. The Originals are almost all

gone, at every level. But the profit sharing plan continues - because the Corporates in charge now revised the
plan slightly to change across-the-board sharing into a
"graduated merit" plan.

Read: The higher you are, the more you get.

OK, so it's Real World now. It's still a good plan, as these
things go. Quarterly, plus an annual dividend, and it
gives us an incentive not to make major screw-ups that
cause the plan to shrink. (Major screw-up #1: Send out a
$100,000 order to the wrong side of the country: lose the
order AND lose the client. It has happened.)

But - with the Real World realities come some Real world
hypocrisies. We've got a plan without the participation
anymore. Never more apparent than yesterday, when 49
people were laid off - including one with 27 years' service
- while the Prez gave a speech about how "We have to protect the profit sharing for those who are still here." Yep,
we are running tight these days, caught in The Squeeze:
just not discussing options in a "share" mode -- like unions might have demanded.

Like the old Guns and Roses song used to ask in a basso
profundo whisper while Axel Rose squealed his falsetto:

> Where do we go from here?
> Where do we go?
> Where do we go?
> Where do we go from here?

Saturday, March 18

The Squeeze 3

Robbing From Peter to Pay Paul.
'Used to be a Marketing only phenomena, limited only to paper credit.

End-of-year comes, book-in the January orders for the "How We Performed" presentation to make the year look better than it was. 'Not really lying, since the numbers didn't translate into Accounting practice. And it was all in-house stroking, marking out your turf, and - in some ways - sort of "reality": the last two weeks of December and the first week of January, no one was really working, Anywhere (obviously we're not in retail). Certainly shipping was clogged up by Christmas commerce (we're not seasonal, either). You could sort of, maybe, wink-wink, pretend that these booked orders represented What We Did This Year.

Now it's expanded to Profit-Sharing reality.

On a quarterly basis.

We have an employee Profit-Sharing Plan, in place for over 25 years. We have a new Executive Management Team, on board for almost 3 years. The Execs quickly understood the benefits of Profit-Sharing, albeit in a Plan revised to have "weighted" participation (read: the higher you are, the more you get). This was a much better plan than those that tie Exec Bonuses to any particular target goals: with our plan, all the company has to do is make a gross profit to get a share.

But this is real money, not paper puffery, so when the first quarter of the new regime rolled around and the profits were not so nifty, a few of the newbies squawked to the new Prez: "But you promised…"

To give him his credit, he held out for a year or two. And then one of the Super Executive Plans accidentally tied up shipments for 3 weeks (one has to assume that they didn't want to have shipments come to a standstill).

This was going to be a hell of a bad quarter. To say that we had "profits" was akin to saying that the sun shines on the North Pole in December. Yeah, there's a hint of hopeful light around the edges, but really …

A bit of a Squeeze.

Well, honestly, we did have hopeful light! All of those June orders that didn't go out the door would boogie down the highways in July along with the regular July flow. Yes! YES! So, let's just book those orders-not-shipped as Profit and Participate in it. YES! (Ummm, and ignore the fact that the Super Exec Plan had laid off a warehouse shift and there was nobody around to step up the pass-through.)

History becomes the present. That was last June. By end-of-quarter September, we needed to book-in October to make the Profit-Sharing Plan for Q3. Then in December, the year-end wasn't quite going to make it, so January (and a wee bit of February)… Now, in March, we need to book-in April, plus a dash or two of May…

The Squeeze.

▶▶▌

Sunday Review

Let's see, it's Sunday afternoon and I'm reading a report on scrap material, analyzing it, translating the analysis to a spreadsheet, and adding color to highlight key data critical to understanding the report.

Critical Analysis: Ask the key questions that will bring out the important points ...

Question: Which color (besides red, which sends an alarm) will bring out the most important points?

Question: Should it be in landscape or portrait layout?

Question: Should it be simplified for the VPs?

Question: Why is a cubicle worker making this analysis when it should be someone with responsibility for the tasks being analyzed?

Question: Will anybody double-check the analysis - or just the presentation format?

Question: Why did I agree to a salaried position, no overtime, when I used to be hourly?

Question: This isn't even in my job description - I could just give the spreadsheet uninterpreted - so why am I doing it?

Question: On a Sunday?

Monday, March 20

Upstairs-Downstairs

Not a new observation, but the Floor-Office divide is growing wider.

Mainly apparent, last week, when the most recent round of layoffs hit the Floor - 42 in a day - while upstairs in the cubes we emerged unscathed. (Not counting two who left under their own steam for greener pastures.)

On the same day, we had the monthly all-company employees meeting. It was here that the divide showed up pretty obviously.

Office People: Laughing at all the President's jokes. Generally upbeat.

Production Floor: Quiet. Waiting to hear what happens next.

Office: Relieved. It's not us.

Floor: It's us.

Tuesday, March 21

Re-Write Rule

A new variation on the maxim: "If you write it, it will not be read."

The new maxim goes: "If you have the power, make them re-write it."

Power. This means that you have to be high enough on the totem pole to "suggest," "request" or otherwise require others to do your bidding. Obviously, this is a given prerogative of the President & CEO, under whom all corporate beings exist. To the Vice Presidents kowtow the horde, too - though they have to play careful with other Veeps. Directors, managers, supervisors - each with descending levels of authority - and so on. It is a corporate pyramid hierarchy after all, not equal-vote democracy.

But Why-Oh-When would this power be exercised?

Easy. Back to maxim 1: When you haven't read the report in the first place.

BUT:

Somehow or other you find yourself in a meeting where the information contained in the report-you-haven't-read(-and-never-will) is a central part of the topic under scrutiny. Perhaps, even, it is somehow proven by some annoyingly efficient cubicle being that this report has been distributed more than once - to you!

Perhaps maybe possibly it was discussed already and, because you have yet (an eternal, never-to-come yet) to crack the covers of that report.

Do not panic. Certainly do not show embarrassment at your failure to know the subject. Remember, not everyone has the talents of Sales' Director Buck, who can talk for ten minutes on anything, whether or not he has a clue to the subject.

No, you are more subtle - and wise. That's the key: Look Wise. Do not make comments that will give away your ignorance. Instead, listen to the discussion for a moment or two, scribble some "meaningful" notes on the report cover or in the margins, then pick up on someone else's question of an issue by observing:

"What we need is a matrix to pull out this information. It's all too lumped together in here. Isolate the key points and prioritize them with a matrix."

The beauty of requesting a "matrix" is that nobody is 100% certain what a matrix is. Most people think of it as a spreadsheet - and, if there's no spreadsheet in the report(-you-have-no-intention-of-ever-reading) - then for your purposes a matrix is the spreadsheet they need to create.

Already a spreadsheet in there? Then:

"We need a matrix to rework the data - give it a graphic analysis."

What the hell does that mean? Who knows? A chart. A new spreadsheet with color?

Time, time, time to delay talking about the subject now.

Let's be candid: this is poker. 50% of the people in that meeting are probably bluffing because, even if they've glanced through the report, they haven't read it for comprehension and, not so deeply in their hearts, they need someone to explain the report to them.

As for those who actually know the subject? Fine: let them feel superior for a moment or two - because, you know, that "superiority" will translate into: It's their responsibility. They'll end up doing it, sooner or later, while your mere attendance at this meeting and wise counsel will buy you a piece of the credit if it succeeds - or deniability if it goes bust.

It's a Win-Win for you, either way.

Wednesday, March 22

Too Competent No-No

Don't appear too competent: you will get more work.

Counter-intuitive to advancement? No - because the type of work you'll have dumped on you will be the busywork of superiors who will receive the credit for your efforts and wouldn't think of sharing that credit with you because it will show up the fact that they couldn't do it. It will not be the planned assignment, not the "I think you are the person to handle this responsibility."

Nope, it will just appear on your desk, outside of your normal workflow, with the briefest of notes describing when it's due.

Lucky you. Too competent.

Thursday, March 23

When You're Trying

> When you're trying
> But they're lying
> And they're dying
> With a sighing
>
> Of loss
> At the boss
> Who's lost
> Heart tossed
> Lost cause
> To do it right
> Why fight
>
> Why fight

Side Notes from The Cube Unrelated:

Sat in a dark conference room at lunchtime with a bunch of co-cubes watching the '99 flick *Office Space.* There should be a special Academy Award for *Office Space.* It is... exactly right.

"Exactly right" is how it felt in that dark room, watching a DVD during lunch break, among the people on the screen transported to the seats we were sitting in. Hope. We laughed. A lot. Could only watch half the movie, but we finished the plot with our own afternoon. We were the last reel of that old classic *Sullivan's Travels*, complete with the prison and, of course, Mickey Mouse.

Always Mickey Mouse. Yea-ah.

Friday, March 24

Form-Fitting Fanny

Pierre Dolet writes his Notes from the Cube ...

Fanny, if truth must be told, loves Forms.

Much like chocolate, cheesecake and the fourth macaroon in the box - all of which she insists "I really shouldn't be doing this" - Fanny is addicted to Forms.

Worse, she is a Form Pusher.

Worse Worse: Fanny is the equivalent of a Form Drug Lord, using her network of connections to push her seductive product onto an addiction-cowed public, from the upper class power brokers of executive management who can afford to "use" the product through their proxy secretaries without actually having to suffer its direct negative effects, to the plebs like moi reeling from its foul effects daily, hourly, minute by minute.

Oh, I know you, Fanny: no situation exists that cannot be corrupted by a Form. Is the process running smoothly? Create a form to record its progress. Does the email one-liner answer the question? Develop a form for the questions. Is it too simple? Complicate it with a form.

In this company, we have 498 employees. We have 504 forms.

And each form requires a work instruction to explain it.

And each work instruction requires training.

Merci, chere Fanny. Mercy.

Saturday, March 25

Paranoia Succeeds

Paranoia succeeds. How do you know? It goes like this:

Create an atmosphere where Buzz feels that everything he says or does is undermined by someone else. Buzz is on the Veep level, so that "everyone else" starts pretty high. Despite 27 years of experience and accomplishment, ignore him when he speaks - or leave him out of the loop entirely. Reduce his staff to a pitiful few. The point is simple: Retire, Buzz, and get out of our way. However, since he's not taking the hint, make him beside the point.

But, being competent, Buzz can still find useful things to do. Annoying, but OK: keep ignoring him and maybe he'll go away.

This is where paranoia works on your side, because no matter how competent and grounded Buzz is, he cannot help but notice what is happening.

So now comes a situation where those few remaining loy-alistas underneath Buzz sometimes, as in the past, disa-gree with him. In the past, this was no big deal. In fact, it led to discussions, exchanges of ideas and often a syn-thesis of new, better ideas.

Now, though, dissenting thought from below is Betrayal if uttered aloud to anyone else.

"We have to present a united front," his voice mail message croaks electronically. "When you disagree with me ..."

To his credit, Buzz is straightforward and confronts the person. Then, after the first few minutes of his angered hurt, when Buzz talks with the person it is back to old times and they are problem-solving, not accusing.

But the bad taste is left in the mouth. Buzz is now looking at everything they say or do with a worried expression on his face. And, from the best motives, Buzz's remaining subordinates worry about hurting Buzz's position. So they start to hold back their opinions. What was the strength of Buzz's management skills is eroding. Oh, it's subtle and slow and certainly not an overnight phenomenon, but it is eroding.

And the paranoia grows.

What a management tactic!

Sunday, March 26

Line-Item Lucy: Form-Fitting Fanny's Sister

Kyla writes her Notes From The Cube to answer Pierre Do-let's Notes from a couple of days ago ...

Cher Pierre,

Yes, Form-Fitting Fanny - I know who you mean. She must have a large family, for her sister is sitting on our floor. Call her Line-Item Lucy.

We have been trying to reduce the forms in our office and, at the same time, make everything electronic as much as possible. Not line-Item Lucy.

Hitting the electronic first: Lucy seems to have a need to have a handwritten version of everything. This makes sense for drawings. And for stick-on notes.

(Hey, I'm not a fanatic - though I know one she-devil wiz who actually has formatted her printer to work with stick-ons. First she has to put them on a piece of letter-sized paper, then hand-feed... I will agree with Lucy here: "paperless" is not for everything.)

Line-Item Lucy has philosophical problems with elec-tronic "masters." Somewhere, sometime, somehow she has gotten it into her head that

Handwritten = Authentic

and so, because Lucy is supervisor over 4 poor souls - and reviews the documentation of another 20 serfs of equal rank below her – Lucy's philosophy has the weight of Official Theology on the subject.

Thus, it cometh to passeth: Every form is handwritten for review by Line-Item Lucy - then, upon approval (with her handwritten initials), it is typed into an electronic table, never a spreadsheet.

(Lucy does not appreciate spreadsheets - traumatized, apparently, by the great rifts between Lotus, Excel, Quattro, and the dozens of local spreadsheet sects of the mid-1990s, when Lucy was just entering the workforce, fresh from college - so her underlings use a word processing program with tables formatted in.)

The newly-typed form is then re-checked by Lucy, whose handwritten redlines are then returned to sender for fixing.

It should be noted that Line-Item Lucy's forte is finding fault - with form: grammar, spelling, punctuation, capitalization. Content is not the issue, BUT, where there's smoke there's fire, and along the way content issues usually get taken care of, too. And the work coming out of her department looks so good!

As for Forms proper, Lucy is a "party girl": the more the merrier.

Right now, for instance, Line-Item Lucy is in the process of creating a process review checklist that is 5 pages long and has over 300 line items to be checked. This will be helpful for those actively involved in the process. A guideline. And, of course, now a requirement.

To be reviewed by Lucy.

Line-by-line.

Bottom-Line Bill

Bottom-Line Bill's got a job to fulfill
And he does his job gung-ho.
As a Finance man,
He's the man with the plan,
The CFO who always says "No."
Not a penny for your thoughts,
Not a dollar if you holler,
Not a dime if you gimme the time.
Bill knows the expense
Of a misplaced cent
No one here's gonna get outta line.
So what if he dunno
'Bout how things go,
'Bout how the business runs?
He knows if it costs
It's gotta be tossed
Shot down with his veto gun.
And value doesn't matter
That's just idle chatter
A dollar is a dollar: that's that.
To Bottom-Line Bill
Gotta mind the till
What is written in the spreadsheet is fact.
Don't know what we do
Don't know what we sell
Don't know about future traction.
Bill's bottom line
Is don't spend a dime:
That's what he calls positive action.
So he makes a decision
With fiscal precision
Ignoring market facts.

Ignoring all things
With a high-priced ring
He gives 'em the Finance ax.
Now we may die slow
'Cause we can't grow
But Bill won't see the crime:
He's sure he's right
He'll always fight
To balance the bottom-line.

Tuesday, March 28

Sardonic Sal

Sardonic Sal has never a word
For anything coming his way
That isn't a snide comment aside
Masking that he has nothing to say.

Yeah it's easy to joke, make a crack, deride,
Raise an eyebrow, shrug a shoulder, smile
To cover up the fact that Sal talks, never acts,
Hasn't added anything for a while.

Oh, he does his job: with a sigh and a nod:
"Well, it's wrong but I'll do it your way."
Got an alternate plan, Sal? No way, man.
There's an emptiness in all you say.

Am I droning on? When Sal comes along
He'll point out how lame this is.
But not to me, no controversy:
Sal's strength is the backstabbing biz.

Now don't get me wrong, we get along,
In the meetings Sal's fun to have around.
It gets to me though, that he's never pro-
That he never gives a shit what goes down.

Now I said "backstabbing," but that's not true:
He doesn't care enough to do that.
No, his jibes are wide, just enough to hide
His general lack of substance and fact.

Still, Sal's been here for many many years
He'll be here long after I'm gone.
When you don't give a crap you stay on the map
Stars fall but the drones linger on.

Wednesday, March 29

Blinded By the Slight

Hank Gerber writes this Note to The Cube ...

Why oh why do I let it happen?

Here I am, working hard on this hand-me-down project: refining, defining, formatting, fitting, making it look feel read right.

But it's wrong.

That's the bugger: the whole thing is wrong to begin with.

And, instead of being able to step back, take the time, take the long view, take corrective action, I am caught up in the details.

"The Devil is in the details," they say - but that's not the Devil's only crime: he makes you blind.

Blinded by the slight:
Caught up in minutia
And losing our sight.
Blinded by the slight -
Those form fitting fixers are pretty twisted trick-
sters
And, baby, you know what I mean:
I mean we don't know what we're doin'
But what we're doin' is we're screwin'
The daylights out of anything with meaning!
Because we're
Blinded by the slight:
Caught up in minutia
And losing our sight.
Blinded by the slight

Thursday, March 30

Passing By

Thursday. Week almost gone. And it feels like I've missed
it. This is it? Week almost gone. Not time passing, time
empty.

Time empty.

Time-

Almost Friday, though.

Friday, March 31

Yesterday Marilyn

Marilyn, admin assistant for both the CEO and his new right-hand President, is retiring. We had our "traditional" cake party today in her honor, when everyone gathers in a large conference room and stands around awkwardly for 30 minutes or so. Because I'm taking over some of her job, I needed to say a few things...

I would like to start out by saying how hurt and jealous I am: the most attractive woman in the company is going away and I have no one to sing my lame "Good Mornings" to with the same daily hope that she will rush out of her cubicle and, like the beautiful Lauren Bacall she reminds me of, whisk me off to a wild romantic adventure. Sorry, other admins, but you're married. And Marilyn, as we all know, can handle difficult men – so while I'm a shy, quiet type, I know that she would make up for all that.

Sigh... so much for my fantasies about Marilyn.

A lot of you don't know that Marilyn, always elegant and classy Marilyn, started off her career as a stevedore and trucker mama. This gave her the perfect training for coming here to work for our CEO, who in his prime was considered somewhat of a strong personality. Now, of course, everyone thinks of him as the cuddle bear of corporation, but when Marilyn came he was known to breathe fire and, occasionally, eat an administrative assistant for lunch, washing it down with an engineer or accountant.

Seriously, the CEO's exacting standards – then and now – met their match with Marilyn who, at least in my personal experience, set a high standard of support performance for the company executives that I've had a hard time matching up to the halfway mark.

Damn you, Marilyn, couldn't you have been a little more snappish, incompetent and sloppy?

You had the perfect chance when the new President came – but Nooo, you had to go and adapt to his style and create a working relationship that, well, for lack of a better way of putting it, works too well.

So now you're going off and retiring. Well, don't think we're going to forget you. Wherever you travel, there will be a little bitty tiny GPS tag in your belongings and we will know, yes, we – will – know, exactly where you are: in our hearts.

And now, because it is important for me to embarrass you and myself with something sentimental, you will have to imagine that there is a full orchestra playing the Beatles' "Yesterday" behind me - Can everyone hum? – as I sing:

(Well, of course 45 people stood there like mutes, but I soldiered on anyway.)

Yesterday
All my files were lost and gone astray
Then you showed me where to put them away
Thanks to you
I wasn't fired
Yesterday

Suddenly
The CEO is not as mad as he seemed to be
And with you he acts so reasonably
Now he belongs,
Sadly, to me.

Our new President came
And you made
Him feel
At home.

There's no one with the same
Patience you have
And now
You're gone gone gone gone.

Marilyn
If you go away it is a sin
What a lonely state you'll leave us in
Oh I will miss you
Marilyn -

We all
Will miss
You
Marilyn...

(Everyone sang the last word with me. Sometimes things work out nice.)

(Sorry to be sentimental today: I'll miss Marilyn.)

April

Saturday, April 01

4/1

Awright, what can I really add today?
I'll leave it to the pros.

Sunday, April 02

Reviewing The System

Supposed to write, this quarter, a proposal for "stream-lining" the department procedures. Meat-and-potatoes assignment: look at a couple of the ones written by people long gone from here (so we don't step on toes) then suggest how to revise them or combine a couple. Basically, decide on my assignment for the next quarter.

I think I made a mistake, tho'. Instead of patching up a couple of holes in the fabric, I decided to step back and look at the whole material. BIG mistake. More patches than anything else.

So now we've gone and made a damn proposal. NO WAY is this getting approved for Q2 - if ever. And I probably stepped on a few too many turfs, no matter how diplomatic I tried to make it. Trouble.

Or, if the rule works ("If you write it, it will not be read."), no one will ever know it exists. We'll see ...

Monday, April 03

Problem-Solving the Procedures System: Introduction

Everyone approaches problem-solving from a particular point-of-view. This is mine:

I am lazy – I hate doing unnecessary work, especially when it is a duplication of someone else's work.

I am egotistical – I like to think that what I do will contribute to the company and loath work that will never be used except to take up space.

I like to teach – I hate teaching subjects that are ignored.

So that's why this analysis was made and the report was written.

That, plus the fact that I was assigned to do a report and this is what came out.

Tuesday, April 04

Problem-Solving The Procedures System: Philosophy

Sorry, folks, t'ain't all fun.

A serious philosophy:

A well-functioning system relies on three cornerstones: Will, Compliance and Understanding. From the top – down.

Without the will for the system to work, especially from the top, even the best system will stutter or fail.

The best intentions and will are worth nothing without

actual compliance with the system's requirements: you have to do it.

If the system is not understood, its requirements will not be effectively defined; its procedures run the risk of becoming meaningless bureaucracy.

Wednesday, April 05

Significant Sampling

Meeting notes:

Based on our present knowledge of the project today, we anticipate ...
(OK, Dan, we have a lead-in, but what are the actual facts?)

Per Barry C: "Systems Solution" = Future
(and the "solution" is ... ?)

MBO = Management By Objective
Define the project
Commit to it
(Die for it?)

Dan C - no interruptions
DC = pain

Thursday, April 06

Something's Happening Not Good

Something's happening today, something not good.

No words, no announcement, just a feeling.

Almost noon and the day still seems tentative.

President absent, Veeps looking around uncomfortably, mid-managers' heads buried in paperwork.

Rumors, of course - lots - but if you live by rumors we have been: bought out, sold, laid off, closed down, the President (Co., not U.S.) resigned, the President (Co., not U.S.) has been indicted, the Co. has been indicted, or the Owner has died. Plus more variations. No "good" rumors (beyond "We're safe - I think"), which is fairly par for the course: bosses don't look like pre-root canal patients when they're happy campers.

A strange electricity in the air and the skin feels tingly. Either mass paranoia, a flu epidemic has hit, or there's bad news a-comin'.

Friday, April 07

As Expected: Bad News Doesn't Smile

So the downcast heads and evasive eyes of yesterday morning had their payoff in the afternoon. Bad news.

Deja vu? No. Just what was expected. More layoffs. We're not losing money, just not making "enough" profit.

Enough for what? "Enough profit margin to compete with 'the future'."

So many words in quotation marks. Must do so, though, to be honest: could not have thought of those words, that reasoning, myself.

Saturday, April 08

They made him cry

They made him cry, the bastards!

Buzz, he's been here 25 years, 26 next month. Once, a few years ago, he was in charge of half the company. Never an owner, never the top Veep, just the man who kept things running and told things straight.

Then the new Exec Team came in. Buzz welcomed them because he knows he's getting old and running out of steam. When they started divvying things up, he agreed, because he knows that one man – even him – should never have had so many departments under him. Besides, he was retiring in a short, very short while.

But this company had been like his extended family. Not a family he wanted, but a family that came to him when it needed help. He saw one owner through two divorces. He saw the security guard through his son's cancer death. He helped keep a line worker's furniture from being repossessed and found another Veep a job after it was apparent that the other guy was too young to retire and too old to meet this company's high-paced needs. Buzz saw children born and accidents rushed to the hospital and houses bought with financing he encouraged the company to arrange. A lot of marriages. There is a photo of Buzz dressed in a Hawaiian skirt singing to the company at an impromptu lunchtime picnic: a little embarrassed, a little embarrassing – speaking of "sing," Buzz can't – but family.

Still, Buzz has his own real-life family and no illusions about which is more important. 'Never did. He saw the big 6-5 coming and knew where he wanted to be when that year hit.

And then he saw what the new Exec Team was doing to the factory family. Even as they were smiling to the crowd they were printing CONFIDENTIAL "lean" strategies for themselves. So Buzz decided to stay on a while longer to help his second family as much as he could. After all, if anyone knows the company and how it runs better than Buzz, it would only be the original founder, Ben. But Ben's in his 70s and admits that he has only enough energy to follow the R&D that was always so dear to his creative heart. Nope, Buzz was who Ben looked to, argued with, agreed with, or overrode when they were both in their prime. There's another owner, but he wasn't a founder only a–

Another story. Buzz's story, now: If you want to know how things run, especially if you're coming from outside, talk to Buzz. From nuts to bolts to shipping to customer care, Buzz knows how things run. All you have to do is listen. He's not even proprietary or egotistical about what he knows: if you've got a good idea, he'll chew it over, subject it to the experience he has, and stand by you stronger than you can yourself. Buzz isn't God, he makes mistakes – and he knows it – but he's a mighty good archangel to have by your side.

All you have to do is listen.

Unless you don't care about facts.

Unless you've come in with your ideas pre-set and your plans pre-determined and, dammit!, if the facts on the ground don't match your plans: Tough. You have MBA-written management books to back you up, seminars from the khans of corporation, the winds of change blowing in your direction, the end of history as your stepping stone. You – can – change – the – facts.

That's what everyone you listen to says: Change the Facts to match the Goals of the Plan.

Certainly don't ask Buzz. He might come up with ideas to meet those Goals via a different Plan. Certainly don't listen to Buzz.

Marginalize him. Divide up his authority into smaller and smaller slices. Keep him around to make Precision Ben feel comfortable, but isolate them by retiring everyone else they know. Make your decisions around them, keep them out of the loop. Precision Ben, well, him you've got to keep around to maintain the cash flow from his reserves. But Buzz: let him know that retirement is a reward well-deserved.

But Buzz keeps sticking around. "I have to try to help my family," he said in confidence one day 18 months ago. "'Lean' means layoff to them. Too many of these people have given us 27, 30, 35 years of their lives. We're not losing money. We don't have to 'lean' that way. We owe it to them."

That was last year. It's not hard to lie to Buzz: he trusts people. So they lie. And they layoff. And, even when they offer "retraining," they can take away the respect from a senior worker, they can make the new job so menial, they can make the company into Just Another Business so that there is no reason to stick around.

And so, Thursday, they even gave a Farewell Lunch to the long-timers going away, along with plaques and presents and a severance package complete with pre-written Letters of Recommendation that are so generically attractive that you almost overlook the fact that it says virtually nothing about the person except for the length of employment. Rosa. Fred. Joybal. Brenda. Carmenita. Who are you?

Buzz couldn't attend the Farewell Lunch. He walked down on the floor that morning and said his good-byes and left to the doctor, his stomach aching, to avoid having to smile at the Last Day.

But a cruel trick was played on them all. The Last Day wasn't the last day – it was just the last working day: everyone had to come back on Friday to sign off on their "voluntary termination" packages. Every ten minutes someone new showed up, trooping past Buzz's office on their way to and from Human Resources.

Where's the Human dealing with these "Resources"? Already young minimum-wage workers are filling out application forms at the same long-desk window where the departees have to stand. Can we make the humiliation more pointed? Marcella, who was beautiful and thin when she came here 30 years ago, stands next to teenagers with glinting eyes of hoped-for employment and no illusions about any sort of loyalty to-or-from this company. Her knuckles crack a little as she holds the unfamiliar pen: Marcella can move product through the machine faster than the automated arm replacing her, but her fingers never had to memorize multi-signature forms. Ah, well, those muscle memories don't matter now. With 17 years to go before qualifying for Social Security (if they don't raise the age minimum), Marcella will have plenty of opportunity to learn new semi-skilled, repetitive tasks (if the jobs don't move offshore). That's why she immigrated to America in the first place: for the opportunities. Oh, darn, forgot! Marcella was born here. She's just brown because... she is.

And, coming back from her awkward moments at HR and the thick envelope of papers they gave her, Marcella stopped at Buzz's office to say good-bye again. Just like Sandy did a few minutes earlier, and Isa will in a few minutes. And Buzz rises from his seat while asking her to sit down, as he has always shown courtesy, and talks about Marcella's two sons, three daughters and five grandchildren now, all growing so fast!, and the changing prices of housing, all so high now thank you Buzz for helping us buy it back when prices made sense, and she suddenly understands that everything she has known outside the home is over, dead, and even though it was "her" choice Marcella has second thoughts – but it's too late now. Isa shows up at the door and Marcella leaves – she and Isa aren't good friends but they hug, this is the last time they will ever see one another – and then Marcella hugs Buzz and leaves, while Buzz and Isa lean against the walls and talk in that old familiar way they fell into back 20 years ago when they worked three straight 18 hour days to deliver a last-minute order that helped the company meet its factor-required payment deadline.

And when Isa left, there was a break. Lunchtime, HR has closed its window, no more processing for an hour. And Buzz has closed his door, turned his back on the window to work on his PC – weekly Veep reports are due by day's end – and in the glint of the fluorescent overhead light, tears glint down the profile of his chin.

I am proud to work for Buzz. And I damn the bastards who are making him cry.

Sunday, April 09

Haiku: Empty Word

> Yeah ...
>
> So what do you say
> after the last few days?
>
> *Shit*
> is not
> enough.

Monday, April 10

Dan's List of Obstacles: Old Regime

Just to keep from getting nostalgic for the past too much, pulled up Dan the Hyper-Active Boss Man's "List of Obstacles" that he compiled when the New Team came in. Of course, as in everything Dan did, he overdid it: we started with "A Summary A, B, C" and ended up at item "R.R.R.R."

This part of the list, detailing the sins of the Old Regime, may explain why the late, great, gone Dan had few fans among the old-timers:

b. Absenteeism of president (70% out)

c. 2 owners, 50/50 vote/fight

d. 1 pro-Us / 1 anti-Us

h. Lack of business plan or direction

i. Lack of continual planning: seat-of-the-pants through

the year, once-a-year thinking

j. Owner intimidation

k. VPs on part-time schedules

l. VPs too involved in petty issues, not enough management thinking

m. Company Culture - Longevity vs. Any Change

n. Longevity employees get away with murder

o. Inequality in Position vs. Title

t. VP conflicts of interest

v. Master Plan used as wish list, not thought out

y. Negative attitudes - say "No" first - justification required even when obvious

z. Positions without Authority

dd. Lack of mid-management accountability

ff. Lack of clear job descriptions & organizational structure

kk. Poor Production planning

oo. Lack of Marketing leadership

qq. Lack of commitment (budget) to consider new product offerings to the company

ss. Micro-management

vv. QC bottleneck - all levels

ww. Elite depts get away with anything

xx. Lack of recognition and commensurate reward among the departments

kkk. Turf issues

lll. Mid-Management weekly meetings: nothing planned

ttt. Lack of vision in existing core products

bbbb. Phone system sucks

cccc. Indeciveness on cubicles - constantly changing

ffff. Too many approval signatures required on documents

gggg. Lack of professionalism

hhhh. Failure of company to provide talent-attracting salaries

kkkk. Lengthy, frequent & aimless meetings

oooo. General decision paranoia

rrrr. Rumors spreading

Tuesday, April 11

High-Concept Analysis

One never listens to inside counsel: the outside voice - paid for profusely - is the wiser one. Always. The receipts say so.

These notes cull the core meaning of our Company's most recent high-concept analysis, distilled from three hours of locked-away seclusion in the meeting room.

It was a motivational meeting. We were inspired, emboldened, prepared to be undeterred in our quest for excellence:

One two, one two,
A snickerdoo: a quicker three or four.
The garboiled fisk has slibbed the klest
Insernate evermore.
Were you to mrew the emptire crew
Impring the brudbund shate,
The instang crash of bouldened snash
Desteers embittered hate.

Wednesday, April 12

Day Before Vacation

There are two ways to approach an impending vacation: with your mind already checked out or as a responsible individual.

If you're honest with yourself, your thoughts are miiiiiiles away from the cube.

Realistically, if anyone else in the company knows you are going - especially management - you ain't got a chance of escaping into the mindworld of travel a minute earlier than the last minute you clock out.

Jeez!, I'll be gone only a week but there are 10 days of "we need this before you go" jobs plopped on my desk. It's funny how, in an economy where every employee is a disposable commodity, until you are tossed out you are indispensable.

I'd like to inflate my ego and think it's me that's so invaluable, but I am fair enough to admit that I have the same stampeding herd instinct as everyone else: when I know that Lucy, Will, Takesha or Jim-Bob Jones is going away on vacation, I home-in on their desk with my own "can you see to this before you go" pleas.

Of course I don't have management clout, but my eyes well up in supplication and ...

And, today, hoping to leave tomorrow A.M. at the crack of dawn, I am still here in the wee hours of the night. Suckered again by sweet eyes, bonhomie and a misguided sense of duty.

Thursday, April 13

Left It Behind - Oh, No

Vacation's begun, job's left behind for a week.

Oh, God, that's the theory, isn't it?

First night's dreams, even before setting out on the road, has piles of papers on the desk reshuffling themselves around. Shuffling themselves around: They - Will - Never - Be - Finished.

This is grade school redux, when the nights before and after a "BIG" report (a whole page! - with a construction paper map!), those nights had the same recurring nightmare: I was throwing out the trash and - right after tearing all the garbage papers in half - I realized that I JUST TORE UP MY ONLY COPY OF THE REPORT!!!

The bad dream followed me into junior high and high school, drifting into adulthood...

The only thing that cured that nightmare was, being in college, seeing a doctoral student have her final draft, typed manuscript blow away in the wind, right out of her hands, as she was walking it to her thesis review. Her real life shock took the oomph out of my nightmare. It was gone. I was relieved.

And now...

I need to find some hard-luck cube worker and watch...

Friday, April 14

Vacation: Countdown Back

Vacation: Day #2

Already counting down how few days are left till time to go back. Not anticipation - feeling oh so feeling life too cliché short (or, at least, vacation too short). Haven't "done" anything yet and already wish there was more time to do it. Small taste is Tantalus' punishment.

Saturday, April 15

Vacation Sleep

Vacation: Day 3

Sleeping later. Major improvement over first two days when arose earlier than normal. Discovered horrible fact: like early morning when not forced to face it.

Sleeping later, then, is perverse sort of punishment: not easy to do, not particularly enjoyable, but know that the body rhythm will change and will forget how to "get up" earlier.

Also, unless you're a hunter (am not) or a golfer (am not not), why the hell get up so early anyway when it's not work-related? Reading t'ain't so fun in the pre-dawn grey morning. And it's too early to sit by a fire with some strong drink in hand. Sex is fun, but it's too early for loved partner who doesn't see reason for pre-work erotic hours when the whole day is free. An excellent idea which we will attempt to implement today. We shall see if ability is equal to ambition.

Sunday, April 16

Offsite Network Access

It is so fun to be able to travel virtually anywhere in the U.S. and find a free internet access. Wireless, usually. I am sitting in a farm country diner in Idaho and keying-in to my friends, to my family, and - stupid, STUPID me - to my work.

I should NOT have looked into my work email. I wrote an Out Of Office message saying I wouldn't. I swore I wouldn't. I even thought I couldn't.

But I could - and curiosity got the better of me. Me and the dead cat.

Now I know what's facing me when I return.

So much for relaxing into my bliss. Sitting in an Idaho diner looking at new-plowed fields with snow-capped mountains in the gorgeous distance and unable to think of anything but forms, reports and filings that I despise. Blisshit!

Monday, April 17

Vacation & Return To Work: Wrong Way

Had the opportunity to drive straight home, have a day off to relax, then return to work at end of vacation. Just couldn't do it. Turned left at Portland and am heading 300 miles somewhere in the wrong direction. The wrong direction...

It will be a long drive tomorrow – probably won't get in till 2-3 a.m. the morning I have to go back into work – but it's not the wrong direction to go.

Tuesday, April 18

Vacation (Still)

Last day of freedom seems the sweetest and saddest.

"Freedom." Wrote it without thinking. Says everything, eh?

Actually, don't dislike working, just the meaningless of so much of it in the cubes. Driving yesterday, meaningless, made more sense than the weekly report that no one reads but everyone demands. The report makes sense, too, actually – but no one reads it. Meaningless.

660 miles to cover on the way home. Too short.

Wednesday, April 19

They Missed Me

It's satisfying to be wanted: the desk piled high with In-coming, the voicemail filled with Requests, the email mailbox filled to capacity, and the gratified looks that say: You've been gone a week - we've missed you.

Actually, they haven't missed me. Not one whit. They just acted as if I was still here and piled all this crap on daily without regard to the email Office Assistant telling them Out Of Office, ears stone-deaf to the voicemail instant message repeating On Vacation, and legally blind to the big Big BIG SIGN taped to the chair with the oh-so-cute-sy message from Ellen, the office secretary, saying He's Gone Fishin'.

But they missed me! They really missed me!

Thursday, April 20

Change, Last Minute

In concert with an earlier mantra, "If you write it, it will not be read," comes now the observation:

If you ask for corrections, they will come - at the last minute.

Corollary to that:

After it is almost too late to do anything without a late-night rush.

Is there anything more to say?

Sure there is.

Let us be truthful with ourselves here: everyone loves to change someone else's work. This is especially true when there is no accountability - i.e., someone else, not you, has their name on the puppy but they have foolishly asked you (or have no choice in the matter) for changes that should be made.

Of course, of course, of course you don't have a lot of time to spend on this dog. but seat-of-the-pants opinion doesn't take much time. And it is so obvious that you, with your last-minute inspiration, can add so much. So much.

And remember: this cur may be mangy, but your 1 or 2 changes can potentially result in a complete makeover of the entire concept, presentation, formatting or whatnot.

Change, Last Minute - it is a powerful tool in the right hands.

Friday, April 21

The Rules & Standards of Hell

Perhaps it is with deadpan seriousness that we will go down in flames. The following list was posted as official Quality policy yesterday:

1. Maintain Quality standards.
2. Discourage non-Quality thinking
3. Enable Quality.

This type of all-company memo complements the company's website marketing literature for a certain Security product, in which the "advantages of the system" are listed:

* Increased facility security
* Personal accountability now guaranteed
* Prisoner tracking enhanced
* Death Row incident reduction
* Terrorist identification
* Inexpensive
* Upgrade-ready
* Easy-to-implement, easier to use.

This puts us in concert, apparently, with the rest of the world, where both liberal and conservative radio stations can boast these statements with a straight face:

Support your Soul and Sheriff Dan Bowen

This store provides you with the revolutionary tools for your next radical feminist meeting.

Saturday, April 22

Weekend Song

Need a weekend song ...

The sun is bright
The day is hot
The wonder of it is
Why do I work so harder now
When this my day off is?

My back it aches
My arms are scratched
My fingers watch them bleed
I sure is fun to sweat and curse
A masochistic need.

The dog barks loud
The cat moans low
The bird squawks in his cage
The morning starts off glorious
Hooray, it's Saturday!

C'mon, now, let's be honest about it: Friday night after work is sooo much better than Saturday responsibilities!

Sunday, April 23

Instant Karma (Advertised)

There's a slogan that you wrote
And the public pays attention,
Now everyone takes note
When you fart with gas retention.
'Cause now you are the man:
Everybody is a fan -
Sell they know you can.
Only problem is,
The product works like shit.
Well, they say, "That's biz,"
But your ad it is a hit.
Instant karma, sudden fate:
Recognition sure is great.

Monday, April 24

Who's On First?

Not being at the meeting, one has only the Rashomon version:

Voice 1 (President emeritus): Marketing decided that they don't like the current OEM deal we have - no profit - and need to revive the old product development that was dropped 3 years ago. That was Harry's decision back then to drop it, no wonder he's gone.

Voice 2 (Veep Engineering): This idea is just from the President Emeritus.

Nobody in Marketing really wants it, they're just going along with him till the idea blows over. We have to think about developing products for the future, not from before my time here, when Harry was running things.

Voice 3 (Director Marketing): We're just exploring ideas, it's one of those on the table. I heard we have an old product ready to go. Harry told me about it but I wasn't in-house back then.

Voice 4: Y'know, I think Harry did a cost analysis and sales projection on the old product development.

Voice 1: This is a top priority.

Voice 2: This is a bottom priority.

Voice 3: We have to explore the priorities.

Tuesday, April 25

Sandbagged

Sat in for my Veep today at an executive meeting.

Things went well for a while, until ...

Until Burt the Bully decided this was a good time for some turf warring on our department. Suddenly there was a new item - not on the agenda: Why was our department engaged in an activity that Burt thought was a waste of time?

"Justify it," he says.

"The executive committee approved this last November, during the budget sessions," I answers lamely, not having been there but knowing when we had to start doing it.

"But why are we doing it now?" Burt bores down.

This is a "fun" situation, because Burt does not believe in "speaking above your pay level" (ex-Army man, y'see) and the look in his eyes is one of challenge.

Burt does not like to hear info he disagrees with - 'learned this from other situations - but now I'm in the catbird seat for my Veep and...

Well, here's the funner part: I actually agree with Burt on this issue - but I don't think it's fair to let my Veep's position get plowed under just because he's not there. And certainly not because Burt is sure he can bully over any old cube worker who happens to be sitting in.

The Prez, as always, acts as if he's never heard anything about the issue before.

It's not his fault: He really truly sincerely prefers to avoid conflict and will agree with anyone he's with when one-on-one - then do what he has to do anyway when they're out of sight. Consequently, these all-together-in-one-place sessions have an awkward protocol: the Prez wants everything smiley friendly and, since the Veeps are wise to his personal preferences, they make mushy mooshy sounds of consensus and then go slug it out in the aisles.

Except for Burt - who, if I didn't mention it before, is also the Prez's hit man: the Heavy to the Prez's Nice Guy persona. No one is quite certain if Burt is always speaking for the Prez but - as in today - when Burt speaks in his definitive way, all others keep silent.

Except for stupid me.

I argued. I voiced the justifications my Veep made when they agreed to this thing a few months ago. I got the dagger look from Burt. And, finally, I kept the group from having a "consensus" by offering, clerical-style, to provide "informational documentation" - a stall tactic till my Veep returns for the next meeting.

'Problem is, I don't think my Veep feels like fighting with Burt over anything.

Stupid me. Time to go back to my cube and not act like a responsible executive.

Wednesday, April 26

Burt Beats Bad

Learned something yesterday: Burt beats bad today.

Burt don' like to be crossed, man.

'Thought I'd bought a week till the missing VPs return and could be part of the decision that Burt the Bully Veep was pushing through yesterday - a decision that would normally be their decision, since it is their departments' activity affected, not Burt's.

Yep, Burt don't like to be crossed.

So I stalled for time with a promise to "provide more information." True promise, too. And provided the info today. Good info, too.

Oh, gawd, Burt don't like to be crossed.

Took me 3 hours to prep the info. 'Took Burt all of 30 seconds to write his Bolded, underlined, no-questions-about-it-at-all response --- to everyone:

"You were not authorized to work further on this: the decision has been made.

Cease all further activity. THIS IS CLOSED."

People walk past the cube with their eyes averted.

Burt is smilin' and laughin', though. Said "Hi!" to me today with a cheeriness I have not seen in months.

Thursday, April 27

Something's Due

Two different people came up yesterday asking for information that I know nothing about.

Well, one thinks, simply say "I don't know."

But that easier answer is a little more complicated by the fact that:

a. The people asking are nice.
b. The people asking are management.
c. The information they want is legitimate.
d. Who the hell does know the answer?

They piqued my curiosity. Now I've got to know. So I promised I would "look into it" and, damn!, forgot that I have a reputation for "delivering."

So now I've got something due and I'm not quite sure what it is.

I'm also not quite sure how much anyone cares: the question could be legit, but the motivation behind it may be shaky. Or forgotten by tomorrow. I have no illusions about the memory retention of the company. Ferrets have more stick-to-it power sometimes. But I promised. And I am curious.

Me and the killed cat: curiosity.

The Deadline That Nobody Cares About

We stayed till 8 p.m. tonight to (unsuccessfully) meet a deadline that nobody cares about.

Oh, the deadline is real. A product cannot be produced and delivered to a new (BIG) client without the deadline met. Which doesn't change the fact that nobody seems to care about that: it is Friday - chance to take a 3-day weekend or go home a little early or, at least, don't stick around past 5 p.m.

Except for our little block of cubes. Nobody gave us The Message. Clueless, we drafted-on through the day, into the night, filling the millions of papers they need, sending them on for the appropriate authorizations on a quarter-hour basis all day long. Going over again and again to retrieve them from --- whom?

All gone or never in. No memo, no relief from The Deadline. We are expected to deliver. They are accountable to none.

So we didn't make The Deadline. Monday we'll try again.

Minions work. Masters bate.

Saturday, April 29

Saturday Sleep

Another weekend song ...

Sleep sleep sleep sleep.
Can't sleep sleep sleep.
Want to sleep sleep.
Why can't I sleep?

Sunday, April 30

Sunday Tasks

It is harder on Sundays.

!

May / June

Monday, May 01

Meeting @ 3 p.m.

16 people in a meeting room meant for 8. Palpable excitement or mis-planned location?

Projector works fantastic but laptop connection to the network dead. Fiddle for 10 minutes. Deader.

Paper now. Economy drive on, so double-sided landscape-oriented spreadsheets, auto-stapled on the wrong corner. The awkward shuffle of upside-down-backward docs.

Font so small you can't read. Economy.

No idea what is being discussed, but assigned to (shuffle, shuffle) help finish (shuffle) ... something. We'll have another meeting later to clarify.

Mtg. over. IS came in. Fixed network connection with flip to function key.

Tuesday, May 02

Made Another Deadline

Made another deadline
Hip-hip-hooray!
Doesn't mean an awful lot
But we had to stay:
Some till seven, some till eight
Some till overnight -
Whew, that's late!
But we did it on time

And we beat the clock
Now they're shipping that order
On the loading dock.
And it doesn't really matter
If there'd been a big delay
But we did it on time -
Though they said we couldn't do it -
Yeah, we did it on time
Today!

Wednesday, May 03

Deadline Workers

Just a little note on yesterday's deadline.

Nancy's a bug, but she's fun to work with on deadlines. Real pain-in-the-ass for everydays, but bright and competent and funny when the pressure's on. Means she's meant for crisis mode, not everydays. Or she's schizo - but it works for us.

Solly's the opposite, though: probably everyone's best friend on everydays - keep him away when there's a deadline. Exactly the things that make him OK to deal with on the daily routine - steadiness, no sense of stress, always a joke, never pressuring you with an urgency - those things seem like such a backwards drag when there's a hard due date and a rush. Solly don't run - never - Solly walks.

So ya live and learn. Too bad we can't swap out Nancy and Solly on an as-needed basis. Then again: What do they think about me?

Thursday, May 04

Selling Ginsu Knives of the Soul

N*ote from The Cube:* Have been required to attend bi-monthly offsite one-day seminars this past year - part of a Company "Improvement" Policy designed to upgrade work skills without actually investing in higher education. There is an entire workbook of programmed "notes," but these are the personal additions in the margins ...

50 clichés in a row - rapid fire - impressive. I bet she sells Ginsu knives on the side.

Who is the audience for her? Us?

Loud.

Chitlin' Circuit entertainment: Energy + Volume

Can we drop any more names? No, because she will be selling their books and tapes later today and this is the set-up to the pitch.

Note that, so far, 40% of this seminar is interchangeable with last seminar on a different topic.

Good idea: Skills not Pills.

Long on generalities that could go with any "motivational" topic.

????Thinking about that: I didn't know that this was supposed to be a motivational seminar.

Asking questions but not looking for answers - already has "answers."

It's a genre.

White noise after a while.

Diva acting. (I suppose I could do this, too - do do it - but get tired of it quickly)

"Motivational" seminars: without context of society - very Me oriented - lip service to religion and culture, but self-esteem is the core.

Very smugly proud of how "innovative" she is. Maybe she's right, since this seems new to so many. But, after only 1 seminar, I already know the slogans for this one - and, theoretically, it is on a different topic.

Friday, May 05

Waiting for Buzz

Buzz has been gone on vacation for almost three weeks - comes back Monday. Not soon enough: the buzzards have been circling his VP desk for the past two weeks, picking at the department in his absence, pulling away bits and pieces of authority, throwing on budget items that they don't want, letting certain "authorizations" slide till their cancellation is a fait accompli. Well, he's nearing retirement - could have retired a year ago. Guess they're just trying to hasten the process or take advantage of the carrion that is us. There won't be a low-up when he returns, just a sigh.

Set-up five meetings for Buzz on the day of his return.

Saturday, May 06

Waiting for Buzz 2

From yesterday:

Set-up five meetings for Buzz on the day of his return...

My guess is he'll leave halfway through the day "for health reasons." He's not a martyr, just an old man not being treated well.

Saturday, May 06 (more)

Starting to think about leaving

Always considered job loyalty a given. Came here for that reason: with a 15-year termer saying "I'm one of the new people," there was a sense of security and family about this place. A lot of problems, true, but like old-time families (before divorce was de rigueur) they worked things out. Or covered them up. Or, at any rate, survived them. Survived them, yes: got here at the tag end of that era and saw how it worked.

Now, since the "new" team has been here for 3 years, loyalty from the company down is certainly no more. Lookit all the old-timers harassed off. I'm new enough to escape that purge, but it still ain't fun to watch.

Job loyalty... Oh, what am I saying: hypocrite - I sure was ready to leave this place a couple of years ago when my "old" manager was getting too oppressive. But that was Dan the Hyper-Active Boss Man, and he had actually only come a couple of years before me - and he was going crazy because the New Team was isolating him, and he reacted in all the wrong ways.

But why leave here? To what? Haven't looked for a better job ever before: there were enough recession-driven lay-offs, bubble-burst collapses and we're-bought/you're-out situations to make most supposedly career-track jobs into just extended short stays. This here is what's out there.

But - what used to be a "family" is maybe now more like a dinner party - and did you ever feel like you've stayed a little too long and it's time to leave?

Sunday, May 07

Avoiding eMails

Last Friday there was a flurry of emails in the afternoon - which I didn't read. It was Friday afternoon, only two hours countdown till time to go, and that flurrying about indicated something that would either:
a. upset me, or
b. give me work over the weekend, or
c. make me feel guilty that I wasn't working over the weekend.

Y'see, I'm taking the advice of the "motivational" seminar they had me attend a couple of days earlier: "You (I) hereby understand that you (I) cannot, will not, and will never be able to CHANGE THE UNIVERSE." So, since I can't, won't and will never - and they paid good bucks to have me taught that - I might as well put the lesson to practice. It'll keep till Monday morning.

Monday, May 08

Avoided eMails Bite the Butt

Ohhh was I smart not to read my late-afternoon Friday emails: they would have sent my head spinning through the roof!

A "flurry" of emails always indicates one of two things:

1. A joke that everyone sends to everyone else, ignoring the fact that their names were already on the distribution list of the email they received containing the joke in the first place; or

2. Accelerating hysteria on some issue that nobody has bothered to get the facts about, opinions being easier to cite than research.

Since jokes don't make my head spin off, accelerated hysteria was the criminal this time.

The head spinning has to do with the fact that I have already written four reports on the topic (in descending order: the original researched info compilation, a summary of the research info, an analysis, and a summary of the analysis). The hysteria came from the fact that Veeps apparently have the collective memory of a ferret: no one appears to remember a thing that was contained in the reports already received.

Wait!, oh, stupid me: memory's not the problem. I forgot Rule #1:

IF YOU WRITE IT, IT WILL NOT BE READ.

We are now scheduled on Tuesday to have a special teleconference with an attorney on the topic. Let's ignore the fact that the research reports were derived from the attorney's analysis of the situation in the first place. He has his own Rule #1, too: At $400/hour, 15 minutes minimum charge, I will listen to any redundant, ill-considered or stupid questions asked.

His Rule #2 makes even more sense: At $400/hour, 1 hour minimum, I will research any topic, even if I have already reported on it.

Tuesday, May 09

Variation on a Theme

The decision was made 2 months ago. Now it's being re-decided. Not "reconsidered." Everyone seems to have forgotten that they made a decision at all.

This is funny (not ha-ha), because we have a memo setting up the old decision-making meeting, a summary of the issue as distributed at that meeting, and a memo issued after the meeting confirming the decision made.

But nobody - nobody - remembers it.

Wednesday, May 10

Accrued Benefits

I still have almost 4 weeks of vacation due to me - the "accrued benefits" of not taking a vacation for over 2 ½ years. (I have to agree with the Counters here: lying in bed sick for a week doesn't quite count as rest).

Almost 4 weeks. Now they tell me I have to "use it or lose it" before the 4th of July.

This is odd, because I just took a week's vacation a month ago. Apparently the Counters reign over the Accountable: the message was filtered down from HR to my VP to my immediate supervisor/lead, who told me this with horror in her eyes, because she knows what is coming up.

Then again, she took off two weeks a month ago at the same time I had my 1 week vacation - mine planned a half year in advance - without particularly caring about accountability for the department. Because she left 2 days before me, she even wrote a company-wide email referring all of her caseload to me. (And me? I had no one to slough it off to, so all I could do was apologize and tell everyone to put it on my desk. Yep, it was there WAITING, Waiting, waiting.)

But now I gotta go on vacation again, starting next week. Wonder how we'll work that out?

Thursday, May 11

The Tragik Komedy of Precision Ben - Part V (finished)

[A Tale in 5 Parts: Part I - 8/21, Part II- 8/28, Part III-9/04, Part IV - 9/11]

This Part V was started on 9/18 ...

Impasse
Standstill
Ben you hate me I hate you we
Love
Hate
This place after forty years
It's been our home our only home our
Child.

Like any good marriage in distress
We sought counseling
  and were counseled
  to seek
  a mediating
Board.

[A Note from The Cube, 5/18: 'have to stop here - for now - too difficult watching it, remembering it - will try to finish ...]

[5/11: So, then, this is how it's playing out:]

I will make my name in futures
I will forget the past

Yep, Ben, that's what you said...

So the Board brought in the Future
  and the Future looked like them.
Found a new President
  one of them.
Found a new Team
  from them.
Started a New Company
  by them.

Don't you know, Ben,
This is your mantra –
You never chanted it quite like this
But this is how they sing it now:
Everything Old is bad
Everything New is good
New is the Future
Forget the Past
(Knowledge)
Steal from the Past
($$$$)
To build the Future.

Isolate,
Prevaricate,
Castrate,
Ben.
The Past is gone.

How could you know the Future
  for them
Was without you?

And me?

Me they lost me first
  with their first lie
  and your first vote.

Me and the 3rd shift:
(but of course they didn't tell you that, still –)
Did you hear us say good-bye?

The office is still yours:
  so big.
The white offices around:
  new faces.
The factories you built:
  farmed out.
They even forced your mistress out:
  so quiet now.

Take your few handful few new clericals
And issue your memos to the wind –

They will report your every word, never fear,
Every word to be discarded

in smiles and yeses and silent ignorances.

50th Anniversary looms:
In honor of the savaged Past
They will honor the Future.
Honored you are, Ben.
Honor for the dead and dying.

Do you hear your voice echo?

I will make my name in futures
I will forget the past

50

And I Stayed Late?

I planned on working late today to clear up as much as possible before I go on long vacation and to prep things for my absence. It was a good, foolishly naïve plan. Forgot that it was a springtime Friday in the middle of the quarter: good weather, no end-of-quarter deadlines, weekend. The Prez and every single Veep was gone by noon (if they came in at all). Half the Management was gone by 3 p.m. 75% of the cubes by 4. By 5 just me and the cleaning lady. Biiiig empty floor.

I left at 8, I prepped it anyway. I like the office when I'm all alone: you get a lot of work done, you can talk loud, and it feels like home since you can raid the refrigerator for leftovers since it all gets thrown out over the weekend.

Saturday, May 13

On Vacation: Cut Off – Intentionally

Started the 3-weeker today. Made a vow not to access my company emails at all during that time. I have even disconnected my cellphone: can't be reached. I will return as if "New."

✳ ✳ ✳

Sunday, June 04

Elsewhere

On vacation.

Noticed something: lived the life of a 21-year-old college student on spring break and have suffered no headaches, digestive problems, carpal tunnel numbness or any of the other daily aches and pains.

Didn't look at company email/voicemail/hardmail once. Wonder what's been happening since gone?

Monday, June 05

Return From Vacation: Déjà Vu

Back from 3 weeks vacation today and – everything – is – exactly – the – same.

Everything.

Not one of the "crisis" issues has been resolved – not even those with "hard" deadlines of 2 weeks earlier.

Desk is piled high with Stuff – expected – but not in a way that indicates any of the Crises were waiting on me. Working my way down the pile(s), I see that the Crises are just going round-and-round in circles.

Maybe that's why I'm here? The impatience of a lowly cube worker pulling things out of the circle brings resolution? Apparently. Responsibility without Authority.

But what if you don't want it?

Tuesday, June 06

Knowing When To Leave

Probably thought that governments were too bureaucracy-laden and private industry would have more room for initiative. Maybe so, but it seems that whenever you get 3 people together there is a bureaucracy.

Have nothing against bureaucracy as a concept per se, by the way – things have to be organized – but the "bureaucracy" complaining about here is just using Organization as an excuse for, for …

For anything, really. For lack of initiative, of course. For ducking responsibility. To cover tracks. To passively aggress. To excuse when there is no excuse. To manipulate by rules. To let rules decide. To forget what the rules meant for. To dance in a circle.

Ten years ago, maybe longer. Just started in the cubes – not here – and worked in an office with Tom. Seemed like an older man. (40? 45? 50? I was 22, who can tell?) Tom always worked hard. Always busy. Tom had been there so long he had an annual 4 week vacation. We were scared: how do we cover for Tom?!? So, each day, 3 of us divvied up his Incoming and… by Day 4… we were caught up! By Day 5 we could finish his work in ¼ day. By Week 2 one person could finish Tom's daily workload in ¼ day. Tom, it seems, was always busy because he never finished anything. He simply worked the bureaucracy, filling up one part of an Incoming and forwarding it on, incomplete, with the assurance that it would come back to him in a circle. 4 or 5 steps per Incoming, when he could have done it in 1 or 2. And no one caught on. When he came back, all went back to normal. The circle dance.

(Funny thing – ha, ha – a half year later I was offered promotion to Asst. Manager over Tom [and over the black guy with more knowledge & skill than me]. First thing a "responsible" Asst. Manager would have to do would be to fire Tom – I knew he was not only not carrying his load but was causing others to work harder. This cube worker can't lay off any middle aged man with a family to care for, so I resigned and found another job elsewhere. Tom was promoted to Asst. Manager. Ha, ha!)

Time to leave here. Give myself 2 months: 30 days notice here and I've still got almost 4 weeks of Sick pay accrued – I can scurry around and find something hopefully. It won't be different anywhere else probably, but I just can't keep the beat to the circle dance.

Wednesday, June 07

Unintended Last Day

So this is how it ended. Gone, Good-bye. Kaput mid-day.

Responsibility repaid: Gave the 30 days notice and the offer to help transition anyone new or old into the duties. Told this to The Lead (she still doesn't have "Manager" behind her name, after 7 years). This was at 8 a.m. She huddled with the Veep at 10 a.m. He huddled with HR at 11 a.m. They called me in at noon – "Can you hold up your lunch for a few minutes" – waited till everyone else had left for vittles, then gave me 15 minutes to clear out my desk. Under supervision.

"Voluntary termination at management request."

Should have known: The Company is "leaning" again –

there's more Budget credit to cutting me out than having me resign: helps meet the 10% Across-the-Boards management goal.

And the transition?

Hey, nobody – nothing's – irreplaceable. There's always someone to take up the slack.

As for the inconvenience, lost time figuring out what's what, and simple monetary losses from an abrupt departure? That's what Overhead is all about.

Pretty much of a normal day.

&

www.ingramcontent.com/pod-product-compliance
Lightning Source LLC
Chambersburg PA
CBHW031824090426
42741CB00005B/118